THINKWELL BOOKS

PITCHSIDE, DOWN IN TENNIS

Jeff Weston was born in 1970, in Bolton, Lancashire. He graduated in 1999 from Manchester Metropolitan University with a degree in English literature and commenced a career in stockbroking the following year. He is the middle son of an electrical engineer and barmaid/housewife and author of three novels (*The Leaf Blower, Mutler, Wagenknecht*), three plays (*The Relationship, Directions, The Broken Heart Ward*) and a collection of short stories (*Homage to Hernandez and other stories*). His writing has crossed over into sports journalism (*Pitchside, Ringside and Down in the Table Tennis Dens*) and book reviews/feature articles for psychotherapy magazines.

"Morning Jeff. Just been speaking to Uwe [Rösler] about your blog. He found it very interesting. He's opened an invitation to come and have a coffee to talk about Nick Haughton and why this situation has come about. Would be a perfect opportunity for you to get behind the thinking"

Will Watt, Head of First Team Operations, Fleetwood Town

"Enjoyed the Burnley report. Jon Parkin as a "beautiful contaminant" is an image that will stay with me. Keep up the good work"

Jon Colman, *News & Star* columnist & SJA Regional Sportswriter of the Year (2008, 2011, 2012, 2013, 2014)

"Top class as always from @jeffweston1970. By far the No.1 Cod Army scribe. Clubs put out enough propaganda around Barton to make him seem infallible, nice to read criticism and a fair, balanced piece"

Darren Dickinson, FTFC and lifelong Liverpool FC fan

"Quiet Friday night in for me so I've gotten that piece out there. Thanks for knocking it together, it's really well written as usual"

Neil Sherwin, Co-editor of *BackPageFootball.com* - Hosting diverse, award-winning original football writing since 2009

"'Paucity' brilliant. An utterly quality article. Good broadsheet standard…As with all your sports pieces, I love the tone and content"

Bill Wood – son of Elgin City 'inside left' midfielder, Colin Wood

"That's one of the proudest things I have read about myself and something I can only say thank you for"

David Ball, Rotherham United striker

"A very well written piece…hope that it gets a decent audience"

Kevin Boroduwicz, Secretary, *Blackpool Supporters Trust*

"I thoroughly enjoyed reading your report on the Wimbledon game last weekend. It is a great read and it is a breath of fresh air to read a report from a supporter's point of view"

Jonathon Swift, Media Manager, Fleetwood Town FC

"What a joy to read, Jeff. Not only because it's typically well-written, full of inventive turn of phrase and ideas, but because of its subject matter…Brought it all back for me – at least the tail end of his career. What I also loved about the article was that you denied the temptation to go balls deep into his big fights, focusing instead on the ones only the hardcore fans would remember, the ones that truly helped create the Carl Thompson legend"

Elliot Worsell, *The Ring/Boxing News* writer & author of *Making Haye*

"Excellent summary of Khan, Humza!"

Mike Casey, journalist, author, editor and boxing historian

"Superb writing, Jeff. Also agree completely with your [Tyson Fury] thesis"

Robert Ecksel, Editor-in-Chief, *Boxing.com*

"Jeff Weston has the beat"

KB, comment on *Boxing.com*

"Now that's a writer!"

Old Yank, comment on *Boxing.com*

"Great Fury-Klitschko piece, Jeff…you did a wonderful job of making me read to the end. Captured the man brilliantly"

Elliot Worsell, Boxing writer

"It goes without saying I am sorry to see you go...The column has been outstandingly well written and hugely insightful for those interested in the Bolton table tennis scene currently and in the recent and distant past"

Neil Bonnar,
Head of Sport, *The Bolton News*

"Just like to say how much I have enjoyed reading your [table tennis] write-ups as posted on Bolton 365 website – they will be sadly missed!"

Steve Hathaway, Bolton & District Table Tennis
League Premier Division player

"Thanks for all your help over the past couple of seasons. I know the players have looked forward to reading your reports and will miss them this season"

Brett Haslam, Bolton & District Table Tennis
League Match Secretary

"It's great to see your articles appearing in *The Bolton News* again. You have a great talent with the pen. Although painful to read [one's stats], [the work is] very truthful, informative and entertaining. Keep up the good work!"

Dave Jones Snr, Bolton & District Table Tennis League
Division Two player & barbershop singer

"The article about Mr Mann...is excellent...you write with both journalistic flair and a very obvious 'feel' for the situation"

Brian Smith, former Harwood Meadows Deputy Head

Jeff Weston

PITCHSIDE,

RINGSIDE

and

DOWN

IN THE

TABLE TENNIS

DENS

THINKWELL BOOKS

For Malcolm Ngouala,

the man from Congo-Brazzaville

who welcomed me into the TT fold

without hesitation and without snobbery

(22.9.2011)

&

Hossein Dobhari Bandari,

my Iranian friend and former teammate (2012)

who taught me that sometimes you wear the

shoes that are too tight, rather than go without

"It's a 'No' I'm afraid" John Hilton, 1980 European Table Tennis Champion Saturday, 5.8.2017 (10.55am)

…upon asking if he would assist in the writing of a biography (*John Hilton: The Forgotten Champion*) given his 1000-1 exploits in Bern nearly four decades earlier.

Hence, I decided to do something else
(*Pitchside, Ringside & Down...*)

Table of Contents

Foreword

Every now and then a man comes along who breaks the rules, but does it enigmatically.

Jeff Weston is a dichotomy of a man - a stockbroker who refused to take the natural next step into London market making in order to carry on with his sports journalism; a man who is so respectfully polite, yet also equally capable of poking the bear in any social situation.

I first met Jeff at Hilton Table Tennis Centre, Horwich, Bolton around 2013. I was a brash southerner, newly-familiar with the area, winning regional table tennis championships that local people didn't want me to attend, let alone enter, beating every local hero in front of their adoring fan bases. I was an alien. I was an illegal alien. I was a Brighton man, too close to York.

Bolton was a cultural mess to me and everything confused me. I was still unsure how to ask for basic bread products; a sandwich now a butty and a roll somehow a cake. Explaining this to most Boltonians made them look at me with a confused expression, like Mike Tyson in a library.

Jeff saw beyond bakery conversation though and wanted to know the man behind the bravado…

Jeff has an unnerving talent of making you feel like the most important person in the room as if there's nobody else around. It feels like he's drinking in your words, studying your motivations and insecurities, whilst drilling down into your soul.

Like many sports journalists before him, Jeff is an ordinary sportsman, but an extraordinary raconteur of events. I remember watching one of Jeff's Summer League table tennis matches, and I don't know if having a regional county champion and B-grade local celebrity in a very niche sport put more pressure on him, but it was certainly a memorable and entertaining match. Jeff is a man who clearly has the odd bit of exuberance or moment of brilliance, but his mind seems to move quicker than his actual hand-eye co-ordination allows. Jeff, as a sportsman, is just as likely to miss a ball comedically as he is to play a running shot off the bounce to win a match at an impossible angle.

But isn't that what sport is all about? Those odd angles of brilliance and timing; the plight of the rising star; comedy in abject failure; the race against the clock; the weaving of underhand tactics and cheating; and the goose pimples of those moments and connections that make you either wallow in despair or celebrate in pure, unadulterated euphoria. Jeff opens, investigates and exposes these moments like Lieutenant Columbo in the last ten minutes of an hour-long special.

I remember reading some of Jeff's early work published in the *The Bolton News*. A typical *pre*-Jeff Weston sports report would consist of an inch of copy and some perfunctory lines; Player A beats Player B-type reporting, a team score and, if you were lucky, maybe even a picture of the current league table standings. When Jeff Weston reported these events they now took up a quarter of a page of copy, maybe even more. They were the talk of the sporting community: "Did you hear what that Jeff Weston said about Rammy (Ramsbottom)?"

Exposing local league match-fixing at the end of his tenure, Jeff 'called out' the establishment and quoted those around them with sufficient damning evidence like every great journalist should. Was the local rag ready for such an investigation? Sadly not. The establishment fought back and Jeff was removed, even on a voluntary basis.

Jeff Weston poked too many bears and the *The Bolton News* probably saved itself a few headaches…but those match reports are still talked and reminisced about by players and officials to this day. And you don't need to know who the personalities are to enjoy them. Why would you? Just look at them as an exploration or foray into investigative journalism, by the king of local bear-pokers.

I'm so pleased that Jeff didn't let the establishment bring him down or forestall his ambition. And I've never really had the chance to tell him, but I'm extremely proud of where he has taken his journalistic career; this foreword almost cathartic in that sense.

If you had told me back in 2013 that Jeff Weston would be writing editorial copy for the prestigious Boxing.com, I'd have suggested you seek advice, help and probably medical assistance. Likewise, if you'd told me that Jeff would take his love of football (Leeds United, Bolton Wanderers and Fleetwood Town) to award-winning site BackPageFootball.com, I'd have responded with a sarcastic smile. But nothing should surprise you with Jeff Weston, as he is the king of surprises, the "Journos' Journo" and, for me, one of the best 'Bear Pokers' in the business.

You may not like or agree with every word or description, but you'll definitely have respect for his craft. And by the time you've finished reading you'll probably have a few more sporting anecdotes that you can share in future, heated debates.

The great beauty of this collection of work is that you get a real sense of what grassroots sports all the way up to domestic, international events, and world title fights, mean to the people of Great Britain. Who would have thought that Jamie Vardy could go from non-league football at the age of 25 to being the Premier League's Golden Boot winner? Without journalism like that produced by Jeff Weston (who incidentally interviewed Vardy's Fleetwood Town successor David Ball), these sports stars, it could be argued, would never get the exposure or opportunities that they have.

We are a small country packing a punch far greater than the sum of our parts and this book and the work of Jeff Weston is the embodiment of that journalistically.

Paul Cicchelli, 26 October 2020

New Journalism

Something vanished in the sphere of journalism in about 1981. Two decades earlier, a different form of writing using literary techniques had sprung up thanks to giants including Gay Talese, Norman Mailer, Tom Wolfe and Jimmy Breslin. Their method was simple: Articles that wrote like short stories.

Mainly furnished for the magazines of the day including *Esquire*, *New York* and *Rolling Stone*, such work was devoured, understood and worshipped by an intellectually needy readership – a group of people that saw the vital link between culture and a highly engaging form of entertainment.

New journalism was a clean way of bludgeoning perfidious politicians, white collar crooks, religious hypocrites and mainstream fakery. It was also a way of exploring wonderfully original angles on big stories instead of the routine dopiness.

And for the *little* stories "giving the mundane its beautiful due" was seemingly in the minds of the great writers before John Updike said it.

Jeff Weston, 2013

Preface

I think it's impossible to say exactly *when* and *why* my desire to write came about – the need to rinse from my mind the half-cocked shuttle of words which would later fall into a novel, a play, a short story or a piece of journalism. I knew one thing though: That I liked to observe. And such scenes, together with their verbal rumbustiousness or subtle arc, were ultimately scrambled and converted into a few paragraphs which had to sing to me before gaining their release into the world.

Alfred Kazin famously referred to John Cheever, J D Salinger and John Updike as "professional observers" in a 1971 essay. This, I immediately understood and related to. For the best writing is a coup of sorts, a seizure of that before you which you hope to god is not pilfered by another person in the vicinity. Ideas, moments, clashes when merging with the brain's chemistry make you giddy – they act as the centre piece of a work, but it's also imperative that restraint and sobriety are employed.

There are a few reasons, I believe, why my brain is wired as it is.

I was the classic failure at school – bemused and perturbed (with the exception of mathematics) by the goings-on before me. I knew I had an unusual take on life, but no one stopped to question my deeper core or the ridges that led to my underperformance.

I joined mail order book club after book club in my teens in an effort to purchase giant hardbacks on the cheap. I had no idea at the time exactly why I continued to do this. I wasn't a prolific reader. My attention span was poor. And the books in question were about art, wine, nature, photography and architecture – hardly my areas of expertise. Something or some*one* told me to buy them, I figured. Look at the pictures, it said. The images – what do they say to you? It was a 'way in' to beauty, I discovered. If I wasn't quite ready for the heavy tracts of literature, then French Impressionism, modern art, wildlife, the natural wonders of the world, vineyards and building design piqued my interest. In the lines, shapes and colours I saw meaning and grace.

Around the age of 25 I started to go to Waterstones' author evenings. I had the privilege of listening to and seeing in the flesh Richard Ford, Tim Willocks, Hanif Kureishi, Julian Barnes, Hugh Laurie, Robert Newman, George Monbiot and Alexei Sayle. These, I felt, were *my people* – full of conviction, not uncomfortable in their idiosyncratic world. To hear them speak tallied with Norman Mailer railing against "slow death by conformity". The last thing I wanted was conservatism and orthodoxy. My grandad used to park his Datsun Cherry in the treasurer's spot at golf clubs for Christ's sake!

Life trundled on. I became a stockbroker. I told myself that it was a temporary state of affairs. After all, Gauguin – that brilliant man of colours – had been a stockbroker. Artists, writers, musicians, sportsmen, dancers, actors – we are all one. We come from the same egg. We despise predictable things, clichéd expression, those souls that engage with the chugging awfulness of bureaucracy and fear.

Artists *can* be "humble and colossal" – the words attributed to Pissarro by Cézanne, eight years his junior. They can produce majestic things but not have to shout about it. In fact, more and more, that *not* shouting is in the work itself – a subtle, humorous, devastating curation of words.

Pissarro liked to call himself "a painter of cabbages". In that simplicity is a lesson for us all. We might be more, but we must be *something* as the race gets underway. When I approached *The Bolton News*' Head of Sport on 1st April 2013 I was armed with nine table tennis articles – pieces I'd churned out between 2007 and 2008 in order to document matches between my friends and I and practise my art. They were rough - *very* rough - vestiges of the style of writing I'd fallen in love with: New Journalism. And on this side of the Atlantic I had Hugh McIlvanney to learn from – his "ably-depicted sporting scenes" and interviews huge in their ability to make one gasp and small in their jostling for position.

Neil Bonnar hired me. I wrote 93 pieces for him between May 2013 and April 2016 – some a little too bouncy, some quite insightful and some significant in what they revealed to the reader in terms of the league's colourful characters, club politics and the minutiae of the sport. That three year relationship – briefly broken and then restored – taught me a lot. I enjoyed working to a weekly deadline. It gave my life structure. I took great satisfaction from visiting all the league's dens or venues; a sixteen-club network at the time with Ramsbottom to the north, Radcliffe to the east, Flixton south and Chorley west. That Division Four teams had to go on a "Kerouacian road trip" each season due to the greater variety of clubs in the bottom rung amused me – the gods taking their petrol, but affording them little limelight.

Frustrations grew alas. With writing comes an editorial overlord and copy editors. The former can, in the main, be hypnotised or made to see the importance of the work you deliver to him. But after a while, you want more. You want the man to embrace your work, be appreciative and ambitious in what he's communicating to the locality. Too many of my bolder plans were knocked back for fear of upsetting the "family audience". And as for the light editing of my articles – when I occasionally went over my 400 or 500-word cap – well, they were often despoiled or ruined; made nonsensical by the 'Welsh cattle house' *The Bolton News* employed.

The "mischievous" reporting of match rigging was principally why I called it a day. The press officer gig at the Bolton & District Table Tennis League and the table tennis column at *The Bolton News* were intrinsically linked, but the fact that both committee and sports editor failed to recognise *why* my penultimate table tennis piece ("Disquiet") mattered I found astonishing. Truth, it seems, is only truth if gentle and cordial.

Producing long reads for Boxing.com and BackPageFootball.com was liberating by comparison. Both editors welcomed my in-depth analysis, my controversial if still meaningful take on that before me – on sport's minor and major protagonists. It is a cruel irony that the likes of Peter Storey at the *Lancashire Evening Post* referred to my work as being more suitable for magazines, thus depriving his own paper of the jaunts and excursions that I desperately wished to communicate to my fellow Lancastrians.

Were they not worthy of a hybrid offering, of articles which tickled them in a different manner? Sometimes I think provincial papers act like vegetable delivery-box schemes, but ignore the fine cuts of meat from the farm which might invigorate the taste buds and take readers beyond largely factual pieces. Writers should have secrets, has always been my mantra. They shouldn't huddle together and follow the house-style. They shouldn't be fearful of expressing themselves. They should explore what intoxicates them and animates their writing. And yet most writers are made to feel like Judas Iscariot if they veer even a few degrees off the prescribed, stipulated path.

Magpie journalism is how I came to know my own style of writing. Whether a myth or not, the magpie's tendency to steal shiny objects I compared to my own eagerness to use beautiful quotes from decades ago – words mostly neglected or deemed redundant by other writers. Such quotes decorate my work or nest – they provide the reader with a cross-generational experience which hopes to infiltrate his/her mind. In utilising numerous archives, I feel that I am giving praise to the work that came before my own, because great, always-relevant quotes are truly timeless and imperishable.

Sports Editors Are Mostly Doormen, I once scribbled down, intending to write such an article at some future point; 'mostly' a convenient way of making a strong statement, but not alienating one's entire black book of peers! Either way, my impression of editors was not particularly flattering. I pictured them stood like bouncers, ready to rough-up new ideas or entrants, ready to batten down the hatches and stick with their minimal, token observations. I saw them as maracas with no sound, men and women whose own work was hardly pre-eminent (in fact, by taking the job of deciding *what* is included in a particular edition, there is an implicit admittance that one has given up thinking one's own abilities are any good).

"[Jimmy] Breslin made a revolutionary discovery. He made the discovery that it was feasible for a columnist to actually leave the building, go outside and do reporting on his own; genuine legwork." I made this suggestion to Michael Holmes at the *Blackpool Gazette* earlier this year in relation to a story I wished him to follow up. He wasn't best pleased. In fact, he was apoplectic. But I think the more noble part of him *would* admit that legwork is a very small part of journalism these days and that dangling something close to your ear and relying on the *Associated Press* is very much the order of the day.

This is what you do when you write – you march up and down in search of your next sentence. You don't jam your legs under an MDF desk and type a pretty piece. That is what I believe as a very minimum. Only you *observe*. You exit the damn building, find the person you need to talk to and stare them down. See if they're rattled. See if they're bullshitting. See if they're unwilling to give you the true line.

Colleges don't teach this. They don't teach interaction. Indeed, part of that undertaking is entirely *your* responsibility, your duty to seek out the more elusive parts of a story. Because only by having that object or subject in front of you can you hope to extrapolate the larger truth.

Without this, without some kind of visual imagery, your endeavour is entirely pointless. *Seeing* lies and hesitation is easier than *hearing* them. And from that your work develops an authentic edge. Your work actually matters.

Jeff Weston, 18 October 2020

Introduction

It still feels remarkable that three sports very close to my heart have silently colluded, nay *demanded*, that I place them together and accord them recognition and space. And that is *before* we begin to see and understand the characters within each discipline who jumped out at me and effectively pushed my pen for me or pressed the keys on my computer. For that is what original sportsmen and women do – they assemble your thoughts for free, they stimulate your brain and provide beautiful, beautiful material often without knowing it.

I recall *knowing* footballers when I was younger through their distinctive ways of running: Tony Dorigo, an ice-skater; David Batty, that battle-hardened, chest-puffed-out cavalier, scampering around; Rio Ferdinand, graceful and stylish; Gary Kelly, like a skipping rodent controlling a piece of cheese. Things like this imprint themselves in your mind. They are hard to explain to people with little knowledge or interest in sport. Because sport is so much more than sport – it is rhythm, camaraderie, joy, suffering, anguish, regularity; it is purpose and a temporary home at times - a retreat.

It is strange in a way because there are sports I now hate to play, but love to watch: golf and tennis in particular. And sports that are in my blood and I could not conceive ever abandoning: table tennis and football. Boxing is something I have never tried (bar the odd Christmas escapade with my brothers), have sensibly stayed away from and not succumbed to courtesy of participatory journalism as per George Plimpton. *Outside* the ring is fine with me, although I'll confess to wanting a scrap with a few contemptible jerks from my school days given the chance.

Professionals *and* amateurs litter these pages, and it is this amalgam which rouses me. Material for my sportswriting has come from – as the title of this book suggests – pitchside, ringside and down in the table tennis dens. But each sport has given me something entirely different. The intimacy of a table tennis evening is truly mesmeric at times – more so when you're one of the six players participating. It is that rare experience – individual pursuit, but also fighting for your team ('dig in' as the common TT expression goes) which separates this unique sport from others. The laughter, the rivalry, the noise, the seriousness, the fitness levels, the skill and the tactics all combine to produce unexpected outcomes at times. And in such random results is hope for those coming through the ranks; a table tennis 'scalp' unequivocally comparable to upsets in the world of boxing and football.

Reporting on table tennis matches was an acquired art form. Furious scribbling, looking up and down constantly (hoping not to miss anything), quoting players' spontaneous reactions to events, absorbing their mannerisms and foibles and giving context to the night's proceedings were all critical to the final picture. And as with any bit of journalism, around 95% of my notes were excluded from the final piece, but could potentially be exhumed or excavated at a later date to be used elsewhere.

Football is different in this respect. I rarely make notes during a match, but recall moments in my head and write them down in a contemplative fashion when I return home. What I deem to be significant on-field events or off-field managerial/player quotes generally form the nucleus of my work. I am an overly-critical observer of the unfolding action (probably because I witnessed both Eric Cantona and Tony Yeboah in their prime), but I do celebrate the few times when something magical occurs at whatever level of the sport.

I have interviewed only a handful of people across the three sports that this book covers, but each experience left an indelible mark: David Ball (Fleetwood Town) at my kitchen table in the summer of 2015; Scott Quigg and Joe Gallagher at the Gloves Community Centre (Amir Khan's gym) in the autumn of 2016; Elliot Worsell, David Haye's brother-in-law, via email between December 2016 and January 2017; and Paul Cicchelli, the senior singles winner, at the Lancashire Closed Championships in May 2015.

It is as Worsell came to realise himself – there is a danger that you can get too close to your subject and thus tarnish or compromise your writing, despite the opportunity for original quotes and nuances. But certainly in the early days of one's career, such experiences are invaluable. They provide a fluid understanding of the character traits that sportsmen and women begin to exhibit in varying degrees: surety, swagger, humility, faith, conceitedness, altruism, joy and concern.

People are never as you expect. Bally was a quietly spoken, down to earth bloke with two sleeve tattoos covered up by the soft material of an elegant sweater. In driving to my house and giving me 75 minutes of his time on a Sunday morning – missing his son's match in the process – he demonstrated that professional footballers *do* often care about public perception and *do* wish to share their back stories and generously enlighten others. Quigg/Gallagher was a different proposition – one I had to wait around for just to get a few minutes, one which came with a harder image and challenge to my naturally shy demeanour. But I had watched all Quigg's fights via YouTube and DailyMotion. I had noticed things – small things which most journalists choose not to focus on or completely miss. And that very act seemed to mollify Gallagher or at least mitigate the unvarnished side of him I had witnessed in the ring.

There are many people I *nearly met* but which real life and earning a living conspired against. Graham Alexander (cup of tea). Uwe Rösler (coffee). But *not* meeting them privately, no longer having that neutral vantage point, was not a bad thing I figured. I had seen Rösler in action at Fleetwood Town's Fans' Forum in 2017 alongside Grétar Steinsson, chairman Andy Pilley and Steve Curwood. And such an encounter – largely anonymous – had provided perfect material for a piece I wished to write concerning one of FTFC's most promising youngsters in recent years, namely Nick Haughton (now of AFC Fylde). This is often the best approach – a surreptitious mingling with others in order to ascertain *who* the person is without the contrived shine of a one-to-one meeting.

People like Joey Barton ("Cigars"), John Sheridan ("Ordinary Man"), Devante Cole ("Horizon"), Steven Pressley ("Lamborghini") and Neil McDonald ("Humble Man") were different propositions entirely. I was intrigued and genuinely fascinated by who they were and what they had become.

Sheridan traced a long line back to my teenage years in the 1980s when I had followed him in his guise as Leeds United legend. Just mentioning his fridge door and desperate need to escape a post-match interview, I found symbolic of "the outer Sheridan, the surface Sheridan". But, of course, there was so much more going on and that's what I wished to get across.

Barton, on the other hand, was the "Antichrist". He had never been a player like Sheridan "dripping in sweet honey". He had a dark past courtesy of a lit cigar and ex-teammate Jamie Tandy. But let's not forget "Provocation. Context. Youth. Red mist. There are many half-defences to such action and behaviour". The words in my article perhaps offered Barton a degree of respite, but they also served to show that people are multi-layered – full of impropriety *and* beauty. So while I acknowledged that "to many [Barton is] a wild, frenzied screwball or cuckoo", I also made it clear that I'll never be part of a mob defining someone narrowly and permanently.

Cole's portrait was indispensable, I thought. I felt the absolute need to give him a fair hearing, unlike most of the fans sat around me at Highbury. There were flashes of brilliance from Cole – speed and awareness of those around him. Certain away matches displayed his lethal ability when Fleetwood played as a counter-attacking side. But, yes, he was far too inconsistent. Sometimes I think he probably needed to confront a few of his own fans just to make it clear that there *was* fire inside of him because calm, quiet players don't always get an easy ride. I desperately wanted to see Devante succeed because he had that latent, well-hidden quality: potential. And I won't hesitate to travel up to Motherwell just to see how he's getting on. Maybe I have a certain affection for the underdog. Let's not forget the *huge* shadow that his father cast, after all – the pressure from which many next-generation players have crumbled.

Pressley was an interesting case – a file that any lawyer would be tantalized by; his "footballing algorithm" wayward, his always-watching a different match to the one in front of him now folklore. And yet, this is the same man who, as Tynecastle captain in 2006, "socked it to [chairman] Vladimir Romanov [when he] threatened to sell all Hearts' players". Respect, though, is lost in an instant. What one previously garnered from a soul can be overhauled in a matter of seconds. But should it be? Does a manager's performance in front of the camera equate in any way to his talent on the training ground? We all want to hear humour, astute lines and the rumblings of an original man, but do we get that with the big names of 2020 when thrust before the camera? Do we get that from those with a supposed presence, those that are manifest in some ineffable way? From the likes of Pep Guardiola or Marcelo Bielsa? I would suggest not. We choose instead to lift them up and take select cuttings from their interviews. We listen to them because of what they've done. But in reality, we are all quite bland and unimpressive at times.

McDonald, lastly, was the apparent puppet of both Carlisle owner, Fred Story and Blackpool chairman, Karl Oyston. His face was the softest to ever emit its glow in footballing corridors. But he had shared dressing rooms with Kevin Keegan, Terry McDermott, Chris Waddle, Peter Beardsley, Neville Southall, Trevor Steven and Graeme Sharp. He had frequented the top echelons. So again comes the great paradox, the seemingly absurd: How can a "soft, cuddly bear" steeped in too much humility mix it with names better remembered from the past? Perhaps because personality doesn't represent skill or talent. Perhaps because one's outer layers only tell a fraction of the tale. And, after all, there are plenty excoriated, egregious extroverts. The McDonald piece was a lovely article to write because it spoke of injustice and Nero-like individuals in the boardrooms of clubs – the same, old pantaloons that still rise to this day.

I should mention boxing in closing – how my birth town of Bolton was "the centre of the boxing universe" for a while; Team Fury Gym and the Gloves Community Centre (Amir Khan's gym) barely a mile apart, with the ripped and scarred Halliwell (holy well) a fitting, residential backdrop to the sweat and grace within both camps. Out of these places came many of my subjects: Amir Khan, Tyson Fury, Scott Quigg and Joe Gallagher. And those that didn't often set up nearby as a post-career disgorging or cathartic release of nervous tension, as in the case of Carl 'The Cat' Thompson (Round 1 Boxing, Horwich, Bolton).

Boxing writing is a studious and meticulous examination of individuals who are not too dissimilar to table tennis players. Competitors hold court through their rangy actions, their weighing up of that before them, their formulating a plan which factors in just seconds of actual experience with a given opponent. In these sportsmen is destruction of a sort, levelling, ruination – an attempt to climb the often lesser-known rungs of society which may or may not lead to comfort. Heartache brings with it great material though – a steady stream of melancholic faces, crushed dreams, the instant betrayal of those once loyal. In the peripheral characters that gravitate around the stars, often provide fodder and take their due amidst blood and ignominy, is immense sadness.

I have seen it in Mark de Mori (David Haye's victim), in Graham Earl (after he met Amir Khan) and in Naseem Hamed (the steel of

Marco Antonio Barrera simply too much). Stories changed. Lives altered. Whatever feeling of impregnability they had immediately broken and rendered false.

I'll confess to having two mentors in the contemporary boxing world: Ron Borges, who wrote for *Boxing Monthly* before its Covid-prompted demise; and the lesser known Stephen Jones of http://mirageboxing.blogspot.com/ who owns a café in Garstang, Lancashire and whose knowledge of the boxing world is quite phenomenal. I am grateful to both men for their polish, deep wisdom and facts which put me to shame. I have a tendency to deep dive into subjects and people that interest me, but Borges and Jones scan everything out there and are a true credit to maintaining memories inside this sometimes vengeful, yet arresting sport; this sweet science which both captivates and continues to shock.

Jeff Weston, 21 October 2020

Joey Barton Reveals a Well-Hidden Humility after Shorting Fleetwood Town's Long

BackPageFootball.com, 16 October 2018

Thirty four seconds into his post-match interview on Saturday, Joey Barton did what head coaches and football managers rarely do. He switched off his delusional gene; a gene very common during the Alex Ferguson era and passed on to numerous managers since.

Barton decided to admit that his 43rd-minute decision to bring on striker Chris Long for the injured central midfielder James Wallace was unsettling:

"…Then we get the substitution and to be honest, errr, err, you know, we were disrupted a little bit by it. It threw us a little bit. Ermmm, I probably made the wrong call. I probably made the wrong substitution which got us on the back foot. We didn't start the 2nd half particularly well. I ended up, ermm, making a further change which I felt stabilised us and then gave us that composure."

The only words that represent a disservice to Barton's candour are "little", "probably" and "further change". What was nearly a full half of focused, committed, intense, hard-working football became, in an instant, a negligent, floating formation.

Not only was the excellence of Ash Hunter's supply line compromised as well as Paddy Madden's purposeful graft, but the smooth, well-oiled 4-3-2-1 engine was whacked with a mallet and expected to grace the terrain in the same manner.

Barton's "further change" was realising his catastrophic, illogical, perhaps maverick-driven error, yet waiting 28 minutes so not to entirely embarrass Chris Long.

Substituting a substitute is indeed a horrible, persecutory act. It is not often that one gets to witness such a voodoo-like deed. And Long's immediate reaction of storming down the tunnel to the dressing room added drama and a touch of upset to a situation that would never have come about were it not for Barton's luxuriant posturing

Interesting to see that Barton's privileged words were left to hang in the air without being challenged by the <u>interviewer</u>, but such is the state of the tentative, soft-shoe media that automatic immunity from tough questioning is mostly granted these days.

The more natural, incontestable substitution on Saturday would have been to bring on the dexterous Kyle Dempsey. None of the midfielders lying in wait (Jason Holt, Harrison Biggins or Dempsey) have the aerial presence of the departed James Wallace, but each would have offered a steadier hand to complement the movements of the experienced Ryan Taylor and Ross Wallace around them.

Alas, Dempsey is no longer part of Barton's inner circle. And that is the case for centre half Cian Bolger and winger Bobby Grant also. Hard decisions have been made during Fleetwood Town's four-month Barton era thus far and it was clearly felt that the current high-octane football was unsuited to the style of Messrs Bolger, Grant and Dempsey.

This, I get, in part. Bolger's towering residency only really works in a back three. And Grant's game, if the shots aren't coming off, tends to impede the team's fluidity. As for Dempsey though – maybe Barton sees him as too much of a star; a star likely to outshine the lacquered hair of the boss himself.

You look around this team now - the starting eleven on Saturday – and curiously begin to see a no-nonsense group of players, a collection of individuals gearing up for a bank job. From Madden, to Taylor, to 21-year-old Nathan Sheron, there is a quiet menace in the air, a team ethic with Ashley Eastham as its centrifuge.

For if one was to mistakenly think that the mould or template from which this team is designed is in the shape of Barton himself, then one need only look across at the 6' 3", Preston-born, ultimate stalwart Eastham and realise that the squad simply undergo daily blood transfusions from the ex-Rochdale great.

To get excited about Eastham would be wrong. He does not require any attention or fanfare or praise. He is just *there*, doing his job, but in such a competent manner that his teammates in the vicinity need never worry. He is an unexpected rock, a diligent, still-young (27) central defender who only really got his career on track four years ago such is the roulette wheel of being appreciated in football.

"A marvellous bit of individual talent," Barton commented in relation to Wes Burns' goal in the 28th minute when Fleetwood were in the ascendancy, two-nil up, against Shrewsbury. So he *does* recognise flair. He *does* recognise finesse and elegance. (There are plenty of precedents here.) And a ski-mask wearing bunch of semi-hoodlums will always require *someone* to crack the safe.

Fleetwood cannot lose someone of Dempsey's calibre. Jon Colman, Cumbria's News & Star football columnist and SJA Regional Sportswriter of the Year winner multiple times will tell you that Dempsey is precocious, such a skilled operator when he watched him as a 20-year-old at Brunton Park three years ago.

And pre-Barton, following the departure of David Ball, Dempsey was Fleetwood's standout player by a long, long way – his artistry in the middle of the park missed by no one.

Respect to Barton for fessing up to his gaff on Saturday. When the substitution board was held aloft in the 71st minute with the numbers 14 (Long) and 4 (Holt) on it, there was collective shock around the ground. Contrition from Barton? Surely not. But, yes, that is what we saw, albeit dangerously close to the end of the match.

What should have been another scalp with four goals or more following the August demolition of Scunthorpe and the recent putting to the sword of Doncaster turned into an unnecessary fairground ride, a helter-skelter with Barton messing around with the mats.

There are noticeably no wallflowers in this team that Barton is constructing. He has taken 34-year-old 'psycho' Ryan Taylor (whose career started to slide three years ago after departing Newcastle United), 33-year-old Ross Wallace (the Burnley/Sheff Wed ever-present, pushed inside after losing some of his pace) – both free agents – and 33-year-old Craig 'Morgs' Morgan (the former Wigan captain), thus adding what he believes to be old heads around the exhilarating '23 and under' youth of Ash Hunter, Nathan Sheron, Wes Burns and Lewie Coyle.

Barton now just has to concede that puffing out his chest and having cult-hero status and undying loyalty amongst a vociferous core of supporters means nothing if his decisions remain capricious and haphazard. And that applies to prompt, instantaneous 'calls' at the side of the pitch and also when thinking long and hard about gifted players' futures.

Overall though, for the first 43 minutes on Saturday, a team was finally born. And that bodes well, in small measure, for the wily Barton. Not so his historic detractors.

No Art in the Gallery for Barton's Fleetwood Town

BackPageFootball.com, 21 August 2018

'They've not got an edge, have they…' a grandma on Row C of the Highbury Stand commented in the 20th minute of Fleetwood versus Rochdale.

She was referring to Joey Barton's second home game in charge and the slightly banal and colourless display before us.

On paper watching a Barton team should be like tripping through the Louvre or Tate Modern or the Museo Nacional del Prado. There should be detail, slick brush strokes, intrigue, captivation and dominance.

This, however, *this* was a torturous circus for the first half hour - a doleful meandering of flesh; not much different to Barton's managerial debut on 4th August versus Wimbledon bar the starting XI which had six different faces.

Joey is still working it out, still tinkering with his formula, still writing his programme notes like his predecessor, Uwe Rösler only without wishing the opposition "a safe trip home".

Perhaps that's what the dead hand of chairman, Andy Pilley does. Perhaps it makes you less benevolent, less gracious, less magnanimous. As, despite the great pals act between head coach and chairman, this is now all about results – garnering, accumulating and stockpiling points, and fleecing the opposition where and when possible.

On first inspection today, Fleetwood Town's side - its splayed Christmas Tree formation (Cairns – Coyle, Eastham, Morgan, Jones – Dempsey, Holt, Marney – Hunter, Madden – Evans) – looked capable. There was no Burns, Biggins or Bolger to offer departmental solace, but what was out there, what wandered onto the field, arguably had nous, experience and talent.

New signings / loanees Craig Morgan, Jason Holt, Dean Marney and Ched Evans were of particular interest given their exploits with Wigan, Rangers, Hull/Burnley and Sheffield United respectively. And in some ways they represent Barton's early vision, his perception, his discernment, his foothold on League One.

Unfortunately, only half of them – at the moment – appear adept and consummate. Only Holt and Evans have shown glimpses of what can be.

Morgan, at 33, seems permanently fatigued as if inside an invisible sauna. And Marney, at 34, is plodding, leaden-footed, sedate not in an unruffled way, but simply because there are no other gears.

Barton, it seems, has chosen to go to the recycling centre but has come back with a couple of broken bikes with the chains hanging off; deceived by the shop attendant standing *in front of* two finer specimens in the corner. He has put his faith in experience, yet Morgan and Marney's squad numbers – 20 and 25 – currently embody not wisdom but figures seemingly half their physical age.

Maybe I expect too much. Maybe I expect League One to be like a rampant, Napoleonic charge. I just know that I like art before my eyes. And Barton promised that – explicitly *and* implicitly. He promised to be a "disrupter...challenge the status quo and shake things up a little". But then his core values are "honesty, humility and hard work" – the fuel for the rocket, but certainly not the hard-hitting hypothesis required; the concept, idea or belief to set us apart.

Barton has tasted three different dishes so far: defeat, victory and a disappointing draw due to a 95th-minute equaliser à la Rochdale's old stalwart, Ian Henderson. His only league victory has been away to Oxford who sit shackled to the bottom of the division in the manner of a penniless beggar.

There *are* positives, but there is no suggestion that these have been mined *by* Barton or that his shrewd, enlightened brain is about to ransack League One.

The effervescent Ash Hunter remains an absolute, unexpected menace to the opposition each game. But then Fleetwood fans have known about the diminutive wonder for years.

Kyle Dempsey didn't quite look himself at the beginning of the Rochdale game – his midfield seniority perhaps compromised by the inclusion of Marney and Holt – but once in full flow, the nuanced flicks and angled running made it abundantly clear that Dempsey is still the creative force we know well.

Ashley Eastham, the 6' 3" vocal tower - once of Rochdale – continues to astonish in terms of his zip, composure and presence. And with Eastham, you get those core values which can be the springboard to any team.

So Barton *has* the building blocks. He also *has* a no.1 (Alex Cairns) who proved in the 25th minute of this game that flinging himself to his right *can* act as a catalyst and example to the rest of the team.

In playmaker, Holt perhaps Fleetwood can grow and echo those poetic days of Stefan Scougall – the much underused and woefully mistreated midfielder during the erratic Steven Pressley era.

Barton at least played Holt as the anchor man versus Rochdale. Somewhat disappointingly though, he didn't get enough of the ball – a major crime when you choose to include such a diddyman but fail to utilise his strengths.

Three games down and it isn't *all* gloom. Fleetwood sit 9th in the table and there have been glimpses of the old fire and lustre (Hunter crosses, Cairns saves, Dempsey ballet movements, Burns going for the jugular). And we shouldn't forget that Rochdale with the giant no.6 Harrison McGahey, cultured left-back Kgosi Ntlhe and the irrepressible midfielder David Perkins *were* organised and *did* offer quality resistance.

One's instinct though says we're still short. One looks at this team and sees that it is *without* rhythm, *without* fluidity, *without* a consistent ethos. Whatever Barton is *trying* to imprint on this side, it isn't there yet - unless that something is a ragged, at times *detached* collection of hearts.

The final 60 minutes were an improvement on the first 30, but even then there was no deluge or explosion of talent. This is still a team hobbled by the lack of a cutting midfield and half a defence. Remove Marney, Morgan and Jones – even temporarily until they're singing in tune with the rest of the choir – and give the deft Holt more of a licence and Fleetwood *might* begin to unnerve and bulldozer teams once more.

This is of course not solely about personnel. It is about tactics, systems, formations and an almost psychic understanding between players. Has Barton the intellect and originality necessary in order to bring to fruition Pilley's dreams? Will *he* explode at some point rather than the latent ability in his squad?

Barton is less animated than one would have imagined. You look at him kitted out in his black garb and see only the mouth moving. With his lacquered hair, he is in many ways a cross between Ernie Wise and a bottle of Just for Men (shade H55).

At the moment, his brief Fleetwood managerial career has relied on the gifts of the old boys Hunter, Dempsey, Burns and Madden, with a snifter of new boy, no.9 Ched Evans.

Barton's major mistake against Rochdale was bringing on a centre-half (Bolger) for a central midfielder (Holt) in the 73rd minute which resulted in Morgan playing at right-back and Jones on the right-wing. It was an act not only of self-delusion in terms of players' abilities, but of saying to the opposition "The barricades are up. We won't need a third goal."

Fleetwood *did* need a 3rd goal, but in the space of 30 seconds that was never likely to happen. Hanging on is rarely an option and interchangeable personnel, if it cripples or enfeebles a team's attacking outlets, inevitably induces optimism in the opposition ranks.

Barton *will* learn, but whether he is savvy enough or has luck on his side is another question. And with Scunthorpe, Charlton, Bradford and Sunderland around the corner – mostly giants in their own right – the tests get harder.

Back to those core values: honesty, humility and hard work. Don't forget flair though, Joey. Don't forget finesse.

Joey Barton: From Cigars to Head Coach

BackPageFootball.com, 4 May 2018

The face doesn't help. It's a baby face, but also a *hard* face – a face not akin to backing down; the sharp nose, intense eyes and waxed hair divisive before a word has been uttered.

Joey Barton can be a charming man, a man that cares, a man that craves knowledge, but to many a wild, frenzied screwball or cuckoo.

The footage of him talking before the Cambridge Union Society a month ago is earnest but a little prim, unremarkable and mewling.

He has a sodden history, a tendentious past – witness to drugs, car theft, a broken home at 14, the disappointment of being released by Everton at 16, nightclub brawls, jail for common assault and affray (Walton and Strangeways) in 2008, red cards, pitch confrontations – but during those 20 minutes we get sensible Joey, polished Joey, bespectacled Joey talking about "challenges" and "journeys" without the earthiness and foul-smelling, feculent detail.

There is the tragedy of his uncle being hit over the head and killed by a pool cue when Joey was eight, but not enough of this honest, forthright history.

'I think you just mature, don't you…that's what we all do,' he stated on *Good Morning Britain* a few weeks earlier.

But is this not the same Barton, at root, who referred to Gary Lineker as an "odious little toad" and Alan Shearer as "a prick…I honestly despise"? Is it not the same man who roughed up his own teammate Ousmane Dabo in training and assaulted a 15-year-old Everton fan? Is it not the same unstable hombre who kicked Sergio Agüero and stubbed out a lit cigar in the left eye of teammate Jamie Tandy?

Provocation. Context. Youth. Red mist. There are many half-defences to such action and behaviour.

Some would like to throw Barton to the dogs, however. Some would like to place Barton, without a weapon, in a Roman amphitheatre in front of 10 gladiators.

There is enough vitriol on-line in relation to Barton to make you wonder how he gets through each day. There is enough rage, bitterness and unforgiving malice to keep hell cranked up for years.

Some think of him as the narrator in Henry Miller's *Tropic of Capricorn*: "I had no more need of God than He had of me, and if there were one, I often said to myself, I would meet Him calmly and spit in His face."

Others think of him higher up the CONTEMPTIBLE PECKING ORDER than a simple, disrespectful, unyielding, blasphemous fellow.

The *Capricorn* phlegm *does* succeed in laying out a blueprint of the supposedly *old* Barton though. It does seem to capture the *Life of Brian* "very naughty boy" (with Barton as "Antichrist" rather than Messiah). It permits us to comb through Joey's past and wonder how the world operates when a man can go from cigar darts to head coach of a prestigious League One setup.

But maybe this is Andy Pilley's way of 'giving back to the community'. Maybe his old mate Joey (or Joe), who played <u>45 minutes</u> for Fleetwood against Kilmarnock six years ago, has displayed extraordinary humbleness, intuition and footballing acumen.

Maybe Barton has regaled Pilley with shrewd, authentic stories, Jack London tales, and the dirt and muster necessary to fire the fragile bones of the young Fleetwood Town squad he is set to inherit.

Perhaps the normally *rash* Virgo, in his brown, Cambridge get-up, has plunged into a parallel never-never land and wishes to make the most of his contacts in the game.

No one could blame Barton for wanting to progress, for jumping life's queue like a nepotistic, well-promoted boxer. But does he have the wherewithal? Does he have the self-discipline and ingenuity required for such a role?

The rather droll Rodrigo Ribaldo wrote in *The Guardian*'s <u>comments section</u> on 18th April: "He couldn't put on a coaching session to save his life. I've spoken to people about him and he can barely lay out cones."

Now, either the bare-faced lie "I've spoken to people about him" gets you here or the visual humour "can barely lay out cones". But underneath both is the serious question around suitability and competence.

Has Pilley hired a human wrecking ball intent on smashing up the impressive Highbury and Poolfoot Farm infrastructure? Has he handed over the head coach keys, complete with deluxe locker, to a truculent psychopath?

You want to believe in the 35-year-old *child manager* Barton. You want to think that standing in the technical area togged up in Italian threads may, ironically, help him focus and grow as a person (responsibility like a spring clean and telling harbinger).

André Villas-Boas he is not though; his 'sophisticates' membership unlikely to be rubber-stamped overnight (nor would he want it to be). He will remain the "reconstructed thug" to large parts of the public. He will find it hard to shake off the contorted image he has projected for over a decade.

Let's not for a second compare him to Eric Cantona in terms of philosophical weight, presence or stature; the 5' 9" Barton five inches shorter than his Marseille counterpart and five aeons from an ounce of the love that Cantona kindled.

What if, though, Barton wins his first four matches of the 2018/19 season? What if the Fleetwood Town players develop a perverse attachment to the man? What if Barton's post-match banter begins to take on a mythical dimension and becomes compulsory viewing?

The media and his detractors may, just *may*, for a *full* seven days regard him differently. They may start to examine his pitch-side body language and decide that people *do* change - indeed *thrive*.

Joey will never be a sensible man, but that does not preclude or disqualify him from being serious. Listening to and reading Barton in his different guises - the conformity he bemoans, the social tool kit he was never given by his otherwise loving father, the public appeal to his cousin and brother to turn themselves in following the 2005 murder of Anthony Walker – it is abundantly clear that he *does* have a conscience.

Perception can be everything though. And the Barton name – by association – in light of the tragic event in Huyton, Merseyside will reverberate in a negative sense for a long, long time.

Joey's own scraps and altercations do not help either. He has been culpable of error after error since turning professional in 2002.

Something in the Henry Winter *Telegraph* article from September 2014 suggests he has finally grown up, however. Something hints that the "saboteur" inside him may finally have departed.

His manner will never be 100% sweet as evidenced by his subsequent, short-lived spell at Ibrox, but *who wants* a compliant drip of a man, an unquestioning automaton? There are enough of those in the office world. God help us if they start to infiltrate the last bastion of working-class honour as well.

Barton has a fluent, cutting grace at times – something shelved and not welcomed during these politically correct times. If this can be gilded with a little humour then who knows what he's capable of?

Football has never actively recruited exemplary, flawless individuals. It only acts that way in starchy, specious circles and in front of the mic. By its very nature it attracts wolves, desperados and the odd genius.

In managerial terms, Barton currently sits in the former camp. He is unproven, untested and has pretty much slipped the wallet from Pilley's back pocket along with the chairman's car keys on the sideboard in the form of a three-year contract.

What *can* he offer though? What *does* he offer? He is refreshingly outspoken. He is not a media-trained bore whose era never truly began and therefore never actually ended.

He is, to break with journalistic convention, not a *pussy* or *sycophant* or *bootlicker*. And if his unhackneyed ideas bear fruit, then other Barton-esque managers may follow, and maybe even the occasional, unequivocal and forthright BME manager.

How Fleetwood Town will cope with Barton though is another matter. Because they are notoriously decorous and restrained when it comes to their public image. Under their last long-term coach, Uwe Rösler it was a little too *unweathered* at times and dainty.

On 2nd June 2018 when the FTFC staff line up to greet the 'Antichrist', some will be thinking that it might free up their own First Amendment concerns within the club, whereas others might simply think "*Fuck*, what have we done here?"

John Sheridan: Ordinary Man, Misunderstood, Underappreciated

BackPageFootball.com, 24 April 2018

He doesn't want to be there…in those early post-match interviews. He doesn't want to be part of the media cabaret.

He looks into the camera as if inconvenienced, as if besmirched by the token, horseshit questions.

It is that flat, bleak indifference that sets Sheridan apart, that says 'Accept me or walk away, because I'm not gonna adapt to *your* world, to this *charade*, this bloody *pantomime…*'

The man from the BBC knows what went on on the field. Sheridan knows what went on. So to pick the match apart, to overanalyse, is futile, insufferable.

Do you want me to be cooperative? Sheridan's ruddy face almost utters. Do you want me in aftershave, smooth as a cat, togged up like a grandmaster?

Disgust would be too strong a word, but Sheridan feels himself in Groundhog Day mode when addressed with flimsy, prosaic probing or debriefs.

I'd like to grip the handle on my fridge door at this very moment, his manner suggests. I'd like to rush out of here and slurp something cool; something much cooler than this mainstream tat.

Sheridan landed on the Fylde coast to cynicism and ire, to fans being underwhelmed by his appointment. *Johnny, Johnny, Johnny, Johnny Sher-id-an* – as the Leeds fans (myself included) used to chant – seemingly represented gruff inarticulacy, a man that meant nothing to the club, a fleeting saviour but with a pretty sketchy managerial win percentage once the hard work had been done.

'I'm very pleased with the performance' were the first words to come out of his mouth after his initial game in charge (1-1 vs MK Dons, 24th February), followed by 'Another good performance from us' (1-1 vs Plymouth, 10th March) and 'It was a good, battling performance' (0-0 vs Charlton, 17th March).

The word 'performance' sits at the roof of Sheridan's muzzle in a similar fashion to how a Cossack's tash drips from his upper lip. It is distinctive, yet worn, idiosyncratic, yet prostrate. The Lancashire/Yorkshire hybrid sees it as his way in though, his pass to the players' souls, his down-to-earth, I kid you not 'This is how we will win' navigation.

After Uwe Rösler's laboratory-run operation with its highs, lows and eventual, stagnant and ruinous 'uncoordinated mice' FTFC team (eight consecutive defeats offering testimony), Sheridan's directness, his unromantic patter, was perhaps needed.

But don't be fooled by the outer Sheridan, the surface Sheridan, the grey-mopped Sheridan who 15 months ago lavished the word 'c***' on match official, Matthew Donohue.

Sheridan's own footballing career – largely at Leeds, Sheffield Wednesday and Oldham - was one very much "dripping in sweet honey". His midfield roaming was exemplary, impeccable, laudable. His grace and fire combined to light up the pitch.

He was the first man – in the late 1980s - to show me what a midfield could be, what a midfield *should* be. Sheridan, the adored no.8, the free-kick specialist, the penalty taker, the linchpin and driving force at the heart of Elland Road, mostly did not need power, because he had accuracy and placement.

He could thread the ball into the net like a seamstress on LSD.

'Listen…listen…' he has a habit of saying, now stripped of those white-shorts days, now dauntless and pluckier in a different way, now festooned in managerial tracksuit and a creaking face.

It is the language of a godfather, of an insensitive baron, of a man born in *Stretford* rather than the Shakespearian *Stratford*-upon-Avon. But underneath that loose-calibre roar is a thinker, a man not completely devoid of his early panache.

Sheridan switched his Fleetwood Town formation on the evening of the 20th March 2018 away to Rochdale. He decided to employ striker, Ashley Hunter as a left-wing back and use *three* centre-halves. He decided to ditch the 4-4-2 that had earned a point a game and at least stopped the rot.

Such a subtle masterstroke is not always obvious at the time. It does not immediately sing to you. It does not lend itself to the whispering suspicion that a hidden door within the club has been found. And behind that door are the toys that Rösler refused to let the players indulge in.

The body language of the players immediately changed upon John Sheridan entering this club. The latter-day bent backs and gloom – depression at the thought of performing uncomfortable and illogical roles – were straightened out and re-injected with pride and a modicum of flair.

Toumani Diagouraga realised once more that he is an imposing figure to the opposition. Kyle Dempsey had his licence to burst forward renewed. And Jack Sowerby, all of a sudden, was allowed to participate and given proper support by his team mates who now digested the effectiveness of his quick-release, accurate passes.

5-3-2 gave Sheridan four consecutive victories and clean sheets leading into April (vs Rochdale, Northampton, AFC Wimbledon and Bristol Rovers). It re-engineered and re-wired a team on its backside with holes in its socks, unable to barely win a game of marbles, never mind a third tier football match.

The new role of Ashley Hunter, although not fully appreciated by the diminutive player himself, although not fully in keeping with the glory a striker seeks (explicitly and implicitly expressed in the club shop recently while signing shirts) *is* actually a win/win for the team: 1) Because it cures Fleetwood's problem at left back; 2) Because such a sacrifice has coincidentally landed Hunter the Sheridan-esque role of set-piece specialist (given the exclusion of midfielder, George Glendon).

It is a trade-off - perhaps not a conscious one, but one that should suit all parties. And this minor, yet significant tweaking of the team (a little like converting Leeds striker, Gary Kelly to right back many years ago) has acted as undoubted catalyst to Fleetwood's short-term transformation.

The stats are interesting under Sheridan. 4-4-2 has brought one win, three draws and one loss, whereas 5-3-2 has yielded four wins, no draws and one loss; the latter against a promotion-chasing Rotherham whose New York Stadium has an enviable record.

Fleetwood look their best when the wing-backs (Lewie Coyle, on loan from Leeds and Ashley Hunter) are in play; allowed to gallop, allowed to penetrate deep into opposition territory, yet also bite where necessary when covering back.

Here's where this story turns though. Because some clown decided to effectively delete this season's cache by announcing Fleetwood's next head coach with three games to play.

Some ill-informed, cerebral halfwit decided that it would be a good idea if the shadow of another man hung over John Sheridan while he was still seeing out the 2017/2018 season.

And while the kit men and laundry women were busy enacting such an incredulous, premature plan (secretly unstitching JS for JB), the players, all of a sudden, lost their new-found impetus and drive; they took Sheridan's very impressive and respectable Won 5, Drawn 3, Lost 2 record and killed it a little, bashed it against a wall; bowed, without effort or guile, to a third defeat under his stewardship.

Watching them in Saturday's penultimate home game versus Wigan (which ended in a dishevelled and dispiriting 4-0 reversal)…it was as if Rösler had snuck back into the building. It was as if the non-animated, hands in pockets, JS had given up (selecting what seemed to be a fluidless 4-5-1), or the players had *already* begun to fear the 2018/19 pre-season under JB (best that we don't say his *actual* name at this point).

Employee/employer relations are a delicate thing, but while the fans are perhaps looking forward to a likely exodus and influx of players, the existing personnel will be wondering just what chairman Andy Pilley has gone and done this time, what heartache is in store.

Because with Sheridan – as per his initial programme notes – you get "tough love", but with the other guy (JB) no one is quite sure. No one is entirely sure whether Pilley has even kept the dice on the table this time.

Fehler durch Technik at Fleetwood Town

Backpagefootball.com, 17 February 2018

They don't come here anymore to be enthralled. They don't come here to bounce around and breathe in wild flowers.

They come here to attend the Highbury wake. They come here to look at the embers of a once good Fleetwood Town side.

Heavy metal football was promised by the East German born head coach. But something got in the speakers. Something took over the strings of the guitars. Something clogged and suffocated the throat of the vocalist.

Local rags, frequented by kindergarten journalists, continue to court the official line, the North Korean-like propaganda ("Rösler salutes spirit"). But we know, *we know*, there is something dreadfully awry.

Six defeats in a row – four of them in the league – naturally stir the ire of the chairman. Make him listen to his lieutenant in a different way. Make him gaze across the boardroom table and begin to smell something other than aftershave.

Sample words do not help Rösler's cause. They do not hint at a pioneer, a trailblazer, an innovator or avant-garde manager. "We didn't want to play balls into the middle because [Shrewsbury] were very strong in midfield with their three players there."

We wanted to play basketball instead. We wanted to seemingly snuff out our strengths before the action had even begun.

Six shots against that latest foe. And only two of them on target.

We are no longer a Cod Army, but rather a tray of mussels ready to be consumed; mussels that we allow the opposition to sip their unoaked chardonnay to.

We have been flung on the back of a wagon. *Rag and bone! Rag and bone!* Disrespected and turned into droids.

For there is little humanity recognisable in this team. Little by way of freedom, risk and flair. Instead, we have *profiles*, high pressing and athleticism apparently.

We have pawned any skill that might have had the impudence to still loiter around Poolfoot Farm. But *hey*, we can *run*, we can *chase*, we can *blink* our eyes before the winter sky and go blind.

There were contaminated personalities on that pitch on Tuesday night. Players that have strayed so far from their identity that it will require a crime scene reconstruction.

Bobby Grant, that heavy oil tanker of a footballer, who once possessed great shooting boots. Now, there appears to be a dash of arrogance and blame.

Nathan Pond, that stalwart and ever-present phenomenon, but the final curtain call is close.

Toumani Diagouraga - still pointing at the floor.

Even the greats – Ashley Hunter, Kyle Dempsey and Conor McAleny - are being asphyxiated by this rotten Rösler railroad, this hopeless hustle towards 'success'.

"In the past, man has been first. In the future, the *SYSTEM* must be first." Has Rösler been swotting up on Frederick Winslow Taylor, the no-good scientific shyster who deadened humanity with the words efficiency and productivity?

One can only sneak into his house and check under his pillow. Question his family. Ask them *how* he eats his muesli.

The substitutions on Tuesday night said a lot about Rösler's frame of mind. In the 78th minute, before that fatal Shrewsbury second goal (82'), he brought on a full-back (Lewie Coyle) for a full-back (Gethin Jones) – the equivalent of picking a blade of grass from the Highbury turf.

What Fleetwood needed at that moment was the galloping Markus Schwabl, the West German buckaroo, the hair-in-your-face earthiness of our *real* protector and tempo man.

For what Schwabl did on Saturday, 6th January against Leicester City in the third round of the FA Cup has been unparalleled so far this season. His is not a *fine* art, but he can tackle. He can impose himself. He can wade into tight spots and come away with the ball.

He allows the craft of Dempsey, Hunter and McAleny to flourish.

When Andy Pilley, Fleetwood's chairman, next shuts his front door and settles down for tea, light banter and contemplation, he must be thinking some of these things. He must be thinking how his axe effectively came down on Micky Mellon after 50 months, Graham Alexander after 34 and Steven Pressley after barely 10.

And now, 18 months into Rösler's reign, how disappointment has manifested itself once more. On the pitch. In the crowd. In the boardroom. And even in the cry of the programme sellers.

One senses with Pilley that he needs to see style and self-belief. And neither of those characteristics are evident at the moment. The players have been drained of their souls. Perhaps over-coached. And if the source of this malaise is not rooted out soon, Fleetwood will fall down the chute into League Two.

Rösler's stats are the only thing keeping him standing at the moment. His 42.6% win percentage set against his predecessors' 38.6% (Alexander), 27.5% (Pressley) and 51.5% (Mellon; although largely non-league).

If those stats soften, however, and the aftershave gets weaker and weaker, then Rösler might find his car turned away at the training ground.

The Mystery of Toumani Diagouraga

BackPageFootball.com, 12 February 2018

In the 37th minute of the recent game against Scunthorpe United, Toumani Diagouraga – Fleetwood Town's latest signing – ran into a pack of players near the touchline and both benches.

Had he come out with the ball, dusted off his shirt slightly and exuded an air of Parisian polish, he would have been officially born as a Fleetwood player.

As it was, he returned to the centre of the park with nothing; a fork without a pea; an unsuccessful Navy SEAL job; a rare gamble that failed to enhance his reputation.

To look at the 6' 2", leggy 30-year-old and central midfielder is to see an imposing ebony wall, a blockade of sorts, a stopper and simple distributor of the ball.

He clearly has two good feet, the required calmness in such a role and the physical stature of a Mali god. And yet, teaming up with his boss of four years ago – Uwe Rösler, whilst at Brentford – has so far failed to yield any noticeable dividends.

One browses Toumani's Twitter feed and can't help but see a unique, compassionate individual set on improving the world. Beaten up 87-year-old grandmothers, Martin Luther King Jr, Cyrille Regis, Clarke Carlisle, #kickitout, Cerebral Palsy/Great Ormond Street Hospital – you name it and the giant Frenchman is adding his voice to the cause.

And look at *any* group photograph and you will notice Toumani's bountiful smile. He quite simply exudes a cheer and generosity we should all learn from.

Has such charity inadvertently seeped into his play though? Has the courteous no.16 forgotten the blessed rule amongst footballers? *Thou shall show no mercy once crossing the white line.*

Mark Warburton, Rösler's successor, said of Diagouraga in April 2015:

"Toumani is almost the pulse of the team. He can keep the shape and pick up the second ball. I can't speak highly enough about [him]."

When Fleetwood Town, as a club, recently fell ill – losing far too many games in a league season – the doctor's prescription read: "Needs a nucleus – a core."

If Toumani Diagouraga (such a poetic, pronounceable name once you get the hang of it) is to be that core, that linchpin, hub and vital component then he needs to find his self-belief once more – something which Warburton referred to in relation to his consistency and dominance.

He needs to remember one of the proudest weekends of his life (2nd-3rd May 2015) when Brentford made the Championship play-offs and he was named Supporters' Player of the Year.

But he also – quite crucially – needs to replace such memories, such award-filled lustre (glass trophies weighing down his arms and shimmering against his slick, three-piece suit and spotted tie) with thoughts of Fleetwood Town and what he can bring to this precocious club.

So far, he has been five yards away from the action. An observer. A twitcher. The soft-hearted General reluctant to rip into the opposition. One could argue that if you're the 'pick up man', the second ball winner, then that's exactly where you should be.

But that would be disingenuous. That would insult the man that Diagouraga was at previous clubs: Hereford United; Peterborough United; Brentford; Leeds United; Plymouth Argyle.

Toumani needs to be *involved*. He needs to show the Highbury faithful that he *is* the action, a script *writer* instead of the passive, unassertive gentle giant we have seen thus far.

He needs to *settle*, get Plymouth out of his head – a clearly enjoyable chapter in his footballing career and a club three times bigger than Fleetwood in terms of fans.

It is perhaps no coincidence that six out of the eight bottom sides in League One currently have the worst attendances in the division (Oldham, AFC Wimbledon, Blackpool, Bury, Rochdale and Fleetwood).

This says much about entitlement, belief and divine right. It also, inevitably, feeds into the minds of the players, makes them question their underlying stature and the level of achievement that is realistic.

Good players live beyond simple reciprocation with a vociferous crowd though. They harness conviction, the dreams of a club irrespective of size, and a deep tenet that insists this is *their* field of play, *their* territory and no sucker from elsewhere is going to drive things.

Fleetwood currently have the fifth worst defence in the division (48 goals conceded). They have an unusually poor home record (Won 4, Drawn 4, Lost 7). Some of the sparkle and pizzazz has gone AWOL.

Head coach Rösler has tinkered with the formation (from 5-3-2 to 4-3-3) yet still been left with a vulnerable side.

New recruits Kevin O'Connor at left back, Paddy Madden up front and Gethin Jones as defensive cover, following the departure of want-a-ways Devante Cole (to Wigan) and Amari'i Bell (to Blackburn), have revitalised the side yet it is *two players*, two *different* recruits, that Fleetwood's short-term future rests in the hands of: 20-year-old centre half, Charles Oliver, on-loan from Manchester City, and the central protagonist of this article, Toumani Diagouraga (who moved up north to be with his family).

If this spine gets it right (with Chris Neal behind it and Conor McAleny ahead of it) then there *is* hope. Oliver, during his brief tenure / few minutes on the pitch so far – serendipitously thrust into the limelight due to a red card – has demonstrated strength, positioning, awareness and skill.

He has instantly looked like one of those centre-halves you dream of in terms of being commanding and confident. If he can keep his head and somehow, through his youthful swagger, inspire the man-mountain ahead of him then Fleetwood might thrive once more.

In the aftermath of the postponed game at Rochdale on Saturday, 10th February, The Cod Army finds itself just three precarious points off relegation. Times are becoming desperate indeed.

But Rösler must know *something* of Toumani's character. He must know that his steel will eventually come through. That the pulse which Highbury has long sought is just minutes away from registering on the oximeter.

Diagouraga has sacrificed a lot by moving up north. He has jettisoned Home Park (capacity 17,800) for Highbury (5,327). He has admirably put family first in what is a challenging and lonely profession at times. In slowly coming to terms with such magnanimity and largesse, however, he must now start to produce.

For this beautiful club in the north west of England. For this tiny, yet impressive outlier on the footballing map.

He must close that gaping hole in the middle of the park and home in on the opposition. For five yards in football is the equivalent of John o'Groats to Land's End.

Haughton Holocaust at Fleetwood Fans' Forum

BackPageFootball.com, 1 September 2017

This is where it happens. Where chairman Pilley switches from orange to beer. Where talk of individual brilliance is strictly forbidden. Where the team mantra is constantly ploughed.

This is where faces and lips give away more than they ever envisaged. Where the subtle demands and immediacy of those present get *something* of value. Between the lines. In the unspoken pauses and hesitations of the Fleetwood Town masters sat shirted and scrubbed.

Steve Curwood. Andy Pilley. Uwe Rösler. Grétar Steinsson. And the fleeting appearance of players Cian Bolger and Bobby Grant. One reserved, Irish and quiet before an audience, the other relaxed and affable – a Scouse comedian.

Forum. noun. 1. a meeting or medium where ideas and views on a particular issue can be exchanged. 2. [NORTH AMERICAN] a court or tribunal.

Which is this? Probably the former given Fleetwood's fine start. No grilling for Rösler. No sharp damnation for Pilley. Just merriment and the intermittent chorus of communal applause.

An easy night. A jokey night. In the wanton racket of FTFC's plot to reach the Championship though something almost dark and poignant (the chairman's head bowed as Rösler powwowed):

"I spoke to Nick [Haughton] at the end of last season. I think every manager or every head coach has a certain way to play…and errm…err…we set out, since I came here, we set out a clear profile on our players we want to bring to the football club, in which age group we wanted to bring to the club and I think that was in line with Grétar [Steinsson] and with the chairman and…and Nick is not really in that profile…

"You talk about high pressing, you talk about quick transition, you talk about athleticism and Nick is a very, very big talent, technically very good….but Nick needs players around him to let him shine and I personally have a different philosophy…errmm…and this is why Nick found it hard to get regular playing time.

"End of last season I spoke to Nick...and said Nick is 23-years-old, I think it's very important now that you play regular football and unfortunately I can't guarantee you regular playing time here...and this is, since then he is looking to find a club...he is contracted with us and I'm sure the type of player he is, the quality he has, I think he has his admirers and...ermm, I'm sure...ermmm...in the near future we will tell you where Nick will play football...either on loan or on permanent..."

That is the problem. When you sit before the hordes. When you get them giddy on discounted £2 beer. Some among them will press. For simple answers that you'd rather lock away. Or code in Anglo-German ambiguity. Press. Better than the press itself. Better than the watered-down fluffballs that emit Value-brand sentences from the offices of *Johnston* Press.

But I admire you. For doing it. For sitting it out. For confronting the often *grunting* public. For allowing us to see the human in you. Your folds and breaks and startlingly even-handed exposé.

We sometimes swim through murky rivers. But then they clear. Then the real sounds and sights hit our ears and eyes. The real, in this case, that macabre word 'profile' – the straight-backed cousin of spew and silt and all those soulless words that cavort before us.

So what of Nicholas George Haughton, born 20 September 1994? *Soon to be* 23 years of age, Uwe, but not there yet. What of his skills and panache? Could his assets not be harnessed, his weaknesses tapered down? His *profile* enhanced?

I agree – he is the kind that occasionally gets busted up, but wasn't he the perfect missile at times, wasn't he the DARPA .50 calibre EXACTO bullet able to turn corners and ridicule dumbfounded defenders when in full flow? Wasn't his balance like that of the Romanian beam great, Nadia Comăneci?

You must know that he *will* come back to haunt us. That when you were speaking Pilley's desperately downbeat mien almost whispered, nay, cried "*Mon amour!!!*"

You have keyed the chairman's finest vehicle. You have ruined and trashed people's desire to sit on the edge of their seats. In anticipation. In excitement. Elation. Delirium. Zeal. Zest. For we had – still have – another Josh Morris, another flair maestro capable of buffeting the ordinary, capable of oscillation and turbulence and fire.

And what have you done? You have thrown him down. Left him on the pavement. Offered him the meagre succour of "important now that you play regular football".

People have been jailed for lesser felonies.

In the conflagration of Nick Haughton, you have wandered over to the dark side and gobbed a fat pool of spittle upon the shoes of every romantic Fleetwood Town fan. You have given brazen recourse to those that would push a world of clones, a *profiled* army, the computerised and sickening sangfroid of the unsentimental.

These are dangerous times, Mr Rösler. More dangerous than your "Two-nil" assertion concerning a team's peak vulnerability. And sometimes the whole of the Fleetwood Town top brass let us down with their Puma/Carling *political correctness*, their miserly and parsimonious interviews.

But not tonight. Tonight you gave us mounds of information. Tonight you were perhaps flummoxed by your own generosity. Away from the tailgating norms of corporate culture. Away from the jejune junk of dutiful jamborees.

Tonight you talked about us having the youngest squad in the league, you talked about long-term contracts, not needing "ten, nine, eight new players each season". You revelled in your worship of Godswill Ekpolo's tenaciousness – our defender's very *honest* bruising of others (even his own team mates!).

It was wonderful to hear. Your respect for the departed David Ball. Your precise understanding that we must "control games" in order to reach "the next level".

I see that. I see it with my own eyes. Billy Crellin, our number three goalkeeper, for England (Under-18s) as well. A significant call-up. A prestigious landmark.

The whisper in Conor McAleny's ear. The future of Amari'i Bell ("We don't get bullied by bigger clubs," Herr Steinsson insisted…for a moment surrendering his Icelandic roots). Scouts. The ground's footprint. The music we come out to – Fleetwood Mac's *Dreams*, a special song to Pilley and *no loud, undemocratic voice will change that!*

It's good. I hear it. And ten years from now – where will we be? Step forward chairman Pilley with a reluctant but coherent answer:

"Awfully long time. My dream scenario would be...I would love to be comfortable in the Championship, with an increased fan base, with local players coming through to the first team.

"I'd like to be a club that can...err...sustain its own...can stand on its own two feet and is not reliant on one man, me, me, writing a big cheque every day because again I just think it's in the best interest of the club that it can stand on its own two feet...and again the model that we have now is we sign players who are on the...that upward curve.

"And what will happen naturally if we continue to do as well as we are. We'll have admirers and it becomes very difficult...errmm...to stand in a player's way. And we had this a few years ago with a certain one in the Premier League...when a club comes along and offers him ten times his current wage and offers him the chance to move up three or four divisions...then I feel obliged as custodian of the club.

"One of the reasons why we sign these players is...we want to be that football club, that stepping stone that can help them to the Premier League or to the very top of the Championship. We want to see them on Match of the Day, we want to see them in an England strip, performing at a top level.

"And that would be my target – to be comfortable in the Championship, to have bigger crowds, to be trading well, and having a sustainable football club."

The mortar in that talk. The mortar between those bricks that you provided us. It had sufficient hydrated cement. But still, the Haughton holocaust concerns me.

Keep him for the damn bench. Put him through his paces. Make him an army conscript. But show the lad *something*. A bean. A conditional contract. A pen with its top off and Pilley's hand wavering at the end of the desk.

You know when he enters the field of play that the uppity defence of the opposition flags and wonders whether it can last those final twenty minutes.

Strengthen him. Throw him in a boxing ring. Hit him with a garden gate. But don't let him go.

The news! The news! Always interrupting long reads! Make sure he returns from <u>Chorley</u>!

Because players with sparkle don't often come along. Those who you love that send shocks through your system, who charm you and fascinate you and engage you – who have you feeling weak and defenceless in the presence of their impalpable magic – are a once-in-a-decade deal.

Don't forget that, Mr Rösler. Don't forget.

The Bally and Proctor Rotherham Roadshow

BackPageFootball.com, 3 August 2017

It is unlikely that the fair-haired assassin – birth name, David Michael Ball – will do an Emmanuel Adebayor knee-slide towards his former admirers this Saturday should he score at Fleetwood Town's Highbury ground.

It is more probable that he will simply hit the mute button, celebrate a little inside – if at all – and then de-mob himself from his new Rotherham teammates before quietly making his way back to the other side of the field.

If there *is* vigour of a kind, then it cannot be criticised as Bally gave this club something it had briefly missed following the departure of Jamie Vardy: a talisman.

Lest we forget that Vardy exited this town on 17 May 2012 and just two months later, on 23 July 2012, Bally arrived in order to take up the grand mantle.

Aura players *do* exist and whilst Bally has plied his trade in the lower leagues, he is not too dissimilar to Eric Cantona or Zlatan Ibrahimović or Edin Džeko in terms of magic and sparkle and scintillating brilliance.

Such words will embarrass him as he is neither the obvious mythical rogue nor the gargantuan presence of those other fellows. What he is, however, is inventive, artistic and resourceful – a player capable of plucking a ball from nothing and laying it to rest in the sheath of the goal net.

Ball, the 2015 FIFA Puskas Award Nominee, courtesy of his sublime, 20-yard lob against Preston in March of that year, is an enigma to some, the man who started off life at Manchester City yet has had to content himself with the less popular brands of Swindon, Peterborough and Rochdale.

When he found Fleetwood, he finally found a home – an audience that lauded his gifts and understood that his celebrations were actually *theirs*; that his bones were merely an extension of their own calcified greatness.

The *everyman* that is Ball, with his slightly arched back and floppy froth of hair, <u>originally left Fleetwood in May 2015</u> before Andy Pilley and Graham Alexander came to their senses weeks later (in time for the 2015/16 season) and slapped a contract of sorts on the chairman's pre-Poolfoot Farm desk.

Such worries have now disintegrated. Fleetwood fans recognise that marginalised ships *do* pass in the night and in that moment, that moon-speckled five years, both club and player had it good.

Bally has been part of some big, heroic matches for the Cod Army. None more so than the League Two Play-Off final versus Burton Albion in May 2014.

The cult hero at the time, Antoni Sarcevic might have scored the decisive goal. The dependable captain, Mark Roberts might have grabbed the Wembley trophy before anyone else. But Ball's name cropped up again and again. He <u>combed the field</u> like a ladykilling grasshopper:

"Ball. Ball. Ball. Half-chances, but you forgave him. Because he was there. Because he had an Ian Rush-like radar. Because he ghosted into positions that other players couldn't comprehend."

Other matches singe the neurons: FTFC vs Yeovil in April 2015 when another promotion was still a distinct possibility. But Fleetwood's debut in the third tier of English football against Crewe (9 August, 2014) is the most significant of all. Not just because such a day was unimaginable when the <u>windows</u> used to fall out at Highbury, but because Bally had – what was to be – a rare 45 minutes with his current strike-partner, Jamie Proctor; a second half in which they *both* scored.

Indeed. This is where 'Procs' comes in – first match for Fleetwood and all.

The <u>BBC</u> claimed Proctor "powered a second [goal]" that day. Such are the scant, indolent reports from the big networks that you could be forgiven for thinking that his shot was a regular, slightly hard hit drive. In the *real* world, away from the champagne journalists, <u>this happened</u>:

"Proctor – hanging around on the left, expending little energy, clever, a quiet ebullience to him, prodigious. Suddenly – bang! The top right corner of the net bulging. Faces amongst the track-suited ranks of Fleetwood's youth spellbound, pleasantly traumatised."

It was the closest thing to a slam dunk in football that you'll ever see.

At that moment I thought *This is the man – the player to steer Fleetwood forward. Slight arrogance, the physique of a Roman gladiator and misunderstood verve.* Why had he tossed away the last few months at Crawley Town after residing at historic clubs such as Preston North End and Swansea City though?

A double hernia it seems during his Deepdale days, plus a bulging Swansea squad.

David Ball once said of Procs: "He can be anything". Swansea chairman, Huw Jenkins – referring to his manager, Michael Laudrup's planned revolution – said: "Our aim is to establish a promising group of youngsters".

But then Proctor was horse traded five months later to the lesser known manager, Richie Barker at Crawley and fell into oblivion.

'Promising' has been the word long associated with Proctor. Even now, aged 25, he simply looks the part – carries himself like a roving executioner. But he didn't do it at Fleetwood, or wasn't allowed to. Bradford and Bolton didn't work out either.

Have Rotherham cannily brought together the strike partnership which was supposed to work three years ago at Fleetwood? Have they understood that modest goal ratios don't always carry through to a player's next side? Has a club *finally* recognised "the best sweets in the pack"?

I have seen many a fine debut in my 30 years of watching live professional football or at least witnessed the entrance of what I would call an 'aura' player: Eric Cantona making his Leeds United bow at Boundary Park on 8 February 1992; Tony Yeboah briefly taking to the field at home to QPR on 24 January 1995; and Rio Ferdinand making his first Elland Road start on 16 December 2000.

With these players there was a mix of the unexpected, the devastating and the supreme. They were on another planet. Bally and Procs are mere earthlings by comparison, but that does not stop me fearing them if they happen to be loitering on the edge of Fleetwood's 18-yard box at the weekend.

Both are capable of jolting the opposition. Both are lower league mavericks that rip up the rule book when necessary.

Saturday, 5 August 2017 will be – although not many people realise it – a titanic day. The return of one former servant is fortunate, if a little frightening. The return of two, an *unusual event* indeed.

Fewer people warmed to Proctor (compared to Bally) during his days at Highbury. The suggestion was that he was lazy – a snoozer from time to time. For the sake of such talent, I hope that motivation is no longer a problem. I hope that he does what he was supposed to do at Fleetwood. Score goals.

The signs are good. In the <u>Yorkshire friendly</u> versus Barnsley on Saturday, 29 July, Proctor bagged a second half eight-minute hat-trick. And Bally is no slouch either having put away six in six pre-season.

Will these stats terrify the Cod Army back three, Cian Bolger, Nathan Pond and Ashley Eastham?

It depends. If Fleetwood have outlets of their own. If we can unearth another talisman on Saturday when the real stuff begins.

Pre-Season Paucity at Fleetwood Town

BackPageFootball.com, 31 July 2017

Is it worth getting up at 6am to write about the lumpen procession that most good-hearted Fleetwood Town fans witnessed on Friday night (versus Preston North End)? Is it worth the analysis and toil in trying to figure out how that same, fetid team the Saturday before against Bolton Wanderers managed to leave the field with a good degree of pride?

"We lost experience [over the summer]. We lost good players with experience. And in those situations experience helps you to stabilise the ship," manager Uwe Rösler commented after the 5-1 drubbing on a rain-soaked night.

Nights tend to be crueller than days when things go bad. A player can hide his honest expression in a dark corridor away from the full gaze of accountability, but what he can't escape is the Dracula-esque sense that he's had the blood drained from him.

What won't come out in a candid way, despite the "young squad…learning curve" rationalising from Rösler, is the fact that midfielder Jimmy Ryan and striker David Ball – players of good repute – were offered meagre contracts to stay; Ryan, the post-injury 'stinker' of an annual income whittled down so much that he could barely afford a new beard trimmer and Ball – the only player to participate in all <u>46 league games</u> last season (39 starts) – top scorer with 14 goals, effectively hit around the chops with a dockside fish when in negotiations.

For Ball and the sake of his career, it was probably time to leave anyway. He has been an incredible servant to Fleetwood – five years of love and the occasional, irrepressible shot which left a keeper dumped on his derriere. This is the moment at 27 years of age when he either 'does the business' in a grandstand season elsewhere (Rotherham) or becomes a squad player kicking his heels in the stands. Such is the spotlight on a striker that each game is critical.

With Ryan, he decided to cross the divide – move from Fleetwood to the somewhat derelict set up at Blackpool. Not exactly like moving from Celtic to Rangers à-la-Mo Johnston, albeit with a two-year stint in between at Nantes, in the late 1980s but still high risk.

You never get a smile from Jimmy. Even when he's shaking hands with Blackpool's chief executive, Alex Cowdy – donned in his James

Dean white T-shirt – Jimmy looks glum. What he initially brought to Highbury though was bite, possession, strength and the eye for a long-range shot. This diluted the longer he was at Fleetwood – for some reason going into his shell and becoming more defensive – but one does wonder what a Kyle Dempsey-Jimmy Ryan partnership could have produced for 2017/18.

Fleetwood have pretty much dispensed with the idea of a roughhouse midfielder it would now seem. Perhaps modern tactics have stolen the show. Perhaps yellow cards are an unwanted consequence of such inclusion (Conor McLaughlin, the yellow card king last season with a total of 10, was the other player of "experience" to leave, but he was a full back).

When you think of the players that have trod the Highbury turf in a proud, battling, partisan fashion, however – Jeff Hughes, Alan Goodall, Matty Blair, Eggert Jónsson, Jimmy Ryan – it is easy to get sentimental over a cruncher, an all-out fighter and tear-up merchant. What do Fleetwood now do when they're being overrun?

Preston danced between our XI on Friday night as if they'd vaporised us, as if we were no longer physical entities or footballers willing to put our bodies on the line. Bobby Grant's out-of-character expletive in the 76th minute ("F*cking tackle back!!") summed up the impotence of the situation, the embarrassing charade, the witless gallops of the team clad in red and white.

What probably came to pass during such a torturous evening was the realisation that 2-0 against Bolton (the previous Saturday) was a smokescreen, a misleading result which reflected the Trotters ineptitude rather than our own velvety greatness. We looked *settled* on that fine afternoon, *established* one might say – not given to panic or chasing unnecessary causes. But…but…looking back, it would probably be wise to stick £100 on Bolton being relegated from the Championship than ourselves making the League One play-offs.

This isn't a massively different Fleetwood team to the one that finished the 2016/17 season against a superior Bradford side. Think Nathan Pond for Ben Davies, Lewie Coyle for Conor McLaughlin, Jordy Hiwula for Ashley Hunter. And Conor McAleny for David Ball. But, in those replacements, despite the quality on show versus Bolton, you sense slightly less polish.

Pond, the old warrior, has been around since Henry VIII and continues to provide grit and leadership of a sort, but against clever opposition does he have the required pedigree to really understand the formation coming at him? Coyle looks tenacious and composed, but he is attempting to fill big Irish boots.

Hiwula appears classy and able to float, but he was a yard off the pace against Preston (message to the Huddersfield loanee: pulling out of dangerous tackles in a pre-season friendly is fine, but you still need to chase things down in a determined manner). As for McAleny – he has looked refreshingly bold, a wanderer extraordinaire with a sweet right foot. But will he be snuffed out of games when given little service from the midfield?

There is a *bigger* question here though: Will Fleetwood be able to cope in a more threatening League One now that Wigan, Blackburn, Rotherham, Portsmouth and Plymouth have joined the fray? Will those first three teams be depressed or looking to return to their rightful spots in the Championship?

And as for the south coast heavyweights promoted from League Two – will they undoubtedly want more success? The simple answer to this is that they will *all* be ravenous – capable of locking Fleetwood in solitary confinement if we allow it by believing that an organised unit is sufficient, enough, ample...resistance when faced with a more skilful opposition.

There were shortcomings on Friday. Yes – it *was* against a team one division higher up, but in that 2nd half massacre a few truths were seen blowing around the pitch and in the stand; facts that Uwe Rösler *had* hoped would stay locked in his personal Fleetwood safe:

1. The heavy metal football, à-la-Jürgen Klopp, has not yet arrived. Sometimes, the opposition has more energy and sprightliness which kind of disrupts such a plan.
2. Left back, Amari'i Bell was awarded the (Fleetwood) Man of the Match award on Friday for effectively NOT bombing forward. Every fan in the ground knows what this man is capable of – indeed, it is the *duty* of a wing back to threaten the opposition – yet we rarely see such a sight.
3. Victor Nirennold, the long-legged Rennes giant, is rotting on the bench and by being played out of position when used as a

substitute (at right back). His bark flakes off in the manner of a neglected tree on a daily basis. If Rösler *cannot* convert him back to his beloved position of central midfield, then this roaming giant deserves a train ticket to a more welcoming place.

4. The purer the footballing technique, the easier on the eye it is, but if there's no stampede up front then such efforts easily descend into the drab, mechanistic ways of international football (boring art with no soul). Fleetwood need to combine liveliness with dominance if they are to truly achieve.

The loss of McLaughlin and Ball has apparently left only Nathan Pond as a 'talker' in the dressing room. This is a worry for two reasons. Firstly, Pond is accepted as part of the old guard and may not be the best man to forage a way forward in what is a different era now. Secondly, there is no longer a commanding voice at the coal face (up front) but rather a gazillion juveniles: McAleny (24), Hiwula (22), Devante Cole (22), Wes Burns (22), Hunter (21).

If these players are incapable of venting or articulating their frustration and requirements to the midfield behind them – Kyle Dempsey (21), Bobby Grant (27), George Glendon (22) – then we are left with a corporate dressing room with too much power in the hands of the manager (head coach Uwe Rössler), technical director (Grétar Steinsson) and director of player development (Stuart Murdoch).

For this is the *real* danger – that kids taught to respect their elder peers, the systems and methods of the management in place and the fortune bestowed upon them courtesy of such rich training facilities will *not* speak up when the tactics are wrong, the player selection wrong and the hunger out of kilter.

Friday night was a spectacle – a spectacle for the wrong reasons (certainly in the 2nd half). Too many sets of feet were taken off the gas. Too many players sub-contracted their responsibilities. I was all set to write a flattering piece on the seamless transition from the McLaughlin/Ball era to the Coyle/McAleny one, but then a bunch of fraudsters wandered out after the half time break as if jangling around in the hood.

Togetherness was absent. Leadership was absent. Penetration was absent. What I saw was a collection of icebergs content to bob along the surface of the pitch in the hope that *someone else* would rescue them or clatter into the land opposite. Even Dempsey was absent at times – now *that is* rare, our most important player, perhaps dispirited, perhaps crumpled by the averageness around him. Dempsey – the 21-year-old, but with the maturity of someone five years older.

Let's hope no one gets hold of a video of this performance which would be on the cutting room floor of *any* self-respecting studio. What it shows is how easy it is to go from satisfaction (vs Bolton) to hurt (vs Preston) – both in the crowd and hopefully in the dressing room afterwards. If you peg your life or general happiness to football then there would have been a tortured scream through the car window driving home Friday night, the feeling that a cull of talent and belief had taken place.

Is it time to maybe bring in a water carrier, a tireless engine in the midfield area in order to free up wave after wave of attack or will Rösler hold firm in the belief that Dempsey, Grant and Glendon are sufficient to orbit around providing the 'flyers' (wing backs Bell and Coyle) are working effectively?

German minds are always efficient. If something is 1mm out of place, then rest assured such intellect usually spots it. The concern for Rösler perhaps is that his team is now short of leaders. Nobody wants a Ryan bollocking a Ball of course as happened in 2016/17 when Ball apparently failed to track back, but a sense that *someone* knows how to turn things around when the storms hit would be nice – immeasurably better than monitoring the directionless zombies that trotted across the Highbury turf between 8.30pm and 9.15pm Friday gone.

Some of the players against Preston, in their heads, were evidently still messing about with paddles or white water rafting in Austria. The bond-forming purpose of such escapism is all well and good, but when you're ripped apart a week before the season begins it's time to put down the paddle.

Against FC United of Manchester on Tuesday, 1st August there will be neediness now – the chance to see if any of the squad's second string can outdo what has become quite a fixed and rigid first team XI (locked down by Rösler's unwavering, yet at times byzantine precision).

There has always been a secret playlist at Fleetwood with the names of promising 'upstarts' ready to swing into position should we require them. Top of that list previously was Nick Haughton – singled out by Alex Ferguson as the player most likely to make great strides.

Perhaps now the names Ashley Nadesan and Jack Sowerby should be bugging head coach Rösler, using up his ink and demonstrating that thrust of a different kind to Friday *does* exist.

Either that or we stash a load of steroids in Ashley Hunter's locker and hope that he doubles in size overnight.

Fleetwood Town – End of the Unbeaten Run

Backpagefootball.com, 14 March 2017

What happened here? Which monster spread its slime over Highbury's immortal turf? Who exactly slaughtered our merry team? Why the subsidence of a 4-2 reverse?

Was it the peculiar line-up with Victor Nirennold as roving, right wing-back and Conor McLaughlin – its usual incumbent – trusted in central midfield? Was it the physicality of the opposition which left us intimidated and shorn? Or maybe Premier League referee and Wiganer, Paul Tierney who chose to stop/start this match like a Hollywood film set?

None of these really. More the set-piece blunders and gaffs which had us imploding, out of character, weak, separate in our aims and team ethics.

Were Bolton Wanderers good? If you consider "stubborn" good, then yes. If you consider morphing between roughhouse tactics and big baby antics effective, then yes – yes they were.

It was a couple of craggy 30-year-olds that had Fleetwood Town unravelling: Glenville Adam James Le Fondre with his "freak" 17th-minute cross-cum-shot and David James Wheater – free to roam the Cod Army's penalty area in the 20th minute like an invisible gorilla.

How did such incredulous cruising come about? Through fear? A normally unflappable defence losing its bearings? Wheater hypnotising our rear-guard?

Perhaps now is the time when reality kicks in. When the loss of 'The Don' Nathan Pond begins to tell. One can't help but wonder that had central defender, Pond and recently-departed striker, Aaron Amadi-Holloway been present on Saturday then we would at least have dished out an equal amount of bruises.

But such a game has now gone. C'est la vie. That is life. "We go again," as the Fleetwood faithful regularly exhort.

The match between The Trawlermen and The Trotters was the most significant at Highbury for an aeon, however, and so post-mortems must be carried out. We cannot just put this 4-2 loss down to mistakes and playing a team who looked and acted as if they were on weekend release.

The forensics point to lackadaisical defending from, first, Cian Bolger, then Conor McLaughlin, then Victor Nirennold and finally Bolger (again).

From the outset, you could see that Bolger was not his usual relaxed self. He had the air of someone conscious of his ex-employer coming to town – an unwelcome visitor scrutinising his current talents and bringing along 1000+ critics to boot.

Fleetwood fans know who the *new* Cian Bolger is. They know how he has grown and filled the immense boots of the injured Nathan Pond in terms of leadership. But Bolton fans do not. Just as they do not know what a wonderful shot stopper and flying ace keeper Alex Cairns is.

If anyone is to be forgiven a bad day at the office though, then it is Bolger. For his efforts thus far. For his commanding performances – headers, goals, the whole gamut of centre half assets including his improved distribution.

What went wrong on Saturday?

It would be ungracious – if sorely tempting – to deny that BWFC have any players of esteem in their post-Zach Clough squad. The returning Darren Pratley – regularly vilified during those days when I had an occasional seat at the Reebok Stadium (now Macron) – seemed to offer composure to this team. His football was always misunderstood to the naked eye, to the non-holistic gaze; his diagonal scampering frowned upon for its lack of end product.

But his polish at the weekend plus Josh Vela's darting silkiness, Gary Madine's Wolverine-like performance and Filipe Morais's flair and obvious self-belief suggests that Bolton might have turned the corner at the right time in order to appease their disgruntled fans who seek a better art form.

As for Fleetwood, they needed a couple of pickpockets on Saturday – players capable of defensive penetration. George Glendon and Cameron Brannagan, introduced respectively in the 51st and 71st minute, souped-up the pinball machine that is FTFC's midfield at its finest.

There was a better sense of stewardship around the centre circle once McLaughlin had reverted back to his recognised position which probably indicated that Uwe Rösler got this game tactically wrong before the whistle.

Sure, Bolton sat back, employed our counter-attacking style together with their unique form of Wimbledon-esque lumping the ball forward, but Fleetwood's inadequate riposte and inability to cut out Morais's skilled deposits/assists to Wheater, Mark Beevers and finally Le Fondre dented – for an afternoon – the Cod Army's invincibility and imperiousness.

Have we been living on luck? Have we conveniently forgotten our hammering at the hands of Bradford City on Tuesday, 14th February which could have ended by the same scoreline but miraculously finished 2-1 in Fleetwood's favour?

No. Because we have become a team. A team without stars. A gang of cloaked assassins who, together, mostly get it right.

"We have got to show [the] character to get back," goal-scorer Kyle Dempsey commented in the aftermath of the Bolton fall.

He is right. And just 10 matches remain now. 900 minutes. Fifteen hours. Two full, merciless days to the average working man. Graft, skill, luck and surety. That is usually the way of things.

The coach ride down to Walsall should provide ample opportunity to train the mind once more.

The Great Fleetwood Town Lunatic Asylum

BackPageFootball.com, 21 February 2017

There are to be no reports of Fleetwood Town's miracle season. There are to be no suggestions that this team of German-guided missiles will go to Scunthorpe soon and blow the bloody doors off their former manager's office.

Nor should there be implicit thoughts around the Cod Army's new cult centre-half, Cian Bolger gaining revenge over The Trotters who failed to appreciate his nutting the clouds (and every ball that comes his way).

Fleetwood! We could say that you are joint third with those Boltonians and that the play-offs are no longer tantalising enough. But we won't. For fear of jinxing the mission. For fear of letting the oxygen out of the players' heads.

For fear of blinding the club coach driver's window with graffitied words sprayed from a canister marked 'HOPE'.

No. There is to be none of this. We must lie flat and quietly regain our true bearings. Mid table! Over the moon to finish mid table. That is what you should hear. You pumper-uppers. You bandwagon fakes. You worshippers of minnows that jettison their small backpacks and circumvent normal aspirations.

We will *not* get promoted. There is no story here. So walk away. Leicester City is the yo-yo you need to follow. Or Brighton & Hove Albion – better sea air. The Fylde coast is particular about who it invites over.

The spine of our team does not matter. Goalkeeper, Alex Cairns probably *could* have joined the circus given his prodigious leaps and poetic, reaction saves. But he opted for the animals here; chief among them and ahead of him – no.12 Cian Bolger, no.34 Kyle Dempsey and no.10 David Ball.

You need not ask how the invisible piece of string keeps these artists together. Suffice to say, they are unhurried in their exploits. And they will be equally unhurried when you venture round with your grotesque suitcases of money.

Like I said – *no story here.* No great goals to speak of. Just the odd, flavoursome pot-shot.

We do not have one of the best training facilities in the country. Just imagine it as a shack or warehouse. Nothing to see here. No Andy Pilley balcony from which to study his troops. No pristine pitches. No spotless interior exemplifying the calmness that Uwe Rösler has instilled.

No. Nothing like that. Just an old seaside town that once had grand plans and the North Euston Hotel to put up posh, travelling guests.

You will see nothing now though. No ingenious formations (3.5-4.5-2). No 'Never Say Die'. No rotation of strikers (the names Devante Cole, Ashley Hunter, David Ball and Wes Burns figments of your imagination).

And no wing-backs already in the clutches and minds of Championship clubs (Conor McLaughlin and Amari'i Bell mere cyphers or ghosts which you should ignore and get back to your winter walk).

So you see – there is nothing to strip. Except your wife if she is in the mood later.

Fleetwood is a barren wasteland with only 27,000 inhabitants and barely 3,000 fans. The M6 will take you past us. We are not even here. Most days there is no one on reception when you ring that great bell.

If you compare us to those brave bastions of former years who rose out of nothing and climbed the heady heights (Yeovil, Scunthorpe and Colchester), then you are confusing nostalgia with the need for a Donald Trump-like headline.

All quiet here. No fuss. No parade. Thirteen games left. And we will lose every one. You will not talk then or romanticise. Instead, you will look on the horizon for a *real* miracle – something to chase, something to attach yourself to that makes you feel marvellous.

Heads down here. We cover our faces with the red and white strip that we do not play in. We eat junk food, not the pasta and corn that you foolishly assume.

We are hearty losers needing no attention. Those sixteen games that the papers say we won – ignore it. It is a misprint.

When our manager talks of Everest, what he's really inferring is the deep valley that we are trapped within.

We have not lost just one game at home, but several. Again – a mistake at the printers.

Our fans do not encourage the team but instead offer up a mere whisper and rasp. They are discontented – unhappy with this rickety ride.

When League One fans point to our unusual recent signings – Ben Davies, Markus Schwabl, Cameron Brannagan and Joe Maguire – we nod in agreement. Yes. Such players will take us nowhere. They are Christmas trimmings that fell to the floor.

Forget their heritage, their strong links to Preston North End, Bayern Munch and Liverpool through family and youth – just push them off your radar because they will be no good for you. They will poison your viewing.

We are not a family, a unified team, players with the same ambition. We have not been on a long, unbeaten run. We are disjointed, a mess, dispirited, envious and weak.

When admirers say we have pace (Cole), guile (Ball), distribution (Dempsey), strength (Bell), leadership (Nathan Pond), professionalism (McLaughlin), promise (Jack Sowerby, George Glendon, Keano Deacon, Ashley Nadesan), shooting prowess (Bobby Grant) and steel (Ashley Eastham), slap them across the face, for they have made a catastrophic error in judging our talents.

We have no talents. If the table still insists that we are fourth, then it is a fluke. We smile and shake our heads at the ludicrousness of it. We are an old, industrial chimney waiting to fall. Waiting for the ghost of Fred Dibnah to come along and put our feet to the fire.

This cannot be. FTFC – what is that? What kind of club emblem has an anchor and rope? Does it suggest we are stuck and ready to hang ourselves?

Ignore the whoops and hollers. We are a tiny club, undeserving. We will fall back into place – our logical position in the pack.

Rest assured. We are not ambitious. We see this whole thing as a scam, a Ponzi scheme, with others temporarily holding us up – the early, gargantuan dividends not likely to last.

You know I am a reliable narrator. And I say: 'Don't worry when we visit you or when you come to ours. It will be easy for you. You only have to blow us over like the straw house and little pig in that tale.'

We are nothing. Just here to help you on your way. There are no masks or humble games or hustling. We really are a shoddy team. Don't you know that? Just look around. Dysfunctional in every conceivable way.

League One. We love it. We are privileged to be amongst the might of Sheffield, Bolton, Bradford, Millwall and Charlton. But to go any higher?! Are you a *fool* or a *stooge* or a *joker*?!!

We were in the Northern Premier League ten years ago; the Conference National five years ago. We are scrappers – nothing more! We still wash our own strips. Believe me! Our players earn £100 a week and that is enough. We do it for fun! Fun, I say!

Have you not seen our £1 match day programme? Who in the top four flights has a *£1* programme?! We barely make back the price of the ink. And the sponsors within – both *official partners* (Puma, Carling, Holland's, Molson Coors etc) and *seasonal sponsors* (Choice Hotels, Evolution etc) – do you think they honestly *exist*?

Come on! Sit down for a moment. Understand that we run onto the pitch and expect to be slaughtered.

Yes, we have the most beautiful woman in England selling our 50/50 raffle tickets before each match, but can that honestly compensate for the miserable specimens that somehow fluke and amass these points?

The fall will come. Believe me. We cannot be the footballing equivalent of Alfie Boe.

Just swagger about and know that we really are in a lunatic asylum and soon our straightjackets will have to be put back on.

It's true. See you back here in August. Or at the hospital.

Devante Cole – Looking Towards the Horizon

BackPageFootball.com, 10 December 2016

With strikers, people *expect*.

On 22nd January 2016 – the day Devante Cole signed for Fleetwood Town – the then manager, Steven Pressley commented: "Devante has got terrific speed and is an exciting player. I hope he brings goals because we need a number nine we can rely on to score goals."

Twenty league matches into his first full season (2016/17) and compared to the healthy striking stats of reinvigorated no.10 David Ball, Devante Cole's figures appear meagre indeed: played 19, goals 0.

Such cold numbers, however, hide a lot.

They ignore the old school way of doing things: Cole's actual 'starting XI' appearances a much more sombre total of nine; his match time – in minutes – well behind that of ten of his teammates. And they flit over the positive fact that he has the most assists at the club.

If there was ever a planned coup in terms of a data provider's statistics resulting in misinformed judgement then the Press Association's brutal 'Appearances' data – perhaps trimmed down and extracted this way by FTFC – is it; the wielder of a menacing sword charging towards Highbury and Poolfoot Farm in an effort to depose the hip and self-conscious Romeo that is, to many, Devante Cole.

This isn't to excuse Cole at all. Grave doubts remain over whether he is cut out to lead the line, whether he has the required je ne sais quoi which ultimately separates Tony Yeboah from Tony Cottee and Alan Shearer from Alan Ayckbourn. But underneath the naked wink of a number is usually a bolder statement.

When he arrived at Fleetwood Town, Devante Cole was a shell of a player, the roughest of rough diamonds, a piece of driftwood lapping at the shore.

Although his previous manager, Phil Parkinson at Bradford City, spoke of him in glowing terms, there was either the disappointment from Cole of having to *yet again* find his way in the world via a fourth lower league club in the space of 17 months (after the grandeur of the Etihad) or general disillusionment with the game.

Fleetwood let go of the mercurial Jamie Proctor and stuffed £75,000 into Bradford's bank account in order to secure the services of an even more irresolute talent, it could be argued. They swapped the delicious jam of Proctor's right peg for the perceived grace of Cole's speed.

In such a transaction was hurt and risk – the realisation that Proctor, no matter what exquisite glimpses we had seen, would never reach the heady heights of 20 goals a season. And the desire – through Cole – to give Fleetwood impetus, drive and momentum.

The initial few months were not good. Fans sensed in Cole the great, footballing crime of indolence. He was seen as work-shy, listless and lackadaisical (or any other L you care to think of) – a man not in tune with the demands of a tiny north-west club with big ambitions. In his strides and failure to close down rickety defences was an ardent lack of regard for the paying public.

To them, he was pampered – the weaning princeling of Newcastle United's golden son, Andy Cole; an offshoot of proven artistry, yet still, in many respects, in his babygrow.

What Fleetwood initially bought was a temperament that needed sculpting, a young man who even though he'd claimed to be a "different type of player to his father" showed no evidence of placing such chips on the table and wanting to "make a name for himself". Graft first – putting a full shift in – *then* the fancy stuff, the Cod Army faithful have always stipulated.

With Cole, suspicion and half-faith from the stands quickly turned into disillusionment. When through on goal, there were numerous gaffes and bloopers. He seemingly did not have the eye of his father, nor the clinical finishes that epitomised Andy's time at St James' Park.

Who can carry the weight of a father's exploits though? And how many alchemists truly reside in a crowd – those patient begetters of developing wonder before them, slowly watching as slight improvements start to unfold?

The two blokes next to me on Row B of the Highbury Stand have already given up on Devante Cole. Normally astute and discerning men have made their judgement and it will take a couple of braces or hat-tricks from the fledgling pupil to potentially turn them around.

It will also take a different type of body language from the 21-year-old, 6'1" striker.

This is perhaps the starkest criticism of all when it comes to evaluating the Alderley Edge-born recruit. Look at Devante as he enters the field of play. There is the touching of the turf and then his making the sign of the cross.

But after that? He swings his arms at the side of him but never fully rotates or windmills them. There is something of the pendulum clock in his expression, as opposed to fairground extravaganza.

He cannot, overnight, transform himself from the slightly inhibited professional novice to the crowd pleaser or man that engages with the fans in the manner of erstwhile employee, Matty Blair.

But the Cod Army devotees expect an *inkling* of his personality, a *glimmer* of the real man who tries to score goals for a living.

They require something tangible to take home, a thought to warm before the fire – the slamming of Devante's arm through the air, perhaps, to indicate passion, indignation and ardour.

They need to know that he is *with them*, that an inflamed and raucous need sits within.

Up for sale. We are all up for sale to some degree. We must, at times, give bits of ourselves that we'd rather keep private, hold onto, lock in a safe, fling down on the hallway floor as we exit our brick houses each morning.

Success demands some of this potency, some of the free-flowing flair that each man and woman has in abundance. Footballing introverts *can* compete with the dolled-up extroverts who don't mind mess and pride and chaos splashed on the floor.

It takes bravery, mettle and an all-too-evident unnatural pluckiness but once through this dark cave, the faces and reckoning of the crowd become easier to digest.

Examining one of the many Andy Cole – now Andrew Cole – goal archives, you get a sense of the pressure heaped upon Devante's shoulders, the mass of history which exudes nonchalance, virtuosity and earned luck.

The Newcastle United and Manchester United machine that was Andy Cole not only possessed an on-field smiling exuberance, but was also the embodiment of justified greed – that striker quality either revered or resented.

AC's prowess and familiarity with the goal when in the six and 18-yard box were notorious in the 1990s. His ability to be slick and squirming in equal measure were instrumental in his effectiveness around goal.

His variety could be quite mesmerising; in his locker were two good feet, the ability to hang in the air à la Les Ferdinand, the dexterity of a ballerina, the uncanny knack of taming the ball with his first touch (however awkward this occasionally looked), breathtaking speed and a straight-shot trajectory which was extraordinary.

There were moments of fortune for sure: bobbled shots that found their way into the net; the ball generously ricocheting to him; an array of superb players around him at the height of his career who appreciated his end product (Rob Lee, Scott Sellars, Peter Beardsley, Ryan Giggs and David Beckham).

But in the main, his sudden sprints, his aerial power, his deft headers and reading the flight or soon-to-be grassy position of the ball were combined qualities unlike anything or anyone that had come before.

What of DC though – the *direct* electrical current, the modern era player yet to reach the dizzying altitude of his father?

On the 23rd August, at the Fans' Forum – just four league matches into the season – manager Uwe Rösler (sat on the head table with Steve Curwood, Andy Pilley and an understandably nervous-looking 'signing' from the *Blackpool Gazette* in the form of Will Watt) answered a simple question I put to him in relation to Devante Cole: Do you believe that you can hone his skills?

"Devante has turned a corner," was the nucleus of his response. To the fans with proper eyes, there was a good chunk of validity in this statement. DC was now much hungrier than the drowsy artefact who first arrived at Highbury to the sound of a mini-fanfare.

He was more certain and had taken to probing defences. He hadn't yet found the football's sweet spot, but was now getting in useful positions, becoming a team player and taking responsibility.

The only thing he needed now was further confidence (through assists and goals) and the respect of the crowd; knowledge that the

2,500 sets of eyes staring down his every move were *with him, in his corner.*

There wasn't going to be the camaraderie of a Nathan Pond or Bobby Grant or Ash Hunter with the hardy Fleetwood fans, yet his prestige was gradually growing – oozing out a better cocktail.

Inside the club it is well known that Cole's progress is "a big project" of the manager's; in many ways, if DC fails, then so does UR. Both of their contracts are up in the summer of 2018, yet since taking over the reins at the end of July it has been very noticeable that Rösler has started to piece together the Devante Cole puzzle.

Gone is the clueless meandering of the fashionista. We now, leading into winter, see a striker steeped in awareness of those around him – an almost psychic quality when you see him break forward with limited-visibility to his left and his right.

Fans, with their head in their hands, still mock and howl in despair when Cole blazes over from short range, yet such occasions are less frequent – the groggy afterthought of a former, unschooled player.

Assists have come to the fore in recent weeks – Cole utilising the byline for his left-footed pass to Conor McLaughlin versus Shrewsbury Town in November and indulging in a lovely right-wing flick past Peterborough United no.5 Ryan Tafazolli before teeing up Bobby Grant a month earlier. And let's not forget the sublime back-heel in August which played in David Ball against Oxford United.

A new Devante Cole is emerging – one capable of pulling multiple defenders away thus opening up useful pockets, one revved up by truly hazardous speed, and one mentally stronger than the unrecognisable Cole Jnr who first set foot in this placid seaside town.

Word from the training ground amongst the goalkeepers is that only the *actual* no.9, Aaron Amadi-Holloway is capable of burning the gloves of those intrepid stoppers, but power and pace are two very different things. First, you have to get there. Counterattacking-wise, Cole (no.44) is a dream ticket.

"Yet to express himself fully @FTFC," I posed recently via a Twitter poll – the four options being Jack Sowerby, Jimmy Ryan, Devante Cole and Aaron Amadi-Holloway. 100% voted for Cole, albeit in neglectfully small numbers.

In that comprehensive answer, I like to think, is hope and belief rather than criticism – the undeniable feeling that this lad can do so much more; zip around, taunt and tease, and eventually rip the net out like his father.

His fast-approaching first anniversary at the club promises a lot.

Honestly Discussing RALF B (Renegades, Atmospheres, Leeds, Fleetwood and Bolton)

BackPageFootball.com, 24 August 2016

I was raised in the Elland Road Kop in the late 1980s. Such an upbringing is comparable to the feral child, Tarzan being among the Mangani great apes.

"Pass him up," used to be the call – latecomers to the match who wished to stand at the *top* of the terrace (the Gelderd End) having their horizontal bodies slowly shifted there by a sea of hands.

You could say there was a bit of Tarzan in that – being suspended, not by a vine, but by faithful fellow fans. I was never 'passed up' because I was only 17 and assumed that the leaders of this song-stirring and rabble-rousing clan were wiser kids in their twenties.

Anyway, I was happy with my slightly less claustrophobic spot – happy to dance with 70-year-old comrades when Leeds scored, content to cudgel the air and roar when Vinnie Jones turned on a sixpence or Gordon Strachan half-volleyed home a minute and 49 seconds into injury time as in the jubilant 4-3 win against Hull City in February 1990.

Noise was seemingly easy then. Free. A manifestation of Yorkshire water and the needy vocal chords of football migrants who gravitated to Elland Road in search of solace.

I was one of those latter fans – a curious attendee following an older sibling who worshipped the Revie years (1961 – 1974) as if they represented a political chapter in British history.

We – Bolton-born lads – had the Frank Worthington 1979 wonder goal versus Ipswich to feast upon but it wasn't enough. Leeds was somehow *more* – the embodiment of an erstwhile giant, a club that would most definitely come again.

Whether that new off and on glory era (1990 – 2001) was triggered by the clamour of starved spectators, the 400-game stewardship of ex-PE teacher Howard Wilkinson, the lucky sprinkle of Lee Chapman's head or the tenacious magic of Gordon Strachan is open to debate.

What *was* clear is that games had an atmosphere – particularly those against the perennial enemy, Manchester United. And the *car*toon army, Newcastle United.

There was reason to shout.

Since then I have drifted, however – become mortgaged-up and without the back pocket fare or wad of a twenty-something.

Hungry for *local*, *cheaper* league football, I have – in the traitorous view of many – turned to clubs just six and four miles from my house: Bolton (the town I originally suckled) and Fleetwood (the team from nowhere).

How is it possible to neuter a decade and a half of over-the-Pennines palpable loyalty, of ripping around the country in a VW Scirocco, Austin Mini and Vauxhall Nova, not forgetting my brother's best man's carpet vans?

The current Leeds players' names never imprinted themselves in my head. A few seasons away from the sport and things alter massively. Allegiance is borne from being *with* players, knowing how they run, what gifts they have and what they do well in your immediate eye line.

Somehow, apart, I felt a kindred glow but nothing more. My attentions had turned to Ivan Klasnić at the Reebok Stadium and, afterwards, to David Ball at Highbury; exhilarating strikers I admired for their flair and felt I knew.

"If you don't witness players close up, they don't really exist" – that had become my maxim.

But with convenience came loss; the loss of noise. Sat inside the Reebok felt like a gig nobody had turned up for. Or if they had, they were timorous, wary of putting the engines at full throttle. 20,000 doesn't generally get you the equivalent fruits of a 40,000 crowd, but these 'exhausted' individuals – *my* locals – weren't even producing half the din.

Yorkshire, that forgotten world, had unfortunately set a horribly high standard in my head – that of crazed, almost rapacious aficionados, keen for good football and willing to do their bit. If I hadn't stood in the Gelderd End or later sat in the East Stand Upper tier, then I might have thought that life inside Bolton's modern stadium was adequate.

We all knew the truth though – understood what a *real* knees-up was. Bolton was comforting, safe, colloquially my ilk – a victim of all-seater stadiums perhaps – but too polite. The occasional burst of "Wan-der-ers...Wan-der-ers...Wan-der-ers" rose from the provincial vocal chords of those scarf-laden Lions of Vienna but the "flapping of gums" overall was insufficient, static by comparison.

Credit to the south-east villains who at least *tried* to muster up a familiar song together with the taunting of the away fans but such a small pocket could not carry the entire stadium.

Atmospheres are interesting phenomena. An April 2013 article raised the subject of engineering noise levels and improving acoustics. Some grounds simply don't carry sound effectively. "The best [grounds] are like ravines," the *Telegraph*'s Henry Winter commented. The Millennium Stadium. Estadio Mestella. Juventus Stadium. "You have the feeling of being on top of the pitch."

Such a problem wasn't relevant to Bolton. The Reebok Stadium (now the Macron), opened in 1997 with a capacity of over 28,000, merely had quieter citizens. A beautiful, distinct place – certainly no aesthetic menace to the landscape, no scourge – it exemplified engineering at its best.

In fairness to The Trotters they were in decline when I began to follow them in 2010. That probably explained some of the hush. Gone was the Bruce Rioch era (1992 – 1995). Gone too were the Sam Allardyce days (1999 – 2007). Bolton had suffered Gary Megson and would, during my time, suffer the maladroit Owen Coyle (despite the early promise of November 2010 tormenting Spurs, then Newcastle) and the lifeless Dougie Freedman.

Such rotten, Scottish souls were capable of killing the most vociferous and well-meaning, bullet-loaded voices of fans.

Was the piping or pumping of artificial sound around a ground the answer though? Did fans want nothing magnified into *something* (like bad alchemy, like an ignoble Old Trafford brew)? Never.

A month after the article I moved house to Thornton-Cleveleys (just outside Fleetwood). Removal van at the ready, I had no thoughts of football, no plan to get involved with such a mistress again. Coyle had strangled what love I had for the game and Freedman had put the final boot in with his nondescript persona and his tangential TV interviews.

Sod football! Let me sit out here on the Fylde coast – marooned.

But then I heard the 'darkness to light' story – from pub team to 'principality' (Prince Pilley in the background). I was curious. Full-time professionals in only 2010. Football league club in only 2012 – the year before I arrived. I had to see it.

The route to Highbury was more scenic and calming compared to Bloomfield Road. And around a mile shorter (which officially stamped me as a local). I foolishly imagined a luscious stand when ordering the tickets.

I mulled over sitting on row K as I had done at Leeds or something higher – say S. The Highbury Stand – opposite the more impressive Parkside – had only six rows, however (A-F). And one quickly realised that despite the draw of A with its proximity to the players, you were in for a front-row soaking via the unforgiving lashings of coastal rain.

B it was then. Beautiful.

Fleetwood, on the field, did not disappoint. I caught them – unlike Bolton – on the upswing. If this was a bandwagon, then I had jumped on serendipitously – witnessed the jovialness of Matty Blair, the inconceivable grace of Jon Parkin and the pomp of Antoni Sarcevic.

Bigger than the individuals, however – and the typical 2,800 attendance – was the belief that this already unimaginable story could get better.

I documented three of the games during that League Two play-off winning 2013/14 season (*Torturous to Some*, *Napoleon at Aspern-Essling* and *Almost Preposterous*); three snippets of history which, looking back, capture the ruddy naivety of certain fans.

Fleetwood's monumental rise was inexplicable in many respects – simply not humanly possible. A tiny fishing trawler community hitting the big time? Was this Queen Victoria and the North Euston all over again?

Fast forward and the splendid, early dessert for me in 2016/17 has been meeting former teams, Leeds United and Bolton Wanderers within a week and a half of each other (the first time competitively).

Both signal a titanic leap forward. Both act as a reminder of how precious playing football at this level is – particularly when you consider the dip in fortunes of the 2001 Champions League semi-finalists and the 2007/08 UEFA Cup prodigies.

Faced with the 'Mangani apes' of Leeds on Wednesday, 10th August in the EFL Cup, Fleetwood fans were surprisingly subdued. Theories abound, it seems that the Memorial Stand had a few key individuals on holiday, the occasion got to them (they had never sung in front of big-time fans before) or they were merely absorbing the moment – gazing into the jungle which had been flooded by a Yorkshire tide.

Ten days later on Saturday, 20th August, a 538-troop Fleetwood garrison made its assault on that Macron castle down the M61. Taking the lead in the match felt...normal. The Cod Army had become composed, filleted of any inferiority complex.

The atmosphere across the stadium was bouncy yet benign, but the importance of the occasion huge; Bolton Wanderers, four-time FA Cup winners, playing the coastal upstarts who by dint of their location would never have a big following.

Mutely sat there amid the Bolton supporters in the Upper North Family Stand in an act of benevolence to my guests, I thought of the word 'renegade' and what it meant. Deserter. Betrayer. Treacherous. Was I traitorous and disloyal – now on my third and final team (Fleetwood) – or were the *real* deserters those motorway punks who ignored their local side?

I recalled, half way into my tenure as a Leeds fan (around the mid-1990s), descending the steps of the then biggest cantilever stand in the world and overhearing a moron behind me castigating the entire team.

I challenged him – insisted that Rod Wallace had had a good game. He took this as an offer to fight. Dialectics or debate hadn't reached Yorkshire if this kid was anything to go by. He preferred intimidation – didn't take kindly to people undermining him.

I weighed him up. He was a little shit. One of those *tough* little shits though – the type that keep going like a Duracell battery. Being a fan but not a local (and still a few flights up), I decided to scurry down the remaining steps away from the truculent titch. Fortunately, he did not pursue me or deem my Bolton bones worthy of crunching.

In the immediate aftermath, while walking to the car, I did not feel like a 100% bona fide Yorkshireman. I felt like an outsider. The chants of 'Ye-ork-sher...Ye-ork-sher...Ye-ork-sher' that I often indulged in now felt a little hollow.

I hung around for a few more years – saw one of the best midfields ever to grace a pitch (Harry Kewell, David Batty, Olivier Dacourt and Lee Bowyer versus Valencia in 2001) and then the egregious nadir of the 2006 Championship Play-Off final against Watford (Leeds outclassed by Ashley Young) – but the love affair was slowly coming to an end.

In going to Yorkshire though, I found Lancashire. And in finding Lancashire, I discovered the best county in England.

This article was written by Jeff in advance of the <u>Fleetwood Town fan forum</u> that took place on Tuesday night.

Andy Pilley Rolls the Fleetwood Town Dice Once Again

BackPageFootball.com, 5 August 2016

Andy Pilley has what could be described as a boxer's nose and a businessman's convenient haircut.

With them come a direct and engaging matter-of-factness, words elucidated clearly, his mission statement willingly rolled out to anyone that cares to listen.

The ex-Enron employee is to football what Harry H. Corbett was to acting – a method actor mimicking the greats that came before him, a man comfortable in his garb, content to talk a good game and hire the right individuals around him.

His local drawl, unashamedly Fylde Coast or full of Wyre warbling, hints at a man still firmly embedded amid his roots.

The saviour or rather messiah of Fleetwood Town – if we ignore for a moment managers Tony Greenwood (2003-08), Micky Mellon (2008-12) and Graham Alexander (2012-15) – has all but transformed this tiny Lancashire club from a ninth-tier outfit into a respected, well run and highly polished third-tier red gem.

Through the state-of-the-art electronic turnstiles and gleaming doors lie facilities merely dreamed of when shy of a hundred people used to show up for matches over a decade ago: modern bars and restaurants, executive boxes and offices, swish team dugouts and spotless loos.

The numbers have gone up in every regard from the £250,000 Percy Ronson 'Away' stand in 2007, to the £1m Highbury Stand in 2008 (550 capacity), to the magnificent £4m Parkside Stand in 2011 (2,000 capacity).

To visit Fleetwood Town now is both a joy and a revelation. It has become an institution of sorts – a place of sustenance and calm filled with the rhythmic running of its modern day doyens.

League One has brought optimism – a gallant first year in the third tier (10th in 2014/15) – but it has also brought, more recently, fear (19th in 2015/16) – the ready understanding that life at this level is precarious, not to be taken for granted, difficult if overloaded with inexperience and the microwaved assumption that training facilities can compensate – overnight – for insight, awareness and effectiveness on the pitch.

Poolfoot Farm – that bastion of pride down the road in Thornton (costing twice what the Parkside did) – is indeed "fantastic", "incredible", whichever superlative you choose to pluck from the air.

What it is not, however, is an instant road to glory or stability or an excuse to cut the Samson locks which ultimately hold this club together.

Such a vexed subject appeared to be at the heart of Steven Pressley's 'resignation' on Tuesday, 26th July. What Andy Pilley described as "an eventful 36 hours" on Wednesday, 27th (on BBC Lancashire Sport) was seemingly a neat way of circumventing just what went on. Pre-season has been…difficult.

None of the concerns overhanging last season have been patently remedied: lack of goals; the underwhelming spine of the team; a distinct lack of flair and dominance (those granite qualities synonymous with FTFC in the 21st century).

Pressley was right to ask for more experienced players and the existing senior players knew it (they did in fact push him towards the chairman's door).

But Pilley was right to question what Elvis would have done with them or who he would want. Last season was harrowing at times. Stubborn tactics. Wrong personnel. Moronic substitutions. Negative football.

The feeling – as Coventry fans will attest – that SP really *was* watching a different game…perhaps via a portable TV in the top pocket of his body warmer. If asking for the money to alleviate such woes was at the forefront of Pressley's mind, then Pilley did not buy it.

Perhaps the chairman felt that temporarily masking a deeper set of problems was not the answer.

This throws up a meaningful question now though following the Elgin man's departure: Has Pilley gone from operating like a miniature sheikh to an impatient chairman with a sand timer in his hand genuinely believing that sustainability should be here just over three months after Sir Alex Ferguson officially opened Poolfoot Farm?

If he has, then Trading Standards appear to have <u>raided</u> the wrong part of Pilley's empire. They should maybe have taken away some of the youth players who have refused to rapidly grow into experienced pros despite the 'generosity' of a dozen pitches beneath their studs.

This is, of course, ludicrous. Becoming good and carrying yourself like a man – an established pro – takes time. Fleetwood fans, for example, know that Nick Haughton is special.

They also know that Ash Hunter is keener than a kid gazing up at The Big One. But does Haughton get hustled and harried off the ball? And does Hunter flag and lose direction at times?

The answer to both questions is 'Yes'. Without adequate quality around them therefore, the starting XI can look fragile with their inclusion. Crazy, but true. The real fattening and fertilising of a player only takes place when skilled architects surround him. And Fleetwood currently don't have such players in sufficient numbers.

Against Wigan on Friday, 29th July – despite the grandiose scoreline (3-4) – there was a sense that the lemonade had gone flat. It did not feel like *the final match* before the real stuff commences. Sure, the friendlies against 5th-tier Gateshead and Scottish Premier high-flyers Hearts have been cancelled what with the turmoil of late, but the players did not seem *together*. This was noticeable in a few areas of the pitch, particularly across the defence.

Right-back Conor McLaughlin, fresh from his European Championship adventure with Northern Ireland, had the look on Friday night of a man disdainfully peering at a judge for wrongly sentencing him; the sentence in this case possibly seeing out his contract at Fleetwood Town.

McLaughlin has been a great servant and no one would begrudge him a 'Pilley blueprint' move to the Championship with Leeds United, Reading or Bristol City – whichever rumoured club happens to be valid (if any) – but having him around, despite his galloping forays, may turn out to be counterproductive.

He still has the presence and accuracy of a top-notch player, yet his wantaway mentality might start to eat into other parts of the squad.

Newly appointed manager Uwe Rösler (as of Saturday, 30th July) will have to address this and so many other concerns which linger around Highbury like a pack of gremlins.

In bringing in the Altenburg-born ex-centre forward – formerly the boss at Brentford, Wigan and Leeds – Pilley has acted quickly and admirably.

He has wisely avoided the trainee megalomaniacs Gary Neville and Ryan Giggs whose attention, given their £200m St Michael's property venture, might not have been entirely on the job.

Good managers can motivate players out of a dark malaise and sometimes beyond their apparent capabilities. They pick up on players' latent talents – re-position them or fuel them with a new-found hunger rarely seen before.

With Rösler one senses that his default position is 'buoyant overdrive' – his staccato English complementing this by softening the blow of his high demands on the squad.

The relationship between a foreign manager and British player has always been an interesting one – easier in some respects, less pride versus pride.

Jack Sowerby, Fleetwood's 21-year-old central midfielder, is an example of how *not* to re-position a budding virtuoso.

Criminally played at left-back during pre-season, the Preston lad is conspicuously dying on his feet, wasting away, his range of passing and tackling neglected (the misspelling of his name [Soweby] on the official teamsheets against Liverpool and Wigan a further insult).

He is not the only professional to be misemployed and mishandled during the languid Pressley era, but he remains an acute illustration of and testament to poor management.

Whether Rösler has the magic touch to overcome this seemingly apathetic or pococurante state is yet to be seen but his stats are, on inspection, healthier than his immediate predecessors (42.5% win percentage versus Pressley's 37.3% & Alexander's 40.9%) and his words somewhat more forceful. "Over time you will see a side that will have a lot of energy, that is willing to attack in numbers, that is willing to press high and fill the box."

It is clear that but for his friendship with technical director Grétar Steinsson, Rösler might not be here. Now that he is, however, talk of energy, numbers and pressing high is to be heartily welcomed.

Fleetwood fans are desperate for a bit of fire, an unmistakable stamp of confidence in the team – something which has slowly whittled away.

There *is* promise in the ranks in the form of striker Aaron Amadi-Holloway and winger Keano Deacon – together a battering ram and tricky workaholic – yet sculpting them and utilising them properly (along with others) has been FTFC's problem of late.

The Cod Army ship has sunk a little but maybe the German hunt terrier, Rösler has started to yap on deck at the right time, warn the previous incumbents that all it takes sometimes is the right spur, personnel and steely tactics.

Rösler comes in with the knowledge of how to score – something Pressley could never impart. During his heyday at Manchester City (1994-98) he scored 50 goals in 152 appearances.

Great stats but not necessarily a harbinger to far-flung management prowess. His self-proclaimed 'heavy metal' attacking football is a style purportedly similar to Jürgen Klopp's at Liverpool and encouraging though.

"The next [manager] I want to be here for a period of years not months," Pilley said, before Rösler was parachuted in. "We've got a Premier League training ground….[we're a] forward thinking, smart football club….[and he would have the] full backing of a very sensible owner," he immodestly continued.

The man above Rösler wants the best. He has a habit of falling in love with managers, but when their time is up he finds them singularly unimpressive.

This isn't perforce a sign of vacillation. It is just that as the dossier on his manager thickens, Pilley begins to have doubts.

Not wishing to be known as League One's Massimo Cellino, Pilley will be conscious of getting this latest appointment right. "Undoubt*ably*," he reiterated last Wednesday in answer to a number of points raised around the subject, not realising his grammatical gaff.

Errors or mistakes are fortunately few with Fleetwood's chairman if we shut our eyes to off-field events, however.

The success story of Fleetwood Town is like a giant rainbow bursting from the murkiest of puddles.

The prospect of relegation back to League Two Pilley refers to as a "disaster". The 2015/16 season was "somewhat alien" to him, he refreshingly admits. Such a mindset is crucial but it must also understand what pushed us to that point.

'Asset stripping' would be too harsh an analysis, yet ridding the club of medium-salaried professionals would be somewhere near the mark.

Quite simply, we have hit the buffers but are keen to stay on the same platform with a smaller wage bill.

This isn't outrageous. Neither is it overambitious. But it takes time. It isn't something, in corporate terms, that can be achieved in one or two quarters – despite the glee such a conference call would bring to the top brass.

Absolute trust in Uwe Rösler must now come in the form of three decent-sized cheques (bar a training ground miracle). Jimmy Ryan, our only marquee signing in the third tier, has long since needed someone of high calibre alongside him.

And the same can be said of the position behind and in front of him (centre half and centre forward). We need steel. We need players proud of the badge. Despite the light crowds. And despite the unique north-west location to which Fleetwood belongs.

"It's about the chemistry…it's about the fit…there is some money still available," Pilley stresses. Let's hope so. Let's hope there are a few safes behind a few works of art on his wall.

We have until the end of August to get the right mix of players in place. But more than this, it is now about Uwe. Will he deliver with his 'heavy metal' football?

Anything to prop up the eyelids of the comatose fans.

Steven Pressley – Driving a Lamborghini on the Pavement

Backpagefootball.com, 28 April 2016

"We dominated," Blackpool manager Neil McDonald said after this Fylde derby as his side played out a 0-0 draw with Fleetwood Town.

McDonald's rotund midriff, it is safe to say, dominated the dinner suit he chose to wear for this encounter, but anything else – even factoring in opposing defender, Nathan Pond's commanding performance – is a fallacy.

Neither manager got it right. Fleetwood's Steven Pressley has a habit of drifting back to his favoured 4-3-3 formation like a nursery kid wanting to constantly play with the tanks. Boom. Boom. Boom.

4-4-2 with Stefan Scougall at the midfield helm had firmly steadied the Cod Army ship at the end of the tax year (2-0 vs. Peterborough), but Pressley seemingly knows more than the blinkered public (that loyal 2,134 Tuesday night crowd); he prefers to ignore the fluidity before him and cosset what must have been the seed of his footballing thesis.

Striding around, looking anxious, he appears at times unsure. Gone is the man that used to shepherd the ball at Ibrox, Tannadice and Tynecastle. On the radio he sounds fine, but visually he is jumpy, out of control or at least separated from his finer faculties.

This was a game that needed the brave. Blackpool are not the once buoyant maracas that terrorised the Premier League with an audacity made of oak but rather a floundering, ramshackle unit – a band still tuning its instruments as the audience reach for their coats.

There was a sense of fear when Leicester's on-loan Jacob Blyth entered the fray in the 77th minute and a deepening paranoia over The Seasiders' voodoo spell, but Fleetwood needed only dispense with the tricycle tactics in order to stamp their authority on this game.

Such a track was too easy of course – not in keeping with SP's footballing algorithm. He is apt to dish out licences, hand players grand hypothetical headlines but with the load-bearing foundations kicked away.

Fleetwood, quite simply, have no midfield, no thoroughfare when operating under a 4-3-3 system. Jimmy Ryan, that normally unbreakable force in Fleetwood's lineup, is running gingerly. He is no longer the master of all that he purveys, but a player cortisoned up due to a broken toe – thrown in because the cod becomes haddock without him.

This wasn't an awful performance, but it was one the likes of former players, Jeff Hughes, Matty Blair, Mark Roberts and Steven Schumacher would have deemed unacceptable. What Fleetwood once had in grit, they now supposedly have in flair and guile (a higher level modus operandi). But badly directed, swagger becomes puff – a distended avalanche of cold air.

"We started the game really well and for the opening 30 minutes I thought we were very good. We lost our way a little bit after that," Pressley conceded. "I didn't think it was a great game of football to be perfectly honest. It was a game where there was a lot of anxiety and a lot of pressure on the players. In terms of the way we played it wasn't our best performance.

"I also thought the effects of returning home at 5am on Wednesday morning [after the Millwall defeat] took its toll in the second half. I will say though that my players showed a mentality and a character when they were tired, and got what could prove to be an important point. The one thing that can't be associated with us is a lack of energy."

For the first time in a while, SP's words *did* actually stack up. In them was an honest appraisal of what went down at Highbury Stadium on Saturday: anxiety, pressure, Millwall and a dogged effort to resist inertia. Nerves, it seems, are understandably starting to creep in.

Blackpool will claim that they had the greater poise, were able to soak up Fleetwood's one-fanged attack, but in reality they stank the place out with their ailing matadors and slow-motion football.

The stocky striker Jack Redshaw looked capable, right-back Hayden White offered the odd Championship touch and their keeper Colin Doyle withstood the Cod Army's modest efforts, but manager Neil McDonald ought to be tried for perjury such is the risible waywardness of his analysis.

"That was a really good performance…We put them on the back foot," he further pronounced, like a drunken sailor finding himself next to Ben-Hur. Managers tend to lie more at this time of the season though – glue the broken wings of their charges and imagine a better scenario than exists.

If Blackpool survive this season and Fleetwood Town fall, then a Vauxhall Viva is officially better than a Honda Civic and George Formby is a more accomplished artist than Frank Sinatra.

Not that Frank has his voice at the moment. There is a croak and a creek to Fleetwood's play. Some of the personnel have ability in abundance, but the cough medicine is evidently being withheld. Off-stage one can silently hear SP extolling the virtues of 4-3-3: 'Stay out on the right, Bobby [Grant]. Scougs, left...you'll be OK – let Jimmy and Amari'i feed you.'

Except, Scougs (Stefan Scougall) is the head chef, the creator extraordinaire. When SP sensibly went panning for gold in Sheffield, he came back with such a nugget and diminutive wonder. Now, however, he chooses to play him out of position. It is akin to driving a Lamborghini on the pavement.

For the final 20 minutes on Saturday, Fleetwood – before a near-capacity gate of 5,123 – went gung-ho; indulged in a 4-4-2 but with four recognised strikers (two of them out on the wings). This is what SP does. This is the random chaos at the centre of his mind. His theatre script, salvaged from an FTFC dustbin, reads as follows:

60mins (1) Scougall the fall guy. Bring Bally (David Ball) on and similarly play him out of position.

60mins (2) Take Bobby off and replace him with Ash Hunter who has pace and tenacity.

70mins (3) Sacrifice Sarcevic for Shola Ameobi. (Note to self: Keep Devante Cole wondering why on earth he transferred to our club.)

Bally, in the 70th minute, did migrate to his more accustomed role of striker alongside Ameobi – with Wes Burns and Hunter running the wings – but by then Blackpool believed they were something; Pressley allowing their egos to thrive. You show fear, you permit the enemy to grow. Blackpool, not exactly gifted with sublime footballing skills, were being sanctioned to pull moonies.

David Ball was clattered on Saturday as soon as he came on. He took some studs on what appeared to be his left shin (a rumoured half a dozen stitches testament to BFC's brutality). This accounted for his uncharacteristic early touches – the ball ricocheting off him twice.

The inevitability of such an incident – a limited midfield roughing him up – was always on the cards. Skilled architects don't belong there. They belong immediately behind the front man. SP believes otherwise. He thinks that Scougall and Ball are interchangeable; oddly tucking Bally inside, placing him in a more vulnerable position.

SP has stayed loyal to his preferred XI of late: Maxwell, McLaughlin, Pond, Jordan, Bell, Ryan, Jónsson, Sarcevic, Grant, Burns & Scougall. Whilst this can often instil consistency and familiarity it does also risk lessening the sharpness of players used to more game time.

Ash Hunter, in this regard, and David Ball looked off the pace. The tempo was seemingly too high. They no longer appear match fit. And given their importance, the flimsy number of minutes afforded them in recent games could rock the notion of super subs saving the day.

If the bookies are to be believed, then Fleetwood are safe. Ladbrokes currently have Blackpool at decimals odds of 1.08 for relegation (a mere £8 profit on a £100 bet), whereas Fleetwood stand at 7.0. Wigan, this coming Saturday, are expected to travel to Bloomfield Road and give Karl Oyston's estranged team a thorough lesson in footballing wizardry.

If Fleetwood better Blackpool's result on Monday, 2nd May when they visit Walsall then the orange slump will continue its shocking, Tango-esque implosion into League Two (barring a mathematical cataclysm).

Certainty in football is like spring beginning in the gardens on 20th March each year though. No one can guarantee that the daffodils won't have already done their stuff. One big daffodil is Jon 'The Beast' Parkin – let go by Fleetwood Town in June 2014.

How that roaming tower built from pasties could be used right now given FTFC's meagre goal output of 49 goals from 44 games. One senses that League One would have been like a kids' sponge pit to the 6' 4" Barnsley man.

The Cod Army battle on without their surprisingly gifted donjon, however. Dreamboat performances are rare but it is hoped that they do not have to take a backward step particularly given the recent official opening of their impressive £8m Poolfoot Farm training complex; the *real* home of the players, as chairman Andy Pilley likes to point out.

Around the corner from Poolfoot sits the Madhatters play centre. One sincerely wishes that Steven Pressley does not need to be housed there once this season ends.

Sowerby, Morris and the Lack of Room Service at 'Hotel Fleetwood'

ItsRoundandItsWhite.co.uk, 11 February 2016

Fleetwood Town have yet to find their Decimus Burton in the dugout it would appear. There are few flashes of genius emanating from the management team and even fewer coherent after-match sentences which might gee up the Cod Army faithful.

Steven Pressley arrived on the Fylde coast four months ago now. He seemed composed and knowledgeable. There were strands of originality in his thinking. A lot of people warmed to him because he seemed to be from the NO BULLSHIT school of managers.

Recent programme notes and comments in the press have detonated this initial interpretation of the Elgin man, however, or at least shattered the wise, Scottish aura. Sample words from SP include:

14.1.2016 (Blackpool Gazette): "I wouldn't swap [our midfield] for any midfield in the league."

4.2.2016 (Programme notes vs Barnsley): "In the last couple of months I don't think there's been a game where we haven't been the better side."

7.2.2016 (Programme notes vs Shrewsbury Town): "At this moment in time the feeling in the dressing room is that from 18 yard line to 18 yard line, we are the strongest team in this division."

It would probably be sensible to admit that Wigan and Gillingham have better midfields and that the former were a much slicker side when they visited Highbury on 28th December. As for being the "strongest team" between boxes, the analogies are endless and each one of them points to desperation and risible effrontery.

We make mistakes in our own area and can't seem to penetrate the opposition's, a simple man might conclude. Why mask such a fact in nonsensical blubber?

Pressley had an opportunity on Sunday to redeem himself in part. The obvious failings against Barnsley in the Johnstone's Paint Trophy Northern final (2nd leg) – starting with the wrong strikers (Bobby Grant,

Jamille Matt & David Henen) – were there to be addressed. In came fans' favourites, David Ball, Ashley Hunter and new boy Devante Cole against Shrewsbury – guile, hunger and pace. But cue the manager's splash of Tabasco sauce.

Pressley has been resolute in sticking with his 4-3-3 system, but within that formation lurks imperilment. Ball, instead of being given his Cantona-esque forward role, was asked to play in midfield. As was right-back Conor McLaughlin alongside the leggy and more natural Victor Nirennold. Such a makeshift jamboree stumps the purist. Times are admittedly hard without the injured trio, Jimmy Ryan, Eggert Jónsson and Antoni Sarcevic but better compromises could have been made.

Managers are apt to maintain a mystique at times so that it sets them apart from the crowd, from the dumb-bell wielding public. Square pegs in square holes are too obvious, too straightforward. They risk the fans actually being able to predict the day's line-up and the manager not earning his corn. Why have a full-back slumming it in defence when you can convert him into Gary McAllister overnight? Why have a striker 'posing' up front when his skills could be adapted for the twisting and turning required in midfield?

Such boldness would be applauded if it looked right and did not leave other areas charred and bereft and supply lines creaking. Hunter, I hear, likes his eggs poached with brown sauce on. Cole, so the rumours go, is partial to a good bacon butty. Room service alas at Hotel Fleetwood is, these days, full of clattering and burnt toast. Wont to eat in *some* form during the 90 minutes, Hunter and Cole have taken to venturing down to the kitchen or midfield in their dressing gowns for supplies.

In short, what *was* a respectable midfield of Ryan, Sarcevic and Jónsson – still without the perfect gleam – has become a slightly ragged outfit. Ball is undoubtedly a striker – the superlative link in the chain up front. McLaughlin is an international full back, but definitely not a midfielder able to spray it about. Nirennold (*One small step for Victor, one giant leap for the rest of mankind*) is a capable French battler, able to cover yards and yards of land in the manner of a John Deere tractor.

On his own though, Nirennold cannot shore up the vulnerable Fleetwood wall.

A glance at the bench on Sunday and at the players warming up revealed two interesting numbers: 20 and 28. The former belongs to 19-year-old Keano Deacon – a wiry, still raw midfield prospect from the youth set up; the latter to Prestonian, Jack Sowerby, soon-to-be 21.

It is Sowerby that intrigues. He has started a mere three times for Fleetwood this season but possesses qualities that are much in need. Considered a striker but with the constitution and make-up of a midfielder, he is the one man in recent months who has shown glimpses of all-round ability. Passing it long, getting stuck in, threading the ball through defences, awareness of those around him, an eye for goal – add to this leadership (which will come with age) and you have a very decent find.

Is it too early for Sowerby? No. Can he bring something to the midfield party that we have been lacking? Yes. You cannot put too much weight on his young shoulders, but why shouldn't he be out on the town with Ryan, Jónsson and Sarcevic?

Ryan, according to Chesterfield FC's Head of Recruitment/Development, Paul Mitchell is "an all-round midfielder [who] can play both [attacking and defensive] roles really well". When pressed though as to Ryan's *main* role before joining the Cod Army, he conceded "Yes", it was as an *attacking* midfielder. Fleetwood fans, fully aware of Ryan's gifts and the energy he brings to the team, have mostly seen him as a sideways marauder. He can shoot powerfully and skip past players with ease, yet these occasions are rarer than they should be.

This leads to the question of why the man from Maghull seems inhibited at times and whether Sowerby can form the perfect tag team with Ryan thus finally engaging with the players up top. Have injuries curtailed Jimmy's forward runs this season? Has he been shackled by Pressley's demanding 4-3-3? Has Sarcevic been given the only pass to the nightclub named Adventure?

The boo-boys have come out in force in recent weeks. On Sunday their disillusionment ranged from the Kop/Memorial Stand's "You don't know what you're doing" upon Hunter being substituted for Grant (87') to the Highbury Stand's consistent jeers at having to witness back passes. The former happened because Hunter runs and runs. His work ethic is phenomenal. It did not diminish in any way the esteem in which fans hold top scorer, Bobby Grant. The latter was down to grumblers and green individuals in the crowd who do not help the team one bit.

Patience and an appreciation of crucial areas of the team being in the physio room seem to be traits that 21st century individuals are no longer blessed with. Grievances with the manager and grievances with the team are two very different things though, it should be pointed out. A manager sits on his throne and is there to be challenged or overthrown. Players are in the immediate firing line and require the crowd to pass them bayonets.

"The fans have to be patient. We *will* stay up. Times are different at Highbury at the moment. They need to bear with it and be the 12th man, not boo!" is the language coming out of the dressing room. Articles like this (*Lack of Room Service*) are meant to *assist* the management and ultimately the club and the players. Boo boys – *during* a game – do the opposite. They destabilise the troops. They cynically get into the heads of the players thus affecting the team's performance.

Highbury is a small ground. Players at times must feel *owned* by the fans, obliged in part to do as their turnstile 'bosses' say. Many a time left-back Amari'i Bell has been *encouraged* to bomb down the left for example. This, on occasions, can help – even if it breaks with express instructions from the management – but what is *un*helpful is negativity and misguided barracking from sections of the crowd.

We know the problems at Fleetwood Town. And Steven Pressley is currently part of them. Crowbarring players into a single, inflexible system and not adjusting his tactics radically enough during a game scores him an 'Average' on the report card. Thirty minutes into the game on Sunday it was clear that Ball needed switching with Chelsea loanee, Alex Kiwomya in order to drive the front line. It was also obvious that Sowerby deserved his chance alongside Nirennold and (ultimately) Kiwomya in the middle of the park.

You can generally spot a midfielder's swagger from 100 yards. McLaughlin, no matter what his qualities elsewhere on the pitch, is not from this school. The complete decimation of one's midfield is not an envious positon to be in, but Pressley – having gambled on utilising players out of position – should then have acted when he knew we were not forceful in the slightest.

Football is about constructing belief. You choose your traffic light colour under the guidance of the manager: Red for Fear; Amber for Realism; Green for Belief. The latter weeks of Graham Alexander's reign teetered between amber and red. Realism is often a good thing, but too much of it – and not enough dreaming – and you fall into fear. Belief, on the other hand, comes about through embedding strong faith in players, allowing them to express themselves. Too much tightening, too much constriction of flair and you have gifted players in rags; footballers over-thinking and unrecognisable.

Pressley's brief tenure is not at the same disquieting level Alexander's was in September 2015, but ideas and certainty need to be churned out fast if Fleetwood are to avoid the ignominious prospect of relegation back to the fourth tier. Chairman Andy Pilley – three years older than his current manager – clearly has trust in the former Rangers and Hearts' centre half, but the goals have worryingly dried up since November. Room service for the strikers is nowhere to be seen and scintillating bellboy, Josh Morris has changed hotels.

A canny chairman would drive up to Bradford and get our principal supply line back whatever the cost. The underused Morris (another Prestonian) seemingly and understandably prefers the red rose of Lancashire as opposed to the white of Yorkshire.

Cod Army fans listen out for the conspicuous cry of "Come on boys! Come on Fleetwood!" at home games which stems from a grey-haired chap in the Highbury Stand. It used to find its voice every seven minutes but of late has become a little arbitrary. Even the words have been edited ("Come on lads!" followed by an empty void) – almost, one senses, in response to the plight before our eyes.

Is Pressley the miracle man Pilley had hoped for? Is he slowly building something few can currently see? He needs a born leader from somewhere or a majestic spark. Without either there may be another coup in the managerial hot seat.

Five Months After the Fleetwood Cull

ItsRoundandItsWhite.co.uk, 14 October 2015

Everything points to the 6th May when Fleetwood Town released a staggering 14 players. It may not feel like it given the less than stellar performances of some on the list or the inconsequentialness of others, but a mood, a group of players was broken up.

Footballers should be able to cope with such mourning. They get used to the removal van pitching up outside their house for the next jaunt. But in that savage act very little was spared. Certainly not sentiment. Certainly not foresight. The knife that often rests at the heart of a chairman's club was wielded without fully comprehending what Fleetwood represents.

Mark Roberts was not the perfect centre half but he was intelligent and undoubtedly loved the club. Stephen Crainey might be an ageing left-back but he is better than what we have now. Steven Schumacher is not Jimmy Ryan, but he did the simple things well. Jeff Hughes could bawl and was often injured, but how he fought. David Ball (who has since boomeranged back) was the club's talisman; his return suggesting an arbitrary mess up between chairman, manager, director of football and technical director.

And so the Cod Army became a machine. On paper a sublime, yet hazardous experiment with new players Eggert Jónsson (age 27), Jimmy Ryan (27), Bobby Grant (25) and Victor Nirennold (24) complementing young talent, Declan McManus (21), Amari'i Bell (21) and Lyle Della-Verde (20); they in turn showing the way to Ashley Hunter (20), Jack Sowerby (20), Vamara Sanogo (20) and Max Cartwright (19).

The cold winds of League One have started to blow though. Fleetwood have drawn two and lost six of their last eight. Highbury is not so much a fortress as a Meccano set plonked between terraced houses and Memorial Park. Fear, courtesy of the drum-banging terrace, is never going to supplant itself into the legs of the opposition; an average crowd of 3,500 cannot become a Sheffield, a Bradford or a Coventry no matter how souped-up those Fylde voices become.

It is the latter – synonymous with industry and Lady Godiva – that most recently visited these parts and in doing so welcomed in the new guard, Steven Pressley following the denouement of Graham

Alexander. How Fleetwood could do with its own naked woman on horseback right now; a brave beauty willing to collar chairman Pilley over his 'oppressive taxation', his too-dramatic shift from well-run club to kindergarten.

That is the concern. No matter what the promise of youth, no matter which privileged prospects trample the turf at their state-of-the-art football centre, Poolfoot Farm, Fleetwood must make the transition steadily. Otherwise, the far more important Highbury turf and tough away venues become grazing grounds for an unbalanced team.

That does not excuse or justify the recent calamitous run, but it signals the shock treatment that is now required and why the funds were found to bring in short-term loan players – specifically centre halves – Richard Wood of Rotherham and Dionatan Teixeira of Stoke (the 6'4" Brazilian-born 'Tex' looking the part and bearing an uncanny resemblance to Irish legend, Paul McGrath). It is hoped the left-footed guile and steel of the 23-year-old Teixeira alongside the experienced 30-year-old Wood will add much-needed stability to the back line.

Alexander's downfall – although unfairly starved of funds and senior rhapsodists – was that he did not know his best eleven or formation. Only three players started each of his ten league matches in charge: goalkeeper, Chris Maxwell and midfielders, Jimmy Ryan and Antoni Sarcevic. The defence was tinkered with too often. He arguably employed four full-backs at times (against Bury, Colchester, Doncaster and Bradford – oddly enough gaining a healthy 7/12 points haul). But he did not latterly respect the old-fashioned commodity that is a winger.

Sure, he lost out massively when Josh Morris became unaffordable and found new digs at Bradford. He also did not anticipate Gareth Evans decision to turn down a contract and shoot off down to Portsmouth. But the shifting Sahara sands formation of those first ten games undid him. The football became negative – far from easy on the eye. The team rarely imposed itself. And the manner of some of the defeats was depressing, like a comatose bar brawl.

Uncertainty does not help players. New manager, Pressley seems to understand that. The troops need to know what they're having for tea. Regularity is often a prerequisite for performance and a good, productive shift. To fashion a team with players that work for each other is a hard business, yet the clues to success are in what has gone before.

The Best Feet in the Team

Three players are currently able to claim this throne at Fleetwood Town: Nick Haughton, Jimmy Ryan and Bobby Grant. Although talked of as 'light', it has become apparent that Haughton has that Beckham-like ability to whip in fast, curling balls. Why the Cod Army do not currently take advantage of this from set pieces or the right wing is an absolute mystery.

On the end of such poetry if not a floundering keeper should be striker, Jamille Matt and the centre halves. Strangely referred to as a "poacher" by *The Gazette's* Rob Stocks on September 23rd (similar to that Merseyside trio Ian Rush, John Aldridge and Gary Lineker?!!), Matt should be trained and trained in the art of heading. Why have a bomber (a capable detonator of high balls) if you do not use him effectively? (Pour over a few videos of the limited-in-skill but highly effective Lee Chapman if in doubt.)

Grant, as a spark from midfield – preferably on the left – simply has to be in the starting eleven. His range of shooting is phenomenal, his personality infectious. If he can shake off a bit of the timber then excellent.

Ryan, when he first walked through the doors of Highbury, was quite obviously a class act – nimble, fleet of foot and controlled. Although that form has tailed off – dragged down in part by an unsettled side – he must switch roles and become the link-up man with the front two, relinquishing his job in front of the back four. This way, his shooting flourishes and his skill at gliding past the opposition is compounded.

The Holding Man

From Alan Goodall (who often sat in between the centre halves), to Steven Schumacher, to Keith Southern, to Jimmy Ryan, to Victor Nirennold, to Eggert Jónsson, this position in the team simply has to be resolved. Goodall has gone. Schumacher has gone. Southern did not work out although he still stalks the corridors with eight months of his contract left. Ryan is destined for bigger things. That leaves Nirennold (the long-legged, French Carlton Palmer) or Jónsson. It is too early to tell if either man can cope in the engine room but a dearth of talent here means we'll have to wait and see.

The Strikers

Fleetwood have an array of striking talent. Unfortunately most of them are misfiring at the moment or seemingly being supplied by slow-moving cargo ships.

Jamille Matt, back from injury and a cautious pre-season gets the nod ahead of Jamie Proctor at the moment purely due to his impressive hold-up play, presence, threat and appetite.

And the little man role must go not to McManus, not to David Ball, but to that wiry charge, Ashley Hunter. Something comes alive when Hunter roams around the pitch. As witnessed in the Johnstone's Paint Trophy versus Shrewsbury for half an hour, his speed, natural ability in targeting the goal and penetrative runs are huge, huge assets. This man can go far – be a Francis Jeffers (without the unfulfilled dreams) or a Robbie Fowler (without becoming a landlord).

Those That Need to be Benched

It is massively disappointing when you know players have it but are 'out of sorts', stirring up the crowd for the wrong reasons and thus needing to be rested or given late cameo roles rather than starting berths. Jamie Proctor, Antoni Sarcevic, Vamara Sanogo and Amari'i Bell all fit into this category.

Proctor, the wonder-goal specialist, the no-nonsense 'push back' player just doesn't look the same. He is like a clogged-up hoover. It is as if the bullying, fandango man is being out-bullied or worse, doesn't want it enough. We know what this man is capable of, but where is it?

Sarcevic is a truly great servant, but recently he has begun to get barracked by the crowd. Not assisted by the over-watered Highbury pitch, he twists and tumbles all too often. A captain he is not, but he does bring something original to the party when on form. Where to play him? Probably behind the front man or wide as we get cut open too much with him in central midfield. Those that have the temerity to call him a "donkey" though – as happened on Saturday versus Coventry – should be aware that we wouldn't be in the 3rd tier of English football were it not for this man.

Sanogo is an unknown at senior level. He has had a mere nine minutes of action for Fleetwood and just three appearances in three years for Metz B. Still very young, he offers a bruising directness and left-footed attack that we do not have elsewhere. One to watch and bring on the field when 2-0 up.

Bell, a natural left-back, has been made to play on the left-wing since signing this summer given the absence of artisans in that area. This he has done with a reasonable level of aplomb, but what frustrates with Bell is his 'gentle giant' manner. For a well-built, 5'11" player, he is awfully kind. Back in his preferred position of late there is still the sense that he is too forgiving to on-rushing opponents when timely, crunching tackles would get the job done.

Concern, Missing Pieces and Solutions

Fleetwood have, so far, in 2015/16 won two, lost seven and drawn a quarter of a dozen. They lie 23rd out of 24 teams. Such numbers are crushing – particularly to a club steeped in divisional success and the mesmeric rise that has accompanied it. The fact that Blackpool are one place above The Cod Army makes such a plight more agonising. There has to be a reality check though. Mid-table *would* be acceptable. Cementing their position in League One over the next few years *would* be tolerable, desirable even. No club can just invest in facilities, lower its average playing age and *expect* the football orgy or odyssey to continue. Even the best kids do not grow overnight whatever the standard of grass under foot. Good facilities can lift expectations and standards like a Rodin, but scruffs will always come and conquer – wreck the finger buffet – knowing that the Cod ego has grown.

One wag on *Twitter* shortly after Pressley's first game in charge – referring to the new manager's checkered shirt and body warmer – asked: "Get dressed in the dark, Elvis?" The hoedown garb was certainly unusual, if practical given the autumn month. What it did signal though was Steven Pressley's insouciant and unruffled demeanour. It was like being back in the Hearts' press room nine years ago in notable bob hat and casual apparel; the former Tynecastle captain socking it to Vladimir Romanov who had threatened to sell all Hearts' players.

There is sometimes the feeling that *all* managers are disingenuous frauds, that they roll out a few soft words for the camera and despise journalists that dare ask pointed questions. Pressley – one game in – isn't even on his Fleetwood honeymoon yet, but one thing he quite evidently exhibits is candour. The size of the job, the mini-rebuild and the metaphorical mopping of the players' brows will require nothing less.

Fleetwood under previous incumbent, Alexander became a club with the reins too tight – the players almost like horses. "Most horses toss their head as a negative reaction to tight reins...Horses are basically claustrophobic animals so they have a lot of trouble with confinement...and tight reins are nothing if not confining. The type of horse most given to head tossing is usually a fairly high-energy, forward-aholic horse."

This is the daft thing: Fleetwood *have* the high-energy players, despite the cull – players interested in romping forward and letting the opposition know they are there. Will Pressley fix the stable and the paddock though, the whole squad mentality – change how the players perform on the surrounding recreational ground? Will he reduce the head tossing which became clear to the crowd?

Certain things need addressing for this to happen – from the cosmetic to the fundamental: 1) Have the players run out to some evocative and rousing music, a <u>club anthem</u> other than the limp, banausic affair that currently makes its way through the speakers; 2) Get the team playing with a sense of entitlement. Far too much fear runs through this tentative, backward-passing team; 3) The slow-moving cargo ship (as mentioned) that is Fleetwood Town's midfield needs to become a speedboat. Speed and supply to the starved strikers *must* improve; 4) When bits of the opposition start to puff hard, as was the case with Coventry's right-back, Sam Ricketts on Saturday after 75 minutes, double up, expose them – exploit the gaps; 5) The defence must, in the short term, evolve from its over-reliance on loan players. Right-back Conor McLaughlin should have his mind back on the job following Northern Ireland's European Championship heroics. Stephen Jordan should be integrated into the team perhaps as a strong, makeshift left-back until Wood and Tex leave. And the return of club legend Nathan Pond – given his composure and elegant canter – would be surprisingly welcomed right now (the 30-year-old Prestonian just goes on and on, comfortable in the thin air of the upper echelons).

Highbury Stadium hosts its Fans' Forum tonight. Perhaps the title of a book by Stephan Pastis should be highlighted to Andy Pilley: *Timmy Failure: Mistakes Were Made.* He has proved himself to be a valuable, ruthless, no-nonsense chairman, but how credible is Fleetwood's journey from here given the recent paradigm shift? Can they really make the Championship or does the shadow of League Two haunt them daily? Without Mr Pilley's assurance that Fleetwood's base camp for the foreseeable future can be the unappreciated glamour of League One, then the club may well find itself susceptible to a landslide (back to the anonymous lower tiers).

On the question of 'What does Fleetwood Town Football Club represent?' the answer is graft, humility, togetherness and daring.

Fleetwood's Iceman Cometh

ItsRoundandItsWhite.co.uk, 4 August 2015

The Return of 4-4-2 and Hearty Optimism: Town 2 Getafe 0

Fleetwood sought forgiveness from their wailing fans this evening – a sixth effort at pre-season victory in danger (on paper) of becoming the sad march of a funeral cortège.

Their recent outing against Burnley was unsatisfactory. Whether experimental, whether an exercise in continued fitness, it undoubtedly stuttered, chugged and offered little by way of optimistic insight.

Out on the pitch though Friday night (against Getafe) walked Eggert Jónsson, the 6' 2" iceman born in Reykjavík – a midfielder by trade, now 'slowing down' as he approaches his 27th birthday by pairing up with Stephen Jordan at centre half.

Calmness, presence, a strong reading of the game and fight are characteristics that do not get bandied around in defensive gene pools too often. Such qualities collectively are rare. Every so often you will see a Rio Ferdinand, a Jonathan Woodgate, a Des Walker and smile. Protection: a self-contained mafia unit almost. Without it, teams are vulnerable, given to squandering leads and pansying around.

Jónsson is no stranger to a tear-up, a bit of dynamite, the capsizing of seemingly impenetrable teams. Seven years in Scotland with Heart of Midlothian (2005-12) has hardened him. He arrived there days after the appointment of 'miracle man' George Burley who looked set to break up the Glasgow 'Old Firm' stranglehold in Scotland before owner Vladimir Romanov's maniacal decision to sack him.

Although Jónsson made his league debut at Tynecastle in February 2007 – a year and a half after walking through the door – he was still a pup, still young (just 18) and slowly being considered as a utility man or Mr Versatile; a defensive prop somewhere on the pitch.

'He impressed our scouts up there,' Jónsson's first English club manager, Mick McCarthy said (in December 2011) somewhat ominously two months before he himself was axed.

This is the thing with Eggert – you hire him and swathes of managers get sacked (or relieved of their head coach duties). Eleven while at Hearts (albeit under the turbulent reign of Romanov). Four while under contract at Wolves. Even two while playing for Portuguese side Belenenses between the summer of 2013 and 2014. The iceman, it appears, haemorrhages managers and yet most speak highly of him.

He has had – as is a footballer's lot – a not-too-straightforward career. Starting out at the unpronounceable Knattspyrnufélag Fjarðabyggðar on the east coast of Iceland as a 15-year-old boy, Jónsson now finds himself – after much shilly-shallying and ineptness from clubs – on the west coast of England in the lightly populated town of Fleetwood. The intervening 11 ½ years have hopefully served him well – taught him how to be resolute.

Do not be kidded by the baby face or the soft parting of hair or the Scandinavian dourness which it is difficult for those of English origin to equate with spirit. Jónsson, if his Highbury debut is anything to go by, is the real deal: graceful, tenacious and blessed with two great feet.

But what of the match against Getafe, against the side that finished 15th out of 20 teams in La Liga?

One got the sense that this is manager Graham Alexander's preferred XI: Chris Maxwell; a defence (left to right) of Danny Andrew, Stephen (Stevie) Jordan, Eggert Jónsson and Conor McLaughlin; a midfield of Amari'i Bell, Bobby Grant, Jimmy Ryan and Antoni Sarcevic; and a strike force of Jamille Matt and Declan McManus. To think otherwise would be to undermine the season ahead, believe that you can casually play with the chess board with just eight days to go.

In terms of personnel there were only three changes from Tuesday night's struggle with Burnley (Matt for Jamie Proctor, Grant for Lyle Della-Verde and Jónsson for Tyler Forbes). Somewhat crucially though, there was no messing around with the formation – just an old-fashioned, no nonsense 4-4-2.

Certain things stood out tonight in front of the 1300+ crowd: the combined belief of the team; Ryan's legal bullying of the opposition; Sarcevic's freedom to express himself now that Grant is in the mix; and the iceman Eggert's composure. The team swarmed back into position when required. There was little profligacy with the ball. And Getafe were made to look average.

But was it actually Getafe (as per the official programme and extensive previews) that trotted out onto the pitch? A cursory glance at Getafe's final 2014/15 lineup away to Real Madrid on 23rd May shows the following XI: Codina, Alexis, Naldo, Escudero, Vigaray, Medhi Lacen, Pablo Sarabia, Pedro Leon, Diego Castro, Juan Rodriguez & Freddy Hinestroza. The line up on 31st July at Highbury was: Megyeri, Roberto Lago, Darlan Bispo, Cala, Alberto, Arcas, Carbonell, Moi Gómez, Campos, Borja Galán & Mbaka.

Getafe's 2013 signing Pedro Leon came on as a substitute – but then he perhaps had to as he was on page 13 of the programme. The starting lineup, however – unless this old dog's eyesight is failing – was 100% different; generally a mix of Getafe B players from Segunda B Group 2 (Spain's third tier: Carbonell, Mbaka), fringe/squad/loan players (Lago, Moi Gómez) and new signings (Megyeri, Cala).

Despite this sense that the team jogging around Highbury was maybe not the team that went in 3-3 at half time at the Bernabéu, there *were* positives. The Spanish season might begin and end two weeks later than the English one (giving the English an advantage) and the intensity might have been lower than a gritty League One encounter, but healthy seeds were finally planted Friday night.

'Pre-season isn't about winning,' Alexander claimed. But didn't he enjoy, didn't he revel in this tidy performance. 'They are starting to gel,' he admitted.

Concerns still stalk the camp: the lack of goals from open play (Sarcevic scoring the only goals against Getafe – both penalties); Danny Andrew rarely braving the shark-infested left flank (erstwhile full-backs Charlie Taylor, Stephen Crainey and Adam Chicksen setting the bar high); the superb prospect Nick Haughton not being utilised (best reposed on the left wing until he develops). But a bad Tuesday has become a good Friday, even if various top-flight Spanish personnel mysteriously went AWOL.

Fleetwood Town's paella and Estrella Damm night was never going to compete with the pubs, penury and promenades in this magical corner of the Fylde – hence the low Friday crowd – yet something clicked while the paella was on the hob; the team finally ebullient and up for it.

The news at this sensitive time of the year can be disheartening (28/7: Gareth Evans signing for Portsmouth), welcoming (31/7: Eggert making his home debut) and remarkably uplifting (3/8: David Ball returning to the club). The mist and gloom hasn't entirely disappeared but the spine of the team has thickened. It just remains for Graham Alexander to ensure that genius is at the edges.

Fleetwood Town – Running Out of Coke and Crisps

ItsRoundandItsWhite.co.uk, 28 July 2015

Fleetwood Frazzled: Town 0 Burnley 2

There was something of the office world in this performance – bland, mechanical, without real invention. Meeting a team two divisions above you (based on 2014/15) is clearly a hard proposition but Fleetwood offered little by way of hunger, impromptu football and penetrative guile.

The worry with just eleven days to go until the blustery, promoted Southend United rock into town is that the Cod Army has been purified too much. No longer do beautiful contaminants like Jon Parkin roam the Dale Frith turf, but rather a collection of automatons – imitation players short on heavy-duty ardour and gusto.

There is still a spine. Chris Maxwell, *Stevie* Jordan (as he is now known) and new signing, Jimmy Ryan offer permanent comfort, but beyond them – particularly under the guise and formation of Fleetwood's occasional 3-5-2 (or is it 5-3-2?) – things look out of whack…screwy and confused. Players, housed by such a system, generally feel lost. Are centre halves centre halves or full-backs? Are full-backs full-backs or wing-backs?

There is the definite sense that on-field lodgings are being provided for Tyler Forbes. A natural winger – albeit with the rustlings of someone still learning his craft – Forbes has jostled Conor McLaughlin from his preferred right-back birth (whether in a 4-4-2 or 5-3-2). Such uncomfortable switches let one conclude that the squad – the real *muscly* squad – has become threadbare, inadequate and short on experienced players.

If you do not have a centre half then do not wreck *two* positions (and consequently the fluidity of the team) – just get a makeshift centre half from the squad or buy one. McLaughlin – it is clear – will suffer in that position over the course of the season. He will be physically grappled with and lose heart and lose faith – even when re-housed in his full-back role. And his international place may well be compromised.

There are other gripes – musings as to what is going on underneath that Graham Alexander beard. You see the face of a man, you see a little of his soul. When such skin is covered up thoughts and facial twitches stay protected. That is OK for a midfield force like Jimmy Ryan – better even – but for a manager wishing to communicate with fans, the full deal, the beef, the tortured picture does not get disclosed.

Fleetwood's pre-season is a harbinger of League One trouble, a waving in of bigger and more skilful teams. Anyone watching the run outs, the recent parades, will have noticed an absence not just of goals, but of a spark – that Frankenstein essence so crucial to performance. The bald facts do not make good reading: AFC Fylde 1 Fleetwood 0; Dortmund 'B' 1 Fleetwood 0; Alemania Aachen 2 Fleetwood 1; Kilmarnock 3 Fleetwood 1; Fleetwood 0 Burnley 2. Five matches – five defeats (goals for 2, goals against 9).

If this was meant to be an exercise in parity, then it has failed. If these were meant to be mere run-outs, stamina sessions, discovering one's best XI, then there is a whiff of bankruptcy about the place. The feeling around Highbury on Tuesday, 28th July was of gloom – an invisible rupture. And as such, the atmosphere – noted by chairman, Andy Pilley ("Generally I've been disappointed") – has tailed off even further.

In matches like this versus Burnley one would expect a 'cup minnows against giants' mentality, a 'This is what we've got!!' and 'You're in *our* paddock now!!'; a stand basically against General Custer. None of it. There were moments – Sarcevic magical turns, Ryan being a yard ahead of his teammates, quality Maxwell saves – but elsewhere (like a disease across the park) there were too many passengers; belted-up individuals perhaps over-managed or under-skilled.

Fleetwood's journey has been enormous. They were bound to run out of crisps and coke in the car. League One is a dangerous division – four teams falling through the trap door each season, more than any other tier. When fans have witnessed great strides they get greedy, they want more – reality sometimes becomes clouded. The frustrations here though are justified. Jogging across the Highbury turf and at away grounds are mostly red and white jerseyed players of promise only. Substance is lacking.

Vamara Sanogo. Amari'i Bell. Jamille Matt. Lyle Della-Verde. Bobby Grant. Declan McManus. Dark warriors followed by pale hopefuls. But Josh Morris (now of Bradford City) and David Ball (that polished artisan) they are not. You lose players of this ilk and you struggle. No amount of youth or blueprint or Pilley whooping can compensate for the hard, merciless arena that is football. The drizzly, echoey chants that barely made it out of the necks of Fleetwood fans on Tuesday were symbolic of this.

Something is amiss and it needs fixing. Even the rough-and-tumble raggedness of the modern day Micky Quinn, Jon Parkin (now of Forest Green Rovers) would be welcomed right now. Pretty football becomes weary if not doled out with equal portions of invention and grit. And not testing the opposition keeper or scoring in such a miserly fashion leaves you with nowhere to go.

Will Alexander sort out his nest or be forced into emergency signings in January despite Pilley's insistence that Financial Fair Play is now king? I'm not sure, but the club's new-style, slim-line match programme which hopes that "the Cod Army faithful will find the new experience pleasing" is perhaps indicative of language being torn apart and shafted. And if language is ruined, if there is a creeping corporatisation when engaging with fans, then something dies, something begins to rot the core of a place.

The message for the FTFC top brass must be: keep personalities in the game, do not strive to homogenise every corner of this wonderful place. And get a bloody goal scorer – it doesn't matter if he breathes fire or wears a dress. Just get him!

When Fleetwood Let Their Cantona Go

FootballLeagueWorld.co.uk, 30 June 2015

Great departures – departures of infinite magnitude – wound a man. They hurt a community. They penetrate the gut and twist it so fiercely that fans must lie down, prostrate, paralysed or fatigued by the news they have just heard.

Thursday, 26th November 1992 prompted such reactionary symptoms when brief terrace hero, Eric Cantona left Leeds United for Manchester United. That such a situation could come about was insane, incredulous, idiotic, surely the work of a mad man. Bill Fotherby and Howard Wilkinson – chairman and manager at the time and immediately up on WANTED posters around the city – had not only sold the club's best crockery, but delivered it lovingly wrapped to the enemy across the Pennines for a pittance (£1.2m).

At 3.29pm on Wednesday, 6th May 2015 as the UK was readying itself for a new government, a similar thing occurred: Fleetwood Town announced that fourteen players had been released. On that list were big names (Mark Roberts, Stephen Crainey, Steven Schumacher & Jeff Hughes) but the name sandwiched between them was Ball…David Ball; surely a mistake; surely a clerical oversight.

Not so. Fleetwood actually wished to ditch the name sung the most from the stands. Spiffing Daleks may have taken over the country on the Friday, but football is supposed to be more humane than politics. People need guarantees. They need reassurances. Thou shall not mess with cult heroes.

"We have had to make some very difficult decisions…We have a profile of the makeup of our future squad going forward and a stronger emphasis on up and coming professionals." For a moment you see the pensive, slightly troubled face of Howard Wilkinson, but you then realise that the words belong to Graham Alexander and will be echoed by chairman, Andy Pilley.

These are good men, men of sound judgment, men who have participated in the Cod Army revolution over the last decade. You wonder for a second though – nay, longer – whether a number of ales were consumed when this particular decision was made. Ball is as far away from Cantona in many respects (if only in kung-fu kicks) as Morecambe was with Wise, or Smith was with Jones. But the crucial parallels are: flair, unpredictability, magic from out of nothing, unique running style, goals from all over the pitch and a hatful of assists.

Cantona was loaned out to Martigues, Bordeaux and Montpellier; Ball to the less glamorous Swindon Town and Rochdale. Both men craved a home though – a real home; a club that would treasure them, treat them like family, understand their foibles and inner workings. Cantona eventually found it under Alex Ferguson between the years 1992-1997. Ball, at a similar juncture (nearly 26 years of age), is about to find his.

"I started out at Prestwich Marauders FC," Ball tells me, kindly allowing me 75 minutes of his time on a Sunday morning. The club, formed in 1972, represented his pre-Man City youth, his initial taste of football. A Whitefield lad, Ball at the age of seven signed for City. "When I was younger I was a United fan. My father was United. I had the chance to go to United or City at the time. I chose City...thought it was the longer route."

By 'longer route' Ball seems to indicate that City offered longevity. Ten years with the kids and then an official youth career (2007-09) and senior career (2009-11) proved him right. "I won everything you could win as a youngster. The Nike Premier Cup, the 2008 FA Youth Cup." Stints in the Premier Reserve League (joint second top scorer 2009/10) further enhanced his reputation but by then City's new owner Sheikh Mansour was two years into his tenure and starting to inject obscene amounts of money into the club. In January the following year, Ball was gone – sold to Darren Ferguson's Peterborough United for a modest £50,000.

The senior debut at Man City never materialised although he did work under three different nationals – Sven-Göran Eriksson, Mark Hughes and Roberto Mancini. Hughes or 'Sparky' is the one he remembers with great veracity. "I think he understood how tough it was to break through. He'd seen something in me. Took me out to do shooting sessions."

With Sparky's departure in December 2009 came six months of thinking, a loan spell to Swindon and the eventual transfer to

Peterborough. Is football a smooth career? "No. You just try to work with it, go with the flow…something comes up, you deal with it."

Ball is an honest chap. He looks you in the eye. There is none of the ostentatious bluster with him. And he is certainly not the unseemly caricature of a footballer often beamed into homes which reinforces the old quote: "Football is a gentleman's game played by hooligans, and rugby is a hooligans' game played by gentlemen." You ask him for his time in a respectful way and he gives it to you. You tell him the angle of the story and he looks genuinely overwhelmed.

Compare this – perhaps unfairly – with Kenny Dalglish (as a manager) in 1988: "There are quite a few men attached to microphones and notebooks up and down the country who will tell you that Kenny Dalglish reacts to interviewers as if they are trying to mug him, that he tends to meet their inquiries with the verbal equivalent of Mace."

Ball seems to be one of those rare people that have made it in life without the need for cynicism. There is no shrugging off well-wishers, critics or earnest journalists. He is straightforward and has retained a sense of conviction and integrity when others might have compromised their personalities and become more guarded. "At times I think it's a very harsh sport, a very political sport. As you grow up, it becomes a lot harder. You see and hear things you're not going to like. If you need to speak up though, you do."

We talk about Clarke Carlisle and the mental side of the game, the 'Get on with it' approach which tends to prevail inside clubs still anchored to the 20th century. "Managers want to get a reaction from you. They also might put their arm around your shoulder, give you praise. It's a great thing in a manager if they can be more personal – tell players what they're really thinking. The mental side – that's a side in football that has to be developed."

Schadenfreude is anathema to Ball. He speaks warmly of former managers and fellow players. On Micky Mellon (now at Shrewsbury Town): "I never really played in my best position under Micky. People sometimes suffered from weekly changes [to the team]. But he's a lovely man, an infectious man." Jamie Proctor: "He can be anything, Procs." Graham Alexander: "He spoke when I left, said 'I'll give you a glowing reference. Get managers to call me.' I'd love to play for

Graham again. To pick his brains at any time, which I'm able to do, is refreshing." Josh Morris: "If you ask Josh, I think he would like to have stayed [at Fleetwood]. I'm sure he could play every week in the Championship though." Jamille Matt: "A fit Jamille is a great addition to any team. He's been working really hard." Antoni Sarcevic: "He can shift, he's strong, pre-season he's up there with the top runners. 2014/15 it was a new league playing against clubs that have the technology to go and look at different players and think 'How can we stop the best players?' Sarc did well, but I'm sure you'll see a better Sarc this season." Mark Roberts: "Robbo is a really intelligent man on the pitch and off the pitch. I'll be friends with Mark for a long time." Jeff Hughes: "It's a learning curve for a young lad playing around Jeff. He plays with his heart on his sleeve." Nick Haughton: "This is a kid learning when to pass, learning when to do his trickery. Again – he can be anything." Matty Blair: "Real. Genuine. Amongst the group [at Fleetwood], I met some really good friends. Those who came to work, wanted to work."

What about 'Bally' as he is affectionately known, however? Where now? "I played with some great players at 18, 19, who are now doing normal jobs. My mum always said if you make a living from football, you've made it. That is my mindset." The grounded comments are sincere – slowly crafted from David Ball's easy-going demeanour. "My mum and my dad are a massive part of who I am now. Dad would never question me. You need to do it this way…"

But what of ambition from this non-hubristic man? And his next club? "When I initially dropped down two divisions into League Two [from Peterborough to Fleetwood in July 2012] it was a big thing, but I wanted to showcase my ability." At 22 a necessary gamble, but now – three years later – less likely even though discussions have taken place.

A total of four clubs are currently on the radar – all of them sleeping giants, one could say, situated in Yorkshire, Lancashire and the south. Huddersfield has been mooted via *The Huddersfield Daily Examiner* due to Ball's links with coach, Steve Eyre who he played under at both Man City and Rochdale. The language in the article of "back-up striker" though is either off the mark or misguided. Ball is no 'support act'. Squad rotation is all well and good, but money is not the thing with this Whitefield man who lives in St Helens – first team football is.

"Personally, I wouldn't sit on a [juicy] contract. It's a short career. If you've got opportunities to play, then play."

Other factors jar with the interesting prospect of Ball teaming up with Huddersfield's 'black, Asian and minority ethnic' (BAME) manager, Chris Powell – one of only six BAMEs in the top four tiers much to the chagrin of <u>John Barnes</u> ("Very few black managers can lose their job and get another."). Ross Wilson, former Director of Football Operations at Huddersfield and "middleman to the boardroom", but poached by Southampton three months ago, knows a lot of young players well courtesy of his network of contacts. Having such a character around the place gives the players faith, belief in the wider dreams of the club. His departure is, in many quarters, a wrench.

Wilson, as scouting and recruitment man, is symbolic of the way the game is going. Financial Fair Play (FFP) austerity has had the effect of modernising clubs, of adding a necessary thrift – putting them on the "cutting edge...with a strong emphasis on player recruitment and analytics". His replacement Stuart Webber is from the same sharp-suited, thirty-something brigade and may just entice similar players and recalibrate the Championship side, however – a nice balance between youth and established professionals.

This takes us back to Fleetwood and the hard truth behind David Ball's exit. Word around Highbury seems to be: You sack the cake lady – ten cake ladies. But you do not do this. You do not oust your main man. But what if your club's average attendance is a mere 3,500? Three thousand five hundred devoted fans full of iron and wine, but nonetheless a trifling number despite the vigorous strides of the club. Downsize, sacrifice and re-model are all ugly words. Graham Alexander, Fleetwood's manager, readily admits: "With some of the players who have left, it wasn't a decision directly linked to their ability. But with age and cost. These are the realities of competing at the level we are at."

Indeed. And Financial Fair Play when reduced to "League One clubs can spend a maximum of 60% of their turnover on wages" compounds the picture further; simplistic analysis points to a club earning £700,000 on tickets per season (3500 x £200). Messi alone would barely survive three weeks were he to play on the Highbury lawn mown by Dale Frith.

So Fleetwood haven't so much gambled on their future as been bound by the FFP Stasi. Memories of Ball though (Bally to his mates) the no.23 maestro…23 because his son Mason was born on the 23rd May? His thoughts on young players tell us everything we need to know: "They should be fearless in their play, showcase their talents…take the game by the scruff of the neck. I know how quickly you go from 20 to 25."

One day this Fleetwood Town great will make a fine coach.

Neil Mcdonald – Humble Man

ItsRoundandItsWhite.co.uk, 17 June 2015

Blackpool FC's fall from Premier League glamour in 2010/11 to League One obscurity five years later is to many the consequence of blinkeredness and a Kafkaesque environment where only the wrong are right. The 2nd June appointment of new manager, Neil McDonald serves not to highlight increased desperation at the club but rather a new-found reality with limited bait.

The Seasiders are no longer the swaggering immortals of yesteryear. Long gone are Stan Mortensen, Tony Green, Ray Charnley, Alan Suddick and the like. Today's players are drunkards by comparison and so low in numbers as to leave ample room at the bar. Such is the recent regression that the 2006/07 stewardship of Simon Grayson and his fellow Yorkshireman (and goal scorer), Andy Morrell must seem like a halcyon glow – the mythical bird in flight from the third tier after nearly three suffering decades.

Ill-fated once more alas (having barely taken to the skies) and preparing itself to run through the lower league trenches, Blackpool FC – along with its famous tangerine strip – is now struggling to retain any sense of credibility. Complaints and unrest over numerous things dog the club: the Bloomfield Road playing surface; the threadbare squad; dwindling crowds; the Squire Gate facilities or "Training Ground & Centre of Excellance" (sic); the removal of the Mortensen statue; and controversial chairman, Karl Oyston.

'*Gloom*field Road' is how this 1953 FA Cup winning club is referred to on popular forums, Back Henry Street, Fans Online and Vital Football. Something appears rotten and neglected – unprofessional and bewildering. And yet into this mire has willingly walked Neil McDonald, the 1980s Newcastle United full-back. He is not recognised by many these days – assistant managers generally aren't. "Who the Hell is Neil McDonald?" was a Fans Network article which appeared in the hours after his appointment. Fans have grown used to recently retired, successful players promising to embody their high standards in a team or foreign names whose after-match interviews are forgiven because flair has been re-denoted as a language of one's tailor, not one's words.

McDonald has so far 'failed' on both counts. There are no bespoke suits – just northern cuts and a chimney-sweep barnet. Some of his quotes have been decidedly trite and banal – taken from the stock cupboard and worn out even more: "This is a great opportunity…a massive club in my opinion…I've got to try and get it back to where it was." Underneath the curdled words rolled out for the cameras, however, is an engrossing backdrop. Neil McDonald *was* somebody – "An intelligent, classy full-back who knew how to take a chance" according to Geordie central; 24 goals in 180 appearances in fact but ultimately "handicapped by injuries", his second club Everton "picking him up too cheaply".

No stranger to the north-west after this (going on to Oldham, Bolton and Preston), McDonald was a former England U21 international earnestly carving out a career. Significantly – and hardly reported – he began his playing career alongside giants like Kevin Keegan, Terry McDermott, Chris Waddle and Peter Beardsley. After that Neville Southall, Trevor Steven, Graeme Sharp and all manner of iconic names crossed his path. You do not sit in such dressing rooms unless blessed with some strength. McDonald can give the impression of being a soft, cuddly bear – leant on by those around him. He is a down-to-earth, likeable fellow seemingly not schooled in boardroom smarts or shrewdness. Interpreting him this way is to miss the bigger picture though.

What of his time at Carlisle United (now an aeon ago, nearly eight years)? "Many players spoke glowingly of his coaching methods and sessions, and his reputation as a coach has always been extremely high," Jon Colman, journalist at Cumbria's News & Star tells me. "It was alarming then for McDonald to be sacked after one game of the 2007/08 season and this is something that has largely been shrouded in mystery for most of the years since." That was until nine months ago in September 2014 when former Carlisle owner Fred Story admitted: "I now regret sacking him."

The BBC archives show that McDonald's squad travelled to Walsall on Saturday, 11th August 2007, "dominated the first half" in front of a 6,933 crowd and came away with a respectable point. Twenty-four hours earlier McDonald had prised away Joe Garner from Blackburn Rovers for £140,000. Forty-eight hours later, the man with the most humble expression in sport was fired. Part of the club's 'generous' statement read: "The termination of the contract is not a knee-jerk reaction, and is not part of any disciplinary action."

So why the sacking? A manager can die on Monday, 13th and be partly resurrected on Saturday, 13th. Colman's exclusive seven years later rinsed out the damp rag that is often boardroom words. Story quite simply broke his silence: "I sacked him because we had differences of opinion on handling the media and on player transfers, and I also thought he had lost the dressing room." Lose the dressing room, he did not. And on the other matters Story readily confessed "I should have worked with him". Implicit in Story's new-found openness is that McDonald – in his first managerial role – was perhaps too raw, a little clumsy (or honest as they used to call it). Hearing him now, you wonder if the Geordie twang interspersed with north-west acquiescence has become too smooth, flat and regulated.

It is easy to see that McDonald is a good man, of the right constitution, but he is evidently holding something back. A nervousness and semi-fear shine through him. He is part actor, part coach. Fred Story has not entirely gone away – just re-clothed himself as Karl Oyston. And men such as these have a litter of former managers scattered around them, souls they have pulled the hand grenade pin on, people they have discarded because they choose not to study themselves (How could Nero ever be wrong?).

This is the worry: Blackpool FC – a club in a more ramshackle state than Leeds, Newcastle and Sheffield United put together; a one-year rolling contract for McDonald hardly an endorsement of his talents and unlikely to seduce the right players to the Las Vegas of the north. Kevin Boroduwicz, Blackpool Supporters Trust Secretary is uncompromising: "Neil McDonald is dependent to a great degree on the quality of the tools he is given to do the job. His predecessors, including Ian Holloway, have not been given proper provision in terms of finances or facilities. The archaic training facilities that have barely changed in 70 years, the contracts issued to players that almost guarantee a huge turnover in staff and a lack of continuity, the lack of any clear footballing philosophy or policy that have ensured a decline in the club's on-the-field fortunes. I could write at some length on this alone but wouldn't want to bore you unduly."

Neil McDonald will turn 50 years of age on 2nd November. The milestone will either represent a first quarterly conference call lauding his appointment or a panicked gathering of the board should Blackpool be slumped near the bottom of League One. Judging from the club's Ashley-esque media commitments (Stewart Hudson informing me "The manager has already agreed to do an in-depth feature piece with a *national* newspaper this weekend" [my italics]), contempt for local scrutiny seems alive and well.

The new manager, one feels, *deserves* to succeed. If he can start regaling the watching public with some *real*, earthy stories and bits of history (the things he tells the players) – away from the staple lines – then all the better.

You just fear that this is a cardboard club with cardboard executives, however and unless they are able to address things on so many fronts, convincingly and transparently, then the doom-mongers will have their day.

Maybe the capture of Brad Potts from Carlisle – the old stomping ground – on 11th June (using actual money) can act as a catalyst. One can only dream or drown in the understandable cynicism.

Amir Khan – Out of Service Concorde

Boxing.com, 3 July 2017

Amir Khan used to be a boxer. In 2007 and 2008, he did what all boxers do early on in their career — he fought a lot; five times in each year. By 2011, he was still climbing through the ropes — a healthy three times — in an effort to show off his wares.

During those formative years, he took some notable scalps which helped him develop: Willie Limond; Graham Earl; Paul Malignaggi; and the giant, Mandalay Bay Hotel fight against Marcos Maidana.

It was this same Las Vegas 'crime scene' which was to disrupt Amir Khan's career in July 2012 versus Danny Garcia after the blip of Lamont Peterson. Khan embarrassed Garcia for nearly three rounds but then got impatient and sloppy and started to fight a 'close up' Philadelphia fight. When the left hook came, it changed Khan's career forever.

"Timing beats speed every time," Garcia apparently said before that bout. He was right, but Khan's profligacy, the nonsensical harnessing of his God-given skills was the real reason for his failure.

Five years on, after the part-time rebuilding or renovation of his career and May 2016's show fight with Saúl Álvarez, Khan has put three dates firmly in the diary: "Next fights will be: November / December 2017. April / May 2018. November / December 2018."

If this 30th May Tweet — perhaps slightly exuberant, given that it came on the eve of his 4th wedding anniversary — is to be taken seriously then it is both presumptuous (that he won't get flattened at the end of the year) and a little naïve.

Set against the rise of the 'superpower' city, Manchester — next door with its many cranes in the sky and endless construction projects — Khan's star and that of his home town, have dimmed.

As I recently overheard a commuter and Mail Box Express employee put it (one of the many Boltonians that seek work further east): "It's everywhere you look, *innit*, yet *our* town's on its ass."

Khan's recent endeavours have, to some extent, mirrored the fate of his birth place. Bolton, despite its surrounding magnificence, has begun to look a little down at heel, perched on its derriere: boarded-up car showrooms, barren multi-storeys, Bradshawgate — its entry and exit point — like a wounded matador.

When Khan was poleaxed by Canelo over a year ago, it not only echoed the relegation of the local professional football team, Bolton Wanderers to the 3rd tier (a place they hadn't been for quarter of a century), but quietly signalled that a new dawn was upon us.

For…with Khan, we are always waiting. For him to understand who he is again. (An undeniable 147lbs welterweight.) For him to pull away from the celebrity choke.

No matter what resplendent circus or opera is playing out in his head Khan needs to give it one last run at his *true* level. He needs to wave on in not money or the servile snippets that still frequent the back pages of *The Bolton News* but rather *proper* opponents.

Harsher critics would claim that he no longer matters. That nobody sees him as significant in *any* weight division. He is, to put it bluntly, the train that never comes despite the grand, tannoyed announcements.

Leaves on the track. Ramadan. Switching disciplines. Having a 'riot' with the Pakistani cricket team. Dubai. Charity gigs. Shisha lounges. Larry King. Channel 5 News. There is always seemingly *something* to keep him occupied, apart from the very thing that created him. Boxing.

Sure, he slopes off occasionally to Virgil Hunter for a handful of intense training sessions. But these hardly represent a Balboa movie. There is no obvious hardship or toughing it out in a meat locker. There is no plan of sorts apart from wistfully chasing the big bucks.

Colossal fights have been mentioned: a domestic blockbuster with Kell Brook; the chance to avenge things with Danny Garcia; and, of course, the meaningless, projected "£30m" scrap with Manny Pacquiao. If Manny was still a vintage wine able to knock over a bottle of Vimto, then it might not matter so much. Alas, he has been exposed badly since 2012.

The last four months in this brutal game have served to demote all these named Khan targets anyway. In the ascendency now are Errol Spence Jr, Keith Thurman and an Australian by the name of Jeff Horn. Would any of these undefeated belt holders consider Khan? Not if they're legacy fighters with an eye on sweeping up the division. And with the welterweights set to absorb Terence Crawford, Mikey Garcia and even the young, 5' 6" Gervonta Davis down the line, it will be no place for glass chins.

Such a label is admittedly unfair and Khan at times, during his career, has been a joy to watch, a bona fide crowd pleaser. But the neglect (maddeningly so), the attention to detail regarding the balance sheet and not so much the boxing, has infuriated his more ardent followers.

Khan can continue to hang out with people who'll tell him he's had a stellar career. That he's mesmerized and transfixed the general public with his speed and footwork. But such people don't help. They merely turn him into a portfolio. They celebrate the paraphernalia and trappings extraneous to the sport.

If Khan is to ready himself for one more assault then he must stop being ubiquitous for the wrong reasons. Shisha lounges. Charity gigs. Talk shows. Worlds where a suit is more important than integrity.

When you fight less than Marlon Brando acts, then there is a problem. Distractions and excuses begin to hold sway. You forget why you put the gloves on in the first place. To outwit an opponent. To gain esteem. To sweat and feel the thrill between risk and adventure.

Amir Khan isn't finished yet. He's just the out of service Concorde on the runway. Perhaps afraid to fly. Perhaps afraid to set aside the blether that crowds out his life and diminishes his aptitude.

Anthony Joshua – Hoping to Avoid the Left Hook

Boxing.com, 29 April 2017

A man's defeats don't always tell us who he is, but they do unmask his vulnerabilities.

Anthony Joshua, the clean-living professional killer with the purposely deceptive and anaemic moniker of 'AJ', has managed to dispel the haunting amateur defeat to Dillian Whyte in 2009, but the dirt and residue of 2011 remain (Mihai Nistor and the unpronounceable Magomedrasul Medzhidov) along with the worry over his defense compounded a year later when fighting Cuba's rangy Erislandy Savón.

Joshua was half the man back then — both in physique and ring IQ — yet pouring over the footage of those forgotten bouts tells us much about what makes him uncomfortable. Nistor, the tough, compact Romanian southpaw walked him down while swinging wildly. Medzhidov recovered from a torrid first round by disorientating and buckling Joshua with a huge, straight right. And Savon simply didn't let up and used his length impressively from numerous angles, albeit in defeat.

Joshua, it seems, does not like wide shots. There is a touch of the shire horse with blinkers to him when unusual missiles come flying in. It is conceivable that because of this errant bullying, he made a conscious decision to bulk up, add essential weapons to his arsenal and improve his resistance. Strength, after all, is the backstop — the roadblock that prevents raw tormentors having their way.

Amateur boxing, it could be said of course, is like kids at junior school still using pencils. When the pens finally arrive, things change. The old, head-guarded crew begin to see a new light. And the stings to body and skull are harder. Some cope with this switch from medals to moolah. Others begin to realise their limitations and the skills and growth spurt of those around them can be demoralising.

With Joshua — half a decade on and a professional 18-0 slate — it helps that he can now walk through opponents and set his feet even better than before. The split purse £30m or £40m fight (versus Wladimir Klitschko on 29th April), or whatever pay-per-view beans happen to be on offer, is testament to his progress, politeness and vim. It does not, however, suggest that he should be considered in the same class as

WBC champ, Deontay Wilder or Luis 'King Kong' Ortiz. Or even WBO champ, Joseph Parker. The method of his victory over 41-year-old Klitschko will decide that.

But *will* he win? Is such an outcome a foregone conclusion for the young IBF lion and former sparring partner of the Ukrainian? The consensus in the UK's *Boxing Monthly* is a resounding 'Yes' by 25 votes to four. Only Glenn McCrory, Paddy Barnes and the anti-Matchroom camp of Peter Fury and Hughie Fury have faith in the gloves of the old master, Wladimir.

"He's been bashing up conventional fighters like Joshua since he was 18 years old," McCrory states.

"Sure, Joshua is young and fast, but Wlad is just as big and a different grade altogether to anything Josh has faced before. Wlad could even stop him and, if he did, it wouldn't be a shock to the serious boxing fan," Barnes adds.

"Klitschko's gonna be very determined to get his titles back. He's got far greater experience and I just see a gulf in levels," Peter Fury comments.

"All the experience is with Wladimir and I see him taking his time and walking Josh on to shots," Hughie Fury concludes.

It is intriguing. And if we rewind five years to Round Two of Joshua's Olympic tussle with Savon we hear the commentator say of the Englishman's flawed jab: "*You bring that hand back quick* before you get burnt."

Joshua has corrected such weaknesses since if only through sheer power and snap. He continues, however, to keep his right mitten low and this is the great hole in the wall making him susceptible to Klitschko's stock-in-trade left hooks. If Wlad can bang a few of these in early on to unsettle the younger man, then who knows?

There might not be much evidence of Joshua being rocked in recent professional bouts — with the exception of Whyte in December 2015 — but he has not been in with many equals. The disparity in the amateur ranks was smaller. When Joshua climbs through the ropes on Saturday at around 10pm, he will instantly know that the former protection afforded him will have evaporated.

That is not to say that he will disappoint. He might indeed be ready. And Klitschko, his aging opponent, can only be categorised now as an unknown: 17 months out of the ring; his desultory performance against Tyson Fury perhaps still fresh in his head; the fear factor against an ox like Joshua maybe even out-stinking Wlad's garbage truck mindset on that horrible night.

Fourteen years and four Olympics separate Wladimir Klitschko and Anthony Joshua. Many see that as an example of youth about to take over. The former has Johnathon Banks as his trainer, the latter Robert McCracken. Sparring partners include Gerald Washington and Malik Scott, and Mariusz Wach and Joe Joyce respectively in an effort to recreate the power and height that will darken the ring.

Whatever the result of Saturday's eagerly anticipated 'no mud-slinging' bout, a multitude of questions will be answered: Is it time for Wlad to walk away? Has Joshua proved that he can make the step up? And most importantly, when will Ortiz and Wilder be let off the leash for a *really* big clash?

The great irony is that Wlad can do *everything* hurtful that Nistor, Medzhidov and Savon did to Joshua. And 'AJ' being a seven-round, over-muscled green might just well run out of stamina.

Discussing Haye, Hendrix, Hacks, HBO, Herzog and Hitting 30 with Elliot Worsell

Boxing.com, 11 January 2017

I originally started corresponding with Elliot back in February 2016 after reading his article *Tyson Fury: Uncut, During Wladimir Klitschko Fight Week*. It seemed to embody the style of the great Gay Talese, have echoes of *Joe Louis: The King as a Middle-Aged Man* and *Frank Sinatra Has a Cold*. I was intrigued that new journalism was still seemingly alive and wondered how such a baton had been passed down the generations.

I put a number of questions to The Ring and Boxing News writer—and brother-in-law and biographer of heavyweight, David Haye—and managed to get great insight with regard to his second, long-awaited book, 'Dog Rounds' which is due out in the summer of 2017.

Elliot—to call you a veteran seems ridiculous given your tender age (just 30), but you've been writing for nearly a decade and a half now, I understand. And it all started with you covering the Howard Eastman vs. Hacine Cherifi European middleweight title fight in Norwich, England in July 2003 for Eastsideboxing.com. Was that a good introduction to the sport and how did it feel hustling your way close to the ring a month before your 17th birthday?

Like the majority of people in boxing, I blagged my way in. Didn't know what I was doing, didn't care. But I wanted to write about boxing and I was passionate about it, and that was enough. I was also willing to write about boxing for free, do it purely as a hobby, which helped a lot at the beginning. Nobody was going to pay me a penny at 16 or 17, but it didn't matter to me. I wanted to do it regardless.

Your first boxing interview was actually the year before that (age 16) with 'Irish' Micky Ward – the legend who fought Arturo Gatti three times at the end of his career and was the inspiration for the Mark Wahlberg film, The Fighter. How did being in the company of such a boxer—albeit on the phone—in the aftermath of that classic first Ward-Gatti fight feel and what did you glean from the man?

I didn't glean much, truth be told. My questions were terrible and Micky, as you probably know, isn't much of a talker. I remember writing down my questions, about 20 of them, on a sheet of paper and reading them robotically to him over the phone, yet he was gracious enough to give me the time and seemed either impressed or a little freaked out that a 16-year-old from England wanted to interview him. He even sent me a signed picture a week later. I was such a fan.

We should get the obvious question about David Haye out of the way. Your relationship with him is not what it was. Are there elements of that bond between boxer and writer that you perhaps miss or was such an ending serendipitous in helping you grow as a writer? You have mentioned being hamstrung by your great knowledge of him in terms of writing fresh material about his career—can you elaborate on this?

It's my preference to be removed and write from a position of insight and relative objectivity. David Haye will always be a boxer I look out for, and I hope he achieves whatever he hopes to achieve, but it's great to write about his comeback with a freedom I wouldn't have had when I was a kid following him from place to place.

I'm 30 now. I don't have the same interest in a single fighter's journey the way I did back then. Following Haye in 2017 would be like listening to the same music I did when I was 17 or 18. I love 'Appetite for Destruction', always will, but you won't find Guns N' Roses anywhere near my iPod these days. I've grown up, moved on.

That said, I know enough about David Haye to write about him without including quotes from him or anyone else, so that's what I'll do from time to time. It's a weightier kind of knowledge, too, deeper than just spending an hour with someone you hardly know and asking them questions.

Piecing together quotes from your articles and correspondence concerning the current crop of paid, boxing journalists (generally newspaper employees) paints quite an ugly picture of the profession. You are refreshingly outspoken about this and perhaps implicitly associate boxing's demise with the dearth of brave writers out there willing to dig properly regarding a story rather than simply pay homage to a fighter's words.

All the guys on the British boxing beat do a great job. Their hands are tied by editors to some extent, so often they can't write exactly what they want, or perhaps as much as they want, but there are far more knowledgeable heads writing about boxing now than there was when I first started getting in their way at ringside 13 years ago.

Of course, a lot of what is written about boxing now is safe. There's a fear of repercussion, a fear credentials might be taken, a fear work might dry up, and that probably makes journalists think twice and turn a blind eye now and again. In a sport as unruly as boxing, that's not necessarily a good thing, but it happens.

My belief is that very little learning is done at press conferences or in arenas on fight night. It's just surface level stuff. And, although I can't match some newspaper journalists for experience or journalistic muscle, I do have an insight many are without. I have been around boxers, been around big fights, been in gyms, been in changing rooms and been places which are strictly off-limits for most journalists and writers. I've seen the true version of boxing as opposed to the director's cut its stars would rather we all saw. That counts for something, I think.

You didn't exactly go quiet after the 2011 publication of 'Making Haye'—what with your article output online and through magazines—but the five to six years in between have been akin to waiting for a Stone Roses or Kate Bush album. There was good reason for this, I believe and plenty of failed projects in the interim which shines an interesting light on the difficulties of getting a book to market even for established authors. Has the hard road been worth it given the imminent arrival of 'Dog Rounds'—your study of the guilt and anguish boxers feel after having killed an opponent in the ring?

Very hard. Boxing is a niche sport, yet fighters are the only sportsmen or sportswomen who really interest me beyond just watching them in action. I want to know the characters and their stories; combat sports stories are the best stories and fighters are accessible in a way most sportsmen and women are not. But try telling that to anyone outside the bubble.

I'm glad I've managed to get another idea off the ground, though, if only because it allows me to put the last book well and truly behind me. It's like anything, I guess, you move on, you get better, you hate that old version of yourself, and 'Making Haye', written by a naïve 24-year-old, was very much a product of its time. It would obviously look completely different if written now. 'Dog Rounds', in contrast, isn't attached to a celebrity fighter nor has it been hurried. It is, I hope, a book that says something and actually means something. It's a book about guilt. The guilt of the boxer and, ultimately, the guilt of the spectator. How does a boxer feel when they do too much damage? And how do we feel when seeing too much damage done?

The current heavyweight division isn't the strongest but it promises a string of difficult-to-call clashes if the promoters and boxing organisations get their act together. Do you see any serious contenders besides the obvious (active) six of Deontay Wilder, Anthony Joshua, Luis Ortiz, David Haye, Joseph Parker and Wladimir Klitschko (whose fate and possible rejuvenation will be decided on 29th April)?

In terms of ability, I don't see a clear leader. I think they are all capable of beating each other. But, certainly, if we're talking marketability, Anthony Joshua is the man the division needs to succeed. He's the one who has something about him beyond just the ability to flatten an overmatched challenger with a single punch. He has crossover appeal, he is exciting in the ring and he is young. Most of the others, to my mind, are either past it or lacking that x-factor that takes a heavyweight beyond just holding an alphabet title that in this day and age means about as much as a post-fight piss test.

Each heavyweight seems to have an Achilles heel: Wilder's windmills leave him wide open at times; Joshua is still learning his craft but looks a little stiff and too muscular on occasions; Ortiz is ageing and doubts remain over his stamina despite his original pedigree; Haye is very much an unknown after returning from injury and one wonders over his ability to go beyond 4-6 rounds; Parker is the new kid on the block with very few fights outside of his homeland; Klitschko—there are big concerns over his ability to judge risk and reward these days. Do you see anyone unifying the division?

At this point, it's hard to say. Some are protected on account of being raw and young, some are avoided and some are buying time and gorging on patsies in the hope of securing one walk-away payday. That was 2016 in a nutshell as far as the heavyweight division was concerned. I'm hoping 2017 will provide some answers.

Adam Booth—Haye's former trainer—once said that a boxer, in order to succeed, needs to be either frighteningly clever or ignorant. Do you see any truth in that?

Absolutely. I think more are ignorant than frighteningly clever, mind you. And in the context of being a professional boxer, ignorance is no bad thing. In fact, it's a kind of intelligence.

"No matter how much I practise, no matter how much I live, and no matter how much I try, I will never ever write like [Norman] Mailer. I haven't been blessed in that way. Others at least give you hope. They seem obtainable. Not Mailer, though. He was a freak." You wrote this in late February in an email. Do you think it's important that writers of all persuasions accept their lot and have a realistic yardstick in terms of judging / accepting what they produce?

I think you've just got to be patient and realistic. I'm only at the start line. I have no idea how good or how mediocre or how terrible I will end up being. But I'm okay with that now. That impatience and delusion of youth has, I think, made way for a bit more maturity, and I only have to look back at 'Making Haye' to realise how far my writing and knowledge of the sport has come. That, for me, is the reminder, that reality check.

"Haye thrived on…the purity of the violence he was about to exact," you observed in 'Making Haye'. Does this, in some way, justify the brutality of the sport? Does a boxer have to be at one with the richness of the game in order to quash some of his darker thoughts?

Boxers definitely view violence—the act of punishing an opponent—differently to how the rest of us view it. To them, a knockout shot is no different than a footballer (soccer player) connecting sweetly with their right boot and volleying a 30-yarder into the top corner. It's what they practised, it's what they hoped to achieve.

Even fans of combat sports view the violence differently to those who refuse to watch combat sports. We also dilute it. We have also become somewhat desensitized to it. Personally speaking, I can look past a boxer getting bashed up and bloodied, his face disfigured, if I know his game plan is to come on strong in the later rounds and outlast his opponent. But most in society won't see it that way. They will see a human being getting pummelled and hurt round after round. They will see straight to the violence.

There's the running battle in 'Making Haye' between your love of Jimi Hendrix and Haye's love of Lenny Kravitz—particularly the song It Ain't Over 'Til It's Over. You see Hendrix as a maestro and original and Kravitz as a copy and mere shadow of such talent. Do you think, looking back, especially with David's eventual words of "Not everybody can be great" that Kravitz represented hope but also a humble fallback in case Plan A went kaput? Do you think Kravitz (and the sadness and regret that happen to lie at the heart of that track) symbolises the doubt that resided in Haye all along despite the apparent confidence?

That was what I was trying to convey. I'd convey the message a lot better now, but I think, even back then, it kind of resonated. Haye certainly wanted to be Hendrix—a god of the game, worshipped, a ruler—but that night in Hamburg was left with no choice but to accept his limitations and realise second best wasn't such a dreadful thing after all. He was beaten by a bigger and better opponent. There's no shame in that.

Also, Haye, though very confident in his ability, was always able to deal with reality in a way few boxers can, which is to say he knew his limitations before they were exposed. David never had designs on having a Hall of Fame-worthy career. He didn't think like that. He wanted to win world titles, no doubt, and he wanted to be remembered, but his primary goal was to make a lot of money and get out by the age of 31 with his faculties intact. That was reiterated to me again and again.

"He's just a boy. Ain't nothing but a little boy," Maurice Core, Carl Thompson's trainer, said after the fifth round TKO and 'upset' back in September 2004 with obvious reference to Haye's foolhardy impetuousness and rush to expend his energy reserves. Preparation, strategy and complacency all seemed to be at the core of that first loss for Haye. And you questioned the legitimacy of the training camp (your first) afterwards: "Haye's cape had ripped while attempting to soar prematurely through skyscrapers." There was talk of light-hearted beach runs, numerous visits to strip clubs

and the like. Even Haye's own words "He might think I'll blow a gasket after four rounds" had a certain, horrible prescience about them, albeit with the gasket blowing earlier. Do you think that experience was a vital and necessary warning to Haye and something that sits in his head to this day?

I'm sure it does. After all, that defeat shaped him. It changed him. It made him realise he wouldn't be able to get by on just talent and punch power. He actually had to knuckle down and train. He had to do what all those other guys were out there doing. And that's what he did. That's why he was able to rebound from the defeat to Thompson and become the number one cruiserweight in the world.

There was definitely something in his head after the Thompson defeat, though. A nagging doubt. He wanted fights over quickly. He didn't want to go rounds. I remember a few days before his European title fight with Giacobbe Fragomeni, a tough Italian known for his durability, he expressed concerns about going rounds and not being able to make an impression on an unbeaten fighter with a granite chin. I then found myself having to remind him that all fighters on computer games—stuff like Street Fighter or Mortal Kombat—have health bars which will invariably and gradually deplete, whether it takes one punch or a hundred. It was as dumb as it sounds, but he seemed to like it and extract some kind of reassurance from it.

The three of you—David Haye (fighter), Adam Booth (trainer) & Elliot Worsell (writer) —together during that special time (2003-2012), do you look back on it with fondness? Do you consider yourself fortunate to have stumbled upon such an adventure (from Tony Dowling and the English cruiserweight title to post-Wladimir Klitschko, at Upton Park vs. Dereck Chisora)?

I do look back on it with fondness. It was an unconventional education of sorts, both in terms of boxing and in terms of life. They both taught me a lot. There were things you wanted to see, things you felt lucky to see, and also things you didn't want to see—bad days, injuries, fall-outs, for example. Sometimes you felt too close. You wanted to be the fan sat in row Z again. At least then you're able to maintain the illusion; when you get close to a sport like boxing, you see the blood-stained masking tape holding it all together.

There was an element of the pariah, the outsider to all three of you: Booth, the former university lecturer and amateur boxer (40-8) "uncomfortable in his role as promising trainer and manager... [certainly] no backslaps from the condescending old guard"; Haye watching Jackie Chan movies as a kid instead of Sesame Street; yourself subjected to snide, journalist comments as a young reporter: "They're even letting schoolkids turn up and cover these things nowadays." Do you think such mutual knowledge helped keep you together even against the backdrop of David being particularly good at engaging with fans via the blossoming online community?

David hated the boxing business and all who claimed to be a part of it. He had no time for promoters, managers or trainers. He saw himself as different to them, more intelligent. He was adamant he knew the way things should be done. He was going to buck the trend and do it all independently. He was going to win titles, make money and then get out. He only wanted a temporary fling with boxing, never a long-term relationship. That was always my impression anyway. Adam was of the same thinking. He too had no time for the characters in the business. He too wanted to do things unconventionally and independently. They had shared goals and mindsets and they worked well together. And by virtue of having me involved, I'd say they were both open to new ideas and perspectives.

Back to the heavyweights. You often get a few moments with HBO's Larry Merchant who confided that the Cuban, Luis Ortiz would beat every single one of his peers. Ortiz, I have to say, reminds me of Riddick Bowe and has so much promise despite only making his pro debut shortly before his 31st birthday. How do you view the 37-year-old King Kong?

I think he is very good. Not good enough to be a star but far too good to be put in with the men considered stars or future stars. That's his problem. If given the opportunity and the right fights, Ortiz could be a nightmare for some of the green heavyweights at the top of the pile. But the longer he waits, the more chance there is that he becomes the next Odlanier Solis rather than the next Riddick Bowe.

Writers have special relationships with certain boxers. I recall you telling me that Steve Cunningham had taken the time to email a "Thank you" back in 2004 following an article you wrote about him and the cruiserweight division. That meant a lot. And since then, besides the Haye years, you seem to have had the ear of _George Groves_, _Tyson Fury_ and Chris Eubank Jr amongst others. Are there a number of 'go-to' fighters you consider more readily than others in their capacity as friends? And if so, who? Also, what do you think brought you together?

I'm wary of getting too close to boxers nowadays, but it's good to have access to a side of them they keep at arm's length from other journalists and writers. Close but not too close is how I see it. You want to be close enough to gain insight and know you can rely on them to provide you with a version of events they won't have already given to someone else with a dictaphone or notepad. But you don't want to be so close that you're unable to criticise them when it's necessary or even write honestly about them. Then you've gone too far. I like to think I can write openly and honestly about any boxer, even the ones I might call friends, and that's important also because boxers typically aren't surrounded by people who are willing to provide them with honesty. Instead, they are often around people who shun honesty in favour of keeping the ship steady and staying on good terms with them. Honesty, therefore, is vital, and is actually appreciated by those boxers secure enough to deal with it.

If I asked you to name five boxers that currently excite you, who would they be? (Fighters that you simply sit in admiration of.)

Gennady Golovkin is the most exciting boxer in the world right now. He's probably the one guy I'd cancel everything to watch live. I also really like Terence Crawford. He's a skilful thinker, a craftsman, who actually looks to entertain and finish. That's a rare thing. Vasyl Lomachenko is the same. He's a joy to watch.

If we're talking UK, I think the Anthony Joshua journey is kind of unmissable right now—he's a heavyweight who looks to finish fights—and I'm also quite fond of Liam Walsh's skills. He has flown under the radar for far too long, but every time I've seen him, whether live or on TV, I've been taken aback by his intelligence in the ring.

You've been in a lot of dressing rooms pre and post-fight. This must be quite an experience and privilege. You must see the REAL

face of a fighter for example, pre-fight nerves etc. Are there any occasions that stand out?

The one that stands out was being with George Groves moments before his two fights with Carl Froch. The second fight, in particular, was almost overwhelming, so big was the occasion, so big was the venue (Wembley Stadium), the changing room, everything. Also, being able to compare Groves before fight one and fight two was fascinating.

At a lower level, I've shadowed amateurs, journeymen and guys in British title fights. They're all different, they all have their own way of doing things. I even spent a night backstage at one of Matchroom's old Prizefighter tournaments—primarily focused on Liverpool's John Watson—and that was a unique and insightful experience; fighters everywhere, fights happening all the time, draws being made, cuts and injuries being assessed.

In all honesty, I don't think there's a better way of getting to know a boxer than to see them at that moment, hours and minutes before the first bell. Often they won't say much, but that's absolutely fine. It's everything you see that counts.

It's extraordinary, looking back, to think that Adam Booth spontaneously trusted YOU to negotiate / phone Carl Thompson in an effort to broker Thompson-Haye II (the clash that never happened). That must have felt a little surreal? I know that David was always obsessed with avenging defeats.

I was always surprised by the trust David and Adam extended my way. Not that I'm untrustworthy, more that I was just a young kid learning on the job. Maybe they saw something in me at a young age. Maybe they had no one else to turn to. Either way, it was very strange to barter with Carl Thompson, a fighter for whom I had enormous respect, in an attempt to lure him into a fight with David. You're right, also, about David's obsession with revenge. Certainly for a while it was all he would talk about. That Thompson defeated haunted him for a good few years.

The journey of a boxer, in many ways, is similar to a writer. Most go from awe to hubris to wisdom. Any thoughts around this?

That's a great way of putting it. What's poignant, though, is often the fighter, unlike the writer, won't stumble upon wisdom until it's too late; it usually kicks in when they've retired. At least writers can capitalise on eventual wisdom.

"Cruiserweights have always been the bastard children of the sport" you once said. Do you mean they occupy quite a unique, unappreciated pocket?

The cruiserweights have always been overlooked. It's a relatively new weight class and even its name triggers confused looks from those unfamiliar with it. The casual sports fan has no idea whether it's just beneath heavyweight or lightweight. It's a shame, too, because the division has always produced decent fights and fighters and is enjoying a renaissance at the moment.

You grew up watching gangster films, then flashier stuff directed by Lynch, Fellini and Kubrick. Such work inspired you to write a number of unpublished screenplays. There are always stories behind a writer's current exploits it seems. What did this early dedication teach you?

It just taught me the nuts and bolts of storytelling, I guess. And that's what I try to do today—tell stories. The screenplay stuff helped in terms of structure and character and it also made me realise, upon looking back years later, that my work sucked and I still had a hell of a lot growing up to do. In ten years I'll more than likely be saying the same when looking back at the stuff I'm writing now.

"I [did not] anticipate how a single boxing match would spook me," you emailed back in April following the tragic events that unfolded at the end of the Nick Blackwell-Chris Eubank Jr fight. I understand that you developed a friendship with Nick over the preceding 18 months and that once out of the coma you "had the privilege of [allaying his fears and] telling him he wasn't knocked out by Eubank, but was instead stopped because of the swelling over his eyes". A sense of pride over and above health from a boxer—to the average Joe in the street, that seems extraordinary. What are your thoughts now?

It was the first injury I'd witnessed live from ringside, so, yes, you're right, it definitely shook me and changed the way I view the sport. It was a jolt to the system, a reminder of what exactly it is I enjoy watching—two men or women beating the shit out of each other. I didn't feel great about it and felt worse when I went to see Nick a couple of times in hospital. The first time I went, when he was still in a coma, was obviously hard, but the second time, the time you mention, was surreal for different reasons. Nick was awake, surrounded by relieved friends and family members, but was convinced he had been knocked out by Eubank Jr. in round ten. We told him the truth and the look on his face—upon realising he hadn't been knocked out and his tough guy reputation remained intact—was one of surprise and joy.

I get the sense that you worry over catch-weight fights such as Khan-Canelo, Brook-Golovkin and, we should say, Bellew-Haye becoming the accepted norm. Are such bouts exploitative and inherently dangerous?

It's not so much the danger—all boxers accept that, it's their choice—more the cynicism behind such fights. Are they fights or business transactions? Do they exist for any reason other than lining pockets? A sign of the times, maybe, all I know is they are not the kind of fights that first attracted me to boxing as a kid.

I think it comes back to the issue of getting too close. So close that the illusion goes. I feel that's what's happening with boxing now as a result of the digital age. There is a transparency the business could do without. We know everything about the promoters and the fighters and the fights, and that's great for us fans, because we've never felt closer, but it shines a bright beaming light on the bullshit of it all. Boxing has always operated from a flimsy scaffolding, but now it's shakier than ever.

Boxers like the once phenomenal Roy Jones Jr struggle to quit this game even once middle aged. How do you view such antics and need?

It's an addiction for some and a necessary evil for others. Some boxers have an inability to give it up because they need the training and the routine and the exposure and the acclaim in their lives, whereas other boxers simply have no alternative ways of making money—big money—in the real world. Both roads lead back to the gym and the arena. Both result in the comeback.

You claim to be quite a cynical person—beyond your years, in fact—having grown up around boxing gyms. Any chance of diluting this distrust and believing the worst in people as you get older?

I'm definitely cynical as a result of being too close. I think anyone would be. It's not a sport to which good people tend to gravitate (which is not to say there aren't good people in it). It's a dark, seedy game, one full of snakes and secrets. That's partly what makes it so attractive to follow and write about, of course, but it will also make you appreciate the virtues of people you meet in other walks of life.

Early on in your career, your dad accompanied you and acted as photographer while you were reporting on certain bouts. Great / funny memories I imagine? Particularly as he once shouted "Get your bloody hands up, David...shattering [your] already flimsy veneer of professionalism".

Before I had a driving licence of my own, my dad, Graham, would drive me to far-flung places like Norwich, Nottingham, Manchester, Liverpool, Derby and Sheffield—hundreds of motorway miles—in order for me to write thousands of words about nondescript undercards played out in empty leisure centres for which I wouldn't be paid a penny. He'd blag his way in as a photographer, just as I blagged my way in as a writer, and for that I will always be grateful. Then, after the event, he'd drive me back down the motorway in the early hours of the morning, elbows on the steering wheel and a KFC bargain bucket between his thighs, and I'd nervously be glancing in the mirror to make sure his tired eyes remained open and focused on the road ahead.

"I was born with a black eye...I looked like a boxer who had [already] done ten rounds...Punching tables and kneecaps was how I spent my early years," David Haye once said to you. Do you think there are significant events behind most people's futures?

Everybody is different. Haye wasn't necessarily born to fight, but he was athletically blessed and could punch hard from a young age. That helps. There are certainly more natural fighters, though, guys for whom a boxer's life is pleasurable. As good as he was, Haye never loved training. He'd probably say he hated it. But he was always more of a scrapper than people thought—tougher, stronger—and was backed up by talent and physical gifts.

Can we associate Haye's failure to beat Thompson with the blue rubber ball you were supposed to be supervising him with all those years ago in order to improve his hand tension / strength and grip?

Yes. Either that or his desire to get to the after-party as soon as possible. Or Carl Thompson being one of the toughest mofos the sport of boxing has ever seen.

"My legs were the problem," Haye famously said following the defeat to Thompson. Do you think most boxers are goners / doomed once the legs go?

It would be wrong to generalise and say all boxers are finished once their legs go, especially when Carl Thompson, Haye's opponent, made a career out of battling back when seemingly finished. Some boxers are frontrunners and are excellent when on top and fresh, whereas others are accustomed to soaking up punishment, going rounds and outlasting their opponent. They're all different. The unpredictability of a fight is what makes us all keep coming back.

You recently broached the somewhat _taboo subject of drugs_ in boxing suggesting that the problem is actually worse in the UK than in the US. How do you think this will play out in the coming years?

It's depressing to think many of the boxers we have admired or currently admire may have benefited from performance enhancing drugs. But it's also the reality we have to face. That was the point I was trying to make in the piece. Either we punish cheats the right way— lengthy bans, if not a life ban—or we simply accept that a hell of a lot of boxers are using and thus resign ourselves to that being the new normal. At the moment we have this weird middle ground whereby we condemn those who have been caught cheating with PEDs yet happily have them fight on our TV screens in major fights. I think that's the result of ignorance and confusion. We don't really know what to think. We want to believe all boxers are honest and genuine and that their excuses are valid. We want to believe the ones who say they were set up or didn't knowingly take anything. We can't fathom being duped, being told Santa isn't real. But the more you investigate, and the more time you spend around gyms and fighters, the more you realise how nothing is as it seems. The drug testing is nowhere near good enough, nor is the punishment served to offenders. We know that. The rest is on us. If we entertain cheats or turn a blind eye to them, we can't then moan when someone gets popped or when, inevitably, a fighter gets seriously injured or killed as a result of their opponent being aided by an illegal substance. At that point we all have blood on our hands.

The effort in writing a book is immense. The research, planning, travelling, desperate need for originality, chapter titles, getting precious quiet time away from the rigours of 'normal life'. How has writing 'Dog Rounds' (2017) been different to writing 'Making Haye' (2011)?

1. I know what I'm doing now, or at least think I do. 2. It's less personal. 3. It's more grown up. 4. It required a hell of a lot more research and that aspect was fun.

Despite your unsparing humour in 'Making Haye' ("Since that [amateur] defeat in 1999 [to Jim Twite], Haye had gone on to excel as both an international amateur and fledgling professional, whereas tiler Twite flunked as a pro and returned to the grout-spreader and spirit level not long after") you strike me as quite a serious person. Has that helped or hindered you in your journalism and writing?

I am quite serious. Anyone who knows me would agree. But I also think, in terms of boxing, that cynicism nicely complements humour. Boxing is a very serious sport, with serious repercussions for its brave participants, but the business side of it is frequently hilarious. That's something I want to tap into a lot more.

"Brutal and beautiful" is how you describe boxing. When, for you, has it been the former and when the latter? Or do you usually mix them together?

When at its best, it's both at the same time. Brutal and beautiful. Mismatches, to me, are just brutal. Worse than that, they make me question why I watch. But then you get beautiful, technical boxers who laugh in the face of the sport's brutality and are somehow able to win fights like it's the easiest thing in the world. Then you're back to seeing it as an art form.

Is there something acutely sad and pitiful about a boxer's life away from the ring? Something inherently ignored by the general public? Something perhaps too unpalatable and indigestible?

Boxers are some of the most admirable yet selfish people you will ever meet. They have to be selfish in order to excel. Spartan-like existence. The loneliest sport in the world. Blah, blah, blah. But what is accepted during the course of their career doesn't necessarily fly when they retire. People become tired of their selfishness, I suppose, no longer willing to give them a pass, and some boxers struggle with this. They get thrown off. They have grown used to having people do things for them for many years—the duration of their career—and that suddenly stops in retirement. The boxing gym and real world are two very different things. You can be the all-knowing king in one and an ignoramus in the other.

When you hear the words "post-traumatic stress" in relation to boxing and not war, what do you think?

I think it's arguably the biggest issue in combat sports right now. I read 'League of Denial' last year and recall scenes of doctors analysing brain scans of American football players and assuming they were the brains of boxers, so horrific was the damage. The book shook up the NFL, yet for boxing, a sport which allows one human being to hit another round the head, I fear this is all par for the course. The sad thing is, all those gym wars, all those fights, they add up, and when you get close to a fighter, and know them over a long period of time, you do notice quite telling changes in their behaviour, changes which were flagged up and explored in 'League of Denial'.

When I mentioned Herzog a while back, there was an assumption on your part that I was talking about the German screenwriter and film maker, Werner Herzog but I was, in fact, talking about Saul Bellow's restless, epistolary novel—itself about Moses E. Herzog and his midlife crisis at the age of 47. What do you think hitting 40 will be about for you?

It seems a long way off right now, but the speed with which I went from 20 to 30 reminds me it's not. I guess I just hope to be ten years better than I am now, in every facet of life; writing, being a husband, one day being a father.

Marc Weingarten in his superb book, The Gang That Wouldn't Write Straight believes that New Journalism's golden era ran from 1962 to 1977, that it was fifteen years of heaven for "thwarted novelists or fiction writers who moonlighted as journalists" and that the three greatest post-war magazine editors, Harold Hayes at Esquire, Clay Felker at the Tribune's New York and Jann Wenner at Rolling Stone were at the centre of this revolution. Do you think there is an equivalent today and if so, does it make you want to raise your game?

I don't know about an equivalent, but the birth of long-form pieces online has certainly provided a platform for that type of stuff to rise from the ashes. And there's plenty of quality new journalism out there if you look hard enough.

You talk about getting a 'real' career at times—perhaps in publishing, perhaps elsewhere due to the pittance that sports writing offers. Do such thoughts ultimately sadden you?

Sure, it saddens me, but you've also got be realistic. Not everybody can do exactly what they want in life. I've been lucky in a sense—right place, right time—but I've also had to do a fair amount of non-writing work that gave me zero satisfaction in order to make ends meet. That's just the way it is. Obviously, though, the dream is to one day write for a living and for that to be enough. If I can achieve that, I'll be a happy man.

From Dickens, Balzac and Fielding and their social realist fiction, to Jack London's advocacy journalism ("minutely observed chronicles"), to George Orwell and George Plimpton's participatory journalism, to Hunter S. Thompson's gonzo journalism and even my own magpie journalism (extracting shiny quotes from other works and placing them in a richer form) — writers have tried in earnest to get to the core or nucleus of a story. They have desperately sought original angles and wished to do justice to the person or people before them whilst hopefully blowing a bugle in relation to their own talents. How do you relate to such history?

I think you have to earn your place in the story. If your presence isn't relevant to the story being told, you shouldn't be there. In saying that, a lot of what I like to read is participatory stuff (and guys like Plimpton, Mailer and Thompson unquestionably earned the right to not only be in the story but to be the story).

Also, a lot of it depends on the interview subject. Some are better than others. Fighters, in particular, cover the extremes. Some are fascinating, others have nothing to say. So, when a subject has very little to say, I enjoy reading the author's observations and insights instead, as it's far more interesting than a fighter giving lip service or combat clichés.

In a sporting context, Hunter S. Thompson's The Kentucky Derby is Decadent and Depraved (1970), George Plimpton's Paper Lion (1966) and Gay Talese's Joe Louis: The King as a Middle-Aged Man (1962) are considered masterpieces of the New Journalism era (and that is without mentioning non-sportswriters such as Michael Herr, Truman Capote, Norman Mailer, Joe McGinniss, John Sack and Joan Didion). Who and what has informed your writing?

W.C. Heinz's boxing novel 'The Professional' is a book I recommend to anybody interested in sports writing or just good old story-telling. It's probably my all-time favourite; definitely, for me, the boxing book which is most relatable and the most realistic. And yet it's fiction.

Like you, narrative non-fiction is my go-to genre. Talese's 'The Loser', an account of Floyd Patterson coming to terms with his second loss to Sonny Liston, might be my number one piece of boxing writing, and obviously Capote's 'In Cold Blood' had a big impact on me when I was a teenager. It sparked a realisation that you could write about real people and places but do so in a manner that was more in keeping, stylistically, with fiction.

I also last year got round to reading Darcy Frey's 'The Last Shot', a brilliant non-fiction account of a number of nineties basketball prospects (imagine the documentary 'Hoop Dreams' as a book), and that stuck with me, as did Andrew Hankinson's 'You Could Do Something Amazing With Your Life (You Are Raoul Moat)' and Gary Younge's 'Another Day in the Death of America', both released in 2016, both great works of narrative non-fiction.

A clue as to the quality of Worsell writing to come was—to my mind—early on in 'Making Haye' when you described Haye's first professional opponent, Tony Booth (41-72-8): "To the uninitiated, Haye might have been beating up a shyster plumber for a job not-so-well done, such was the disparity in athleticism and ambition." Have there been moments in your career when you've sensed that your writing needs to ramp itself up and follow what you see with fresher, evolving eyes?

Of course. I want to rewrite shit all the time. There are things I wrote last year that I'd write differently now. But that's the hard thing about wanting to be a writer, I suppose. You never really know when you're writing good stuff.

All I do is observe how other people cover and write about combat sports and then try to do it differently.

Where do we find new ideas? you once asked somewhat rhetorically. I, nonetheless, told you to hoover the house, do mundane tasks (like washing the pots), go for a walk—anything that is undemanding. That is when ideas ferment, when they are born. Did you take any notice of my words?

Yes. And my wife is both shocked and delighted by the emergence of her new domesticated husband.

"At least he was drinking cranberry juice," you wryly observed of Haye in the run-up to the disastrous fight with Carl Thompson as he was sat in a Bournemouth city centre strip club. Looking back and seeing yourself at the time as "Burt Reynolds in Boogie Nights" does such preparation seem incredibly complacent from a boxer looking to scale the heights? Does it remind you, to a degree, of English footballers in the 1970s and 1980s boozing and smoking?

He will admit himself that he was complacent in those days. And he had every reason to be. Most of his early professional opponents were there to lose, there to be knocked out, and Haye duly delivered. His whole reputation was built on power and knocking old men out and Carl Thompson was hand-picked by Haye and Booth to go the same way. They assumed he was over-the-hill. They believed the timing was right. But, of course, they were wrong. Thompson was fresher and tougher than they hoped and Haye had yet to mature. Lessons were learnt.

One of the finer compliments I've read of yours in relation to Haye is that when watching boxing videos of himself there were "the uncontrollable reflexes of a man programmed to fight...a form of fistic Tourette's". Haye often re-watched his worst and best moments, "relived it in slacks" but apparently "has never re-watched the first three rounds of the Thompson fight" such is the discomfort and embarrassment. Do you still see that naturalness in him?

Definitely. Haye, like countless others, doesn't know anything else; fighting other blokes is what he does best, it's what he's done since the age of 10, and that's why he's still doing it in 2017.

Interview by Jeff Weston conducted between December 2016 and January 2017.

The Changing Landscape for Scott Quigg

Boxing.com, 4 November 2016

Put mittens on the two lads behind reception at Gloves Community Centre – James Shorting and Carl Dyer – and you'd expect a TKO in round six or seven; an austere uppercut from the stockier Dyer. Neither man boxes. Neither man professes to want to step in a ring (although Dyer is taking his ABA coaching badges). Yet this is the thing about boxing, its pre-bell, thin definition – you see two specimens side by side and foolishly think you know who's the hardest.

Scott Quigg would have been downed in his sixth and eleventh fight if that was the case – against Gheorghe Ghiompirica. He would have succumbed to Rendall Munroe twice in 2012 and been chewed up by Kiko Martinez – his "first big-name win" – only last year.

Except, the heart isn't always visible. And ugly doesn't always execute the menace that its face promises.

On the outside, Prince Street, Bolton is ugly, unprepossessing. The home of Joe Gallagher's legion of champions feels like a piece of post-2008 Detroit. An eight-story block of flats sits opposite. Faded double yellow lines shimmy in front of the similarly colored gym front. Half a dozen old, wooden crates stand pointlessly propped up against a nearby wall. The boarded up Cotton Tree public house down the road – "another lost pub" – symbolizes retrenchment of a sort.

At 7 am, sat outside what was boldly heralded by the local rag – post-Carl Frampton – as "the centre of the boxing universe" (what with the Team Fury gym just a mile around the corner), there is a kind of beauty, however – a mishmash of humanity preparing itself for another day. All potter and weave beneath the prominent B&Q orange lights in the distance. All look minuscule in the shadow of the self-storage warehouse behind this boxing hub.

'No Ball Games' blares the red and white sign in the housing association gardens across the road. If not, then there has to be *something* – exhalement and focus quartered in meaningful barracks; a group of kids and young men directing their angst *somewhere*.

James opens up at 8.45 am on this late October Monday morning. He refers to himself as a "caretaker", the odd job man, the man with the keys. He loosens the necessary doors in time for the pro boxers who invariably train between 9 am and 1 pm. It doesn't appear to be a taxing job, but he has to smile and greet all manner of people – some of them warm-hearted, some of them overweening.

Looking around it is clear that this is Amir Khan central. Thirty-four framed snapshots of his fights line the wall. "Just the Canelo fight to go up," James says, almost six months after that heavy night in Las Vegas.

Saúl "Canelo" Álvarez is the man that links Bolton's famous son with the current Scouse (and Mancunian) occupants. Past the two Toshiba televisions, leather suite and greenhillsport.com boxes, and through a maze of conference rooms and staircases, reside Gallagher's often maligned crew including Liam "Beefy" Smith, Anthony "Million Dollar" Crolla and Scott Quigg.

It is just Gallagher and Bury pugilist, Quigg when I arrive – sat on the humble, slat benches of the beige-tiled changing room in their archetypal black gear. Gallagher has his usual scorched smile; Quigg, his always-alert eyes and indoor skin. The Manchester twang of Gallagher is noticeable although less striking – a little softer – close up. He seems reasonable, more approachable in the flesh than he does on TV; his backstreet haircut a sign that intensity and fitness are at the forefront of his thoughts, not la-di-da smoothness.

It is five years now since these two hooked up – Quigg's super bantamweight Lonsdale belt win against decade older, Jason Booth to many the start of the ride. Gallagher got him at the right time (fight number 23). And Quigg's part of the deal is that he's no longer sprayed in the face between rounds by Brian Hughes, but instead has a damp, white cloth placed on his head.

"You're a Bolton fan?" I say to Gallagher after getting some poor information on the way through.

"Who told you that?" is the retort, the appalled counter to such a statement.

I get the names mixed up: "Carl." Blame the imagined, uppercut specialist instead of the guy on the canvas.

Gallagher shakes his head. He likes to work in the provinces, away from the bright, imposing lights of Manchester – following a "surprise" phone call / agreement with Khan's dad, Shah over four years ago – but his football team is firmly "Man Utd. Him too…" he nods in the direction of Quigg.

Quigg is supposed to be loyal to Bury as well, but there is no interjection, no roar from the younger man. He doesn't mind Gallagher taking the lead. When he feels like speaking, he'll speak. There is a quiet weighing up of things from Quigg – mature counsel. By his own admittance he lives a very isolated life and so perhaps trust takes a little longer to come by.

I discuss Carl Thompson with Gallagher as Quigg continues to wrap his hands. "I think I read [your article on] that. Was it a two-parter?" he asks.

"No," is my flat response, knowing that these boxing doyens have a lot of fishing lines in their head and sometimes tie bait together mistakenly – cross one story with another.

We move on – talk about the weekend's boxing and also the discernible, up and coming mismatch between British and European super middleweight, Callum Smith and Luke Blackledge; Smith putting Rocky Fielding to sleep within one round in November 2015 and Fielding doing the same to the "Malik Scott," mask-wearing Blackledge two years earlier.

"The British Board have ordered it…we'll do it." Gallagher seems more respectful than I anticipated. He's aware that Blackledge took a blow to the side of the neck that evening – something you can never legislate for. But maybe only Lee Markham has been of decent caliber / opposition since. And Elvis Dube didn't exactly raise Blackledge's stock on Saturday night.

I cut back to Quigg: "I think Scott's had three outstanding, career-defining fights – Jamie Arthur…" Before I can rattle through or recall the remaining names of Yoandris Salinas and Hidenori Otake (and avoid mention of the malfunction versus Frampton), Gallagher is bubbling over upon hearing Arthur's name.

"That was our Jamie Arthur moment [on Saturday]," he says, verbally nudging Quigg, briefly shaking off his regular, utilitarian voice.

It's not clear if he's referring to Blackledge (down in the 1st), recent recruit, Paul Butler or serial headbanger, Jamie Cox (cut in the 5th) on the Bolton Whites Hotel card. Everybody loves Arthur, the Scottish Welshman though it seems. And for good reason. The "give it your all," free-swinging fighter embodied much of what Gallagher preaches: tenacity, grueling gym sessions and heart. He epitomized a ring attitude that many trainers these days see as high risk.

Gallagher too would worry over the lack of a high guard, a proper defense. "Engage when you want to engage. Work the jab," were his words to Quigg after Round Two on that night back in February 2012; ironically the 24th professional gig for *both* boxers.

How a fighter's career trajectory can change in the space of a few seconds. Quigg – down in the 4th, possibly about to lose the first defense of his British title, the ringside commentators referring to the "first crisis of his professional career," but then employing the front foot, boxing at a better pace.

"You push Arthur back and you take away a lot of his assets," was the boiled dictum from outside the ropes, the cue to Quigg to change his approach. Imperative there's a Plan B.

Frampton significantly said of Quigg in the run up to their fight four years later: "He has to train hard because he is not a natural. He is manufactured." This is undoubtedly the central, salient point about Quigg and one that I can't help wondering over as I attempt to draw out a sentence or two from the 28-year-old now.

Is he manufactured – lacking in flair and quintessential ability? Such a question brings in and lassoes many facts and observations concerning the 5'8" super bantamweight, soon-to-be featherweight.

Gallagher knows he has a good one. He has previously bemoaned the training regimes of Ricky Hatton and Michael Gomez – north-west fighters who unnaturally shed the pounds in the gym pre-fight, unable to stop their weight from ballooning. To Quigg, the gym is a church. And every day is Sunday. When away from the congregation, he is out hill running, swimming, consuming his Science in Sport strawberry protein. But does that make him a potential great and can he live with the skilled architects of the weight divisions around him?

"You know more about my fights than me," he self-deprecatingly states after an initial lull, perhaps healthily looking to the future, perhaps trying to forget the Frampton mist that descended at the Manchester Arena back in February.

Some of it I buy. Some of it I don't. The Quigg Diaries – six, seven, eight years of monitoring and evaluation – are well known. And if every facet of his training – sparring, bagwork, padwork – is videotaped, watched and re-watched, as has been reported, then the fights that prompt such tweaks and preparation must be in his head. "It's a disease…it's obsessive," he once said.

The archive shows that he has skittled over Angelo Villani, Andrey Kostin, Santiago Allione, Diego Oscar Silva, Tshifhiwa Munyai, Stephane Jamoye and Kiko Martinez. From these fights we learn very little, however, except that there are stuntmen, wide open Russians, weight dodgers, boy-like boxers with red Mohicans, fragile atomic spiders, those prepared to be bullied (offering a mere ragged jab by way of muster) and those without a reverse gear.

The fights that best provide a semblance of insight and information on Quigg's potential, alas, are his longer escapades: Arthur, Salinas and Otake; encounters largely responsible for the birth of Brand Quigg. The Bury maestro, it seems, only convinces the purists every fourth outing.

Reference is made to Quigg's boxing hero, Wilfredo "Bazooka" Gómez in the Arthur scrap – the Puerto Rican turning 60 this very month. What a delight with his angles, brawn and unmitigated appetite Gómez was. In entering a ring with Arthur (18-5-0), Quigg got a taste of that – full-blooded confrontation. But then for Gómez, along came Salvador Sánchez – one of the finest talents the sport has ever seen (tragically and briefly).

Sánchez – **killed in a car crash a year later** – taught Gómez an important lesson in August 1981: You can't out-tough all your opponents. If Quigg is to take this track – he possesses, after all, a quite dazzling level of stamina and indulges in plenty of behind-the-elbow tree cutting with his axe-like arms – then he needs to be aware of technically adept bruisers, "natural[s]" to re-quote his nemesis, Frampton.

Quigg gets up and ambles toward the ring. "I wanna do it properly," he says regarding a fuller interview. "I have my trainin' and my eatin'…I'll phone you later." Gallagher chips in: "He can talk a lot."

Properly is his performance against Salinas (20-0-1) – a majority decision draw. Behind in that fight, Quigg managed to summon crucial reserves from the tank. Gallagher's corner advice shifted from "You're waitin' and waitin' but you're not seein' it comin'…you wanna just lay back – feint, little twitches of the head, alright. Just don't let him turn, poke that jab. Alright. OK. Get your legs going, alright – your legs should be gassing. You've not got 'em goin' yet" (after Round One) to "You're breathin' smart…Stay disciplined…Chin down" (after Round Eight).

You learn a lot from Gallagher's tone, his sense of urgency. When the words are more spaced out, then he's generally happy with his fighter. Quigg's volume punching, self-belief and initiative saved this and his comparable lack of an amateur pedigree was pushed aside.

Otake (22-1-3) posed a different challenge: always down on points, but a great example of an Asian fighter being able to handle the body shots; Quigg's finest weapon, like a patter of chopsticks to the ribs. "…the old story of levels," the commentary ran a little unfairly, dismissing the Japanese fighter's chances, but Otake – cut above the right eye at the end of the 9th – showed himself to be a gladiator.

Three times the doctors check him out. And three times he is sent back into the war zone. Quigg, you can tell, is in absolute admiration. Such respect reinforces the peddled sentiment that emanates from his camp. "This isn't hardship…Inside the ring is my home…There's nothing more enjoyable than having my hand raised at the end of a fight."

One worries about his expected step-up, his joining the nine-stoners. It'll be like fleeing a gang only to find himself in a tougher neighborhood. (Nothing like Tony Bellew moving from light-heavyweight to the comfort of cruiserweight.) Gary Russell Jr., Lee Selby and Léo Santa Cruz – not to mention that Irish chap – are hardly generous opponents, but then neither is Guillermo Rigondeaux, the man Quigg has sparred and messed about with at Freddie Roach's Wild Card gym.

If Quigg can stop the unnecessary scouting missions (à-la-Frampton) and find some new tricks then anything is possible. He knows that boxing can be a "dirty, horrible business" yet it gives him a thrill, provides him with a place in the world.

There's some **old footage** of Wilfredo Gómez stood against a wall having a soft ball repeatedly thrown at his head; a chance to perfect his bob and weave; a chance to augment the defenses. Quigg needs some of this old school chicanery and hardness if he is to thrive. He also needs refining – absolving of boxing impurities and stiffness.

"He hasn't had his BoxRec t-shirt yet," Gallagher announces, referring to the gift in relation to Quigg's ranking. Little things. It's the little things with Gallagher, the serial talker.

"Four world champions out of two gyms literally a mile-and-a-half apart – that is some going. There must be something in the water in Bolton," he said back in March.

The Aldi Shepley Spring water, lined up in the Gloves' fridge and sourced from next door, would beg to differ.

All Heart: Boxing's Finest Gentleman, Carl 'The Cat' Thompson

Boxing.com, 28 September 2016

"Don't just swing it. Measure it. Time it. He's open to the right hand. You've gotta put him in his place. He's getting too brave. You hear me? He's getting too cocky now. Show him what you've got. He cannot take your punches…"

It started then, in June 1994, after a brief round three Akim Tafer onslaught. Not with the evangelical words of celebrity minister, Billy Graham but with the impromptu monologue of an altogether rougher, 'say it as it is' Manchester trainer; a 1955 Billy Graham UK vintage.

Such a ubiquitous name. A dozen and a half of them on BoxRec. But this one in Carl Thompson's corner, in a French backyard; his own record during a short, fighting career (12-2-0) eerily similar to The Cat's eventual slate (34-6-0).

You win six, you lose one – that keeps things tidy, just about respectable.

Thompson didn't start round four of his mid-career 19th fight anything other than ragged, playing possum as was his stamp, but the words in his ear perhaps heralded an inner truth: When The Cat missed, he missed big – like a drunk reaching for a Walmart trolley. Hone this somehow and you have a different fighter – one that can pick off an opponent with a single, blistering shot.

For the truth is Thompson's right hand is one of those bar cocktails that send an unconscious shiver through a man's very being, induce a blackout from which few properly recover. His story is thicker and more taut than the average man's, his dedication mostly unsurpassed. He is the only boxer to defeat both David Haye and Chris Eubank and yet these wins are mere specks on a rich, 17½ year canvas.

The initial chapter is widely known: Master Sken Kaewpadung, the knackered shins and the rude awakening or first professional loss to Crawford Ashley in October 1989. Thompson came into this bloodied sport (June 1988) having gained a solid reputation as a Muay Thai practitioner, but the "more upright stance and wide open guard" were deemed bad habits in boxing circles, akin to jab-eating madness, naivety and unfettered generosity.

Fixing such defects would take time. And Master Sken, for all his wisdom, would have to go. Enter Moss Side/Champs Camp stalwart and "left-wing political activist" Phil Martin, and later on the irrepressible Billy Graham and Maurice Core.

Thompson, after tip-toeing through the club and hotel circuit, got an early taste of foreign soil courtesy of his fight *after* Ashley against the relatively green Franco Wanyama (3-1-1). Sint Amandsberg, Oost-Vlaanderen played host to the "rebound bout". Belgium's municipality, known for its manicured lawns and fine architecture, was not beholden to The Cat's temple-like body and prowess, however.

The Wanyama fight was to end with a six-round points decision against Thompson, despite The Cat's claims that he "offensively shut [the Ugandan] down...had that guy rocking and rolling". Thompson was, nonetheless, "floored" and the Ugandan curse was to strike again two fights later in more dramatic fashion versus Yawe Davis (26-6-2) inside Monaco's Stade Louis II; a controversial TKO in round two of eight.

A glamorous venue. The wide-mohicanned Thompson forcing the pace rather than demonstrating the phone-booth credentials by which he would later be known. But such openness suited the Italian-adopted Davis. A fierce, flying right hook from him set the tone.

Thompson must have had blurred vision during this fight. Yellow stadium seats, yellow shorts, everything but The Beatles' yellow submarine sailing towards him. The decision which ended the bout did not provoke the same hot-coals, apoplectic dance that would unfold after The Cat's fight with Johnny Nelson years later but it did prompt incredulity, the sad feeling of being a victim of maniacal refereeing.

Ref Francis Risani may have been French but one sensed that there was some Italian blood in the family – a bit of partisan waving off of a still-fresh fight.

Crazy that Thompson would later admit: "What people always forgot was that I loved fighting away from home. I loved the crowd cheering for my opponent. And when they came to lay me out I put up resistance and broke their hearts. I took their best shots and wouldn't go."

Later experiences would justify this, but in the immediate aftermath of the Davis scrap The Cat stayed at home. He fought on English turf only for nearly three years. Perhaps waited for the sourness to ease. Perhaps waited for a proper referee (who would know him and his ways) once he was more established.

The defeated fighter is prime meat for others though – sometimes *foolish* others, hubristic revellers. What Thompson lost in his April 1991 fight to Davis, he quickly found – and more – versus Welshman, Nicky Piper five months later. The carefully groomed Cardiff-born bruiser (10-0-1) – ironically his only setback to Thompson stablemate and former Strangeways Prison 'guest' Maurice Core – more than likely anticipated a vulnerable foe; an opponent who had lost three of his last four fights. What he did not envisage was resolve and tenacity.

But then, how could he? Thompson was deemed a 9-3 dunce on the circuit; a boxer who had finally walked into the inevitable, punishing haze of the sport. To many he was shot – just another fumbling trier who had, early on, discovered his limitations; that awful realisation that thwarts most men.

To interpret numbers is to ultimately gamble though. And the Piper camp had not accounted for the 10lb weight difference. Nor had they allowed for the tough, physical specimen before them – something of the polite Clubber Lang about Thompson that night at York Hall in Bethnal Green. "A bit of a hard nut," ITV's Reg Gutteridge commentated with his usual brio.

When the "wild" right hands came, in the third round, they demolished Piper. He looked dazed – like a genius who'd just come out of a pub quiz after being defeated by a high school scoundrel.

And so, just 39 months into his professional boxing career, Carl Thompson was off, launched, at the age of 27. He would win all his fights over the next seven years with the exception of his first World Cruiserweight title tilt against Ralf Rocchigiani at the G-Mex, Manchester in June 1995; a cruel, dislocated shoulder in the 11th confounding the scorecards which had The Cat cantering: 99-91, 97-92, 97-92.

The fight against the six-foot German for the vacant belt was significant for many reasons. Manchester had not had a world champion for 60 years since Collyhurst flyweight, **Jackie Brown**. The occasion showed The Cat in his prime, utilizing great variety and poise, and going beyond eight rounds for the first time. And the faces in the crowd – Frank Warren, Naseem Hamed, Graciano and Christine Rocchigiani (*check out that holler!*) – all said something, be it "Do it for your city, Carl" or "Schnell, angriff, Ralf!"

"Show me that jab and left hook, Carl," was the constant phrase seeping into the ring in the second round of this fight. Such purgatory, such interference opens a window on and perhaps explains The Cat's preferred away days. Best not to jinx it, best not to have multiple passenger seat drivers twisting the game plan. (Unless the cry is from the corner.)

But that is what happened. And the pre-bell commentary, heightening expectations, asking of Thompson four lungs instead of his usual three ("Well, everything else that's happened in Carl Thompson's career crystallized really into one night") was an appalling curse, a Ramadan with two sun rises.

Thompson steadied the ship with a trio of 'nothing' fights after this disappointment – versus Albert Call (6-4-3), Jason Nicholson (13-7-0) and Keith McMurray (16-38-2) – but it was effectively two years down the pan like the post-Ezra Sellers era late in his career when Phill Day (8-7-2), Hastings Rasani (11-8-0) and Paul Bonson (18-66-6) inexplicably appeared on the radar.

Chunks of a boxer's life you cannot get back. They must readjust, change the oil, take a few spanners to the engine, fight the ridiculous fights. Or maybe style fights, suitability fights. Examining Thompson's forty gigs in the ring one is drawn to two sets of lottery balls: fights 12 (Davis), 13 (Piper), 18 (Massimiliano Duran), 19 (Tafer), 22 (Rocchigiani), 26 (Rocchigiani II) and 27 (Eubank), 28 (Eubank II), 29 (Nelson), 34 (Sellers), 38 (Sebastiaan Rothmann), 39 (Haye).

Four of these The Cat lost, but only Sellers (23-4-0) wiped him out in what was a **"knockdown festival"**. While the erratic Johnny Nelson was suited up at ringside two days after his victory over Alexander Vasiliev, expecting a spring re-match and WBO defence against Thompson, boxing did what it always does: it KO'd the script.

"I twisted my ankle in the fight and had to make a decision. I had to go at him. He was a southpaw and I knew it wasn't going to last long. If my ankle didn't go, I [would] have boxed him. But he was a tremendous puncher," The Cat explained at the time.

Whether the pensive-looking Nelson was disappointed or now fearful of the Roy Jones Jr-sparring Sellers wasn't clear. What *was* clear is that The Cat would have to build again…in the twilight of his career, aged 37.

Money – that elusive fiend – had hardly cosseted Thompson during his finer days. He had famously earned a mere £3,500 against Steve Lewsam for the British Cruiserweight title in 1992 and a tidy, yet extremely modest £100,000 against David Haye 12 years and 25 fights later when defending his IBO World title. In between there had been abiding slugfests against Duran, Tafer, Eubank (twice) and Rothmann but his clenched fists had failed to morph into able fingers ready to exploit the till.

"I just wanted to live a normal life and make some money, but it doesn't happen that way," Thompson told Elliot Worsell in 2005, weeks before his final fight. "I'm not naturally outspoken, but I feel as though I have to be to get people to notice me and pay the bills. I'm not going to change now, because that would be phoney, but if I knew that from the beginning, I would have opened my mouth more. I just don't understand why you should have to disrespect other hard-working boxers to make money and get people to sit up and listen to you."

This is the essence of The Cat. He is a gentleman – as far away from the **"shrewd realist"** and showman as you can imagine. And yet on these often imbecilic shores (both the UK and the US), people seem to crave that otherness, that ersatz, synthetic personality. It stirs things up, it whets boxing's invisible blade. Without bogus controversy, how can we possibly get on?!

A pleasant dip into the 1994 Duran fight with its 200-year-old ref, old-fashioned coats and old-fashioned faces shows pugilism in another light. There is a feeling of authenticity not just from the Italian's renowned jab and high, white socks, but from the navy-blazered Mario Guerrini gabbing at ringside.

Thompson's first European Cruiserweight brawl in Ferrara, Emilia Romagna emits a bit of everything: a studious, admiring public; magnificent style from the home-town fighter; and Duran's mother playing Mary Magdalene (her boy slumped, crucified in the corner of the ring following The Cat's clinical combination finish in the eighth round).

Such a fight was bound to end after a brief moment of vanity – Duran, guard down, adjusting his trunks, succumbing to the Thompson march, clubbing hooks, short chops and overhead rights. Duran (19-4-0) resembles a confused child once down, unable to grab the top rope at the first attempt, his mother resuscitating him with familial words. As he is walked backwards to the opposite corner and an apparently non-portable stool, the feeling is that Thompson has brought devastation to this northern city close to Bologna, ignored its heritage and ripped the European title from Magdalene's bosom.

The Cat's corner in their yellow, Champs Camp jackets, seem content, semi-jovial. Trainer Phil Martin smiles, assistant Billy Graham looks to have his mind on the next fight. And for good reason, although he wouldn't know it: the man who initially brought him into the fold, Phil Martin, would die from cancer just over three months later aged 44.

It hurt them all.

Tragedy can seemingly do two things – lay a man low or lift him to strengthen the memories, the legacy. Thompson had three more fights that year (Akim Tafer, Dionisio Lazario Nascimento and Tim Knight), but it is really only the first that is remembered: Tafer (19-4-0) in Epernay, Marne, France.

"Please, God – don't let me disgrace myself," were The Cat's thoughts after taking a hiding in round three.

They are a measure of the man. Despite the *Eye of the Tiger* ring walk. Despite being the European champ. You can tell, in that walk, in that face, that Carl is a reserved chap, a relatively shy individual. He is the opposite of the bombs that he throws. He does not crave attention – just a living, a livelihood.

He is, in many ways, the soulful singer-songwriter, Lisa Stansfield. Nothing, absolutely nothing like you imagine once the artistry ceases. Look at the fire in the ring, on stage, and then compare it to the ordinariness outside, the colloquial grain; an extraordinary ordinariness – a kind, affable, man of the people.

Tafer looks brutal. He is built of the finest French granite. The chants of "A-kim! A-kim! A-kim!" around the arena are enough to blow over a lesser opponent. Referee, Franz Marti from Switzerland, to his credit, lets this fight flow. He recognizes that he is in the company of two men of steel – one enormously humble, the other so revved up inside that he punches a towel off the top rope in the first round.

This isn't a 75" versus 75½" reach in favour of Tafer as the stats suggest. It is much more. One examines the Frenchman early on and believes him to have extra-long, bludgeoning forearms. The ceremony, the pomp now over, Thompson must wonder why he has agreed to meet this opponent, *La Marseillaise* and all that comes with it.

"He's gonna keep throwin', he's gonna get fucked, he's gonna get tired." The words from new no.1 corner man, Billy Graham somehow dissolve and don't register. Before The Cat is a wall put together with Napoleon mortar. Ashley, Davis, Piper, Arthur Weathers, Duran – all the fights that came before this do not matter. He is hostage in a ring with a Gallic blunderbuss – precision lacking at times, but a slugger, a dangerous over-the-channel charger who, unlike Thompson, would only fight on away turf twice during his entire career.

No "have gloves will travel" attitude from Tafer – just the stirring home crowd, willing him over the line, praying for an early evening.

"The toughest fight of my career," The Cat would later reflect, just as he would label the second Rocchigiani encounter "the fight where I showed my all" and Sellers "the hardest puncher I ever came across".

Tafer, alas, fatally allows Thompson to fight in the pocket, to lean in on his opponent and when the murderous ending comes via a right upper-cut and right cross in the sixth, he is bewildered, outwardly not aware of the count.

The Cat, quick to honour his opponent, quick to show concern and warmth – like a modern-day Canelo – does all he can to alleviate his professional work from just seconds before, but the smelling salts, exhaustion and possible missing tooth in the French camp tell another story.

Thompson's applause and bows to the crowd from each side of the ring, after having his arm held aloft, speak of a distinct grace, a depth to the man that the world would come to know following his cruiserweight titles in 1997 (Rocchigiani), 2001 (Uriah Grant) and 2004 (Rothmann).

It is undoubtedly The Cat's pivotal night, an early inauguration. Without Tafer there would be no Rocchigiani, no Eubank, no Grant, no

Rothmann, no Haye later on – those giant, defining fights central to his legacy.

Asked about a rematch ("One more time"), Thompson responds: "I'll sit down, think about it, have a rest, next time…thank you, merci." Such simplicity – tinged with ambiguity - but when he gets hold of the trophy, and turns to the press and the crowd, it is the proudest, the happiest you are likely to see him in a ring.

Recognition. The French know how to spoil you a little. Unlike the sport itself which can be unforgiving, ruinous and far from equitable in dishing out its rewards.

Is there an epithet for The Cat besides "Come from behind fighter"? Yes. You hear it at the end of the Rothmann fight in the ninth round a decade later – the last sentence:

"Just needs a little bit more variation, Thompson…Got the left up just in time…Well, Thompson's absolutely exhausted. Thompson is exhausted. He's tired and Rothmann's really going for him now. Thompson, on the ropes, and Rothmann's actually stepped back and maybe let him off the hook. I'm not sure Thompson has a great deal left. Richie Davies is having a good look. He certainly won't allow Thompson to get himself hurt. He may just survive *the end of this round. Oh, what a shot from Thompson. Right hand. Oh, what can you say. Oh, ye have little faith…"*

Fury-Klitschko II:
Better Burgers to Flip?

Boxing.com, 18 July 2016

The more you know a man, the softer you are on him. Tyson Fury — Bolton associations aside — does grow on you, he does draw you in, engage one's curiosity. In him is the suffering animal, the occasionally and startlingly honest dual-personality.

Winning, he says, is ephemeral, short-lived. After the smoke of a fight, it is still him. His demons are still there. The temporary high and cerebral blast of victory does not sort him out. It does not reframe who he is.

Tyson Fury is simply on a trip — some would say a gypsy adventure. The caravan door is ajar and there is singing, play-acting, brawling, the smiles and sadness of life. The boxing ring to him is a false square of virtue. Inside it arbitrary decisions prompt his arms and legs into action. One night he might be effective. The next he might wing it — put his success down to God.

Angels. Angles. They are both Fury's calling cards. That is why he is good, they say. Opponents lose their bearings, they become disoriented. No one expects a heavyweight to have such guile. One audacious line referred to Fury as a "heavyweight Mayweather"; his angles *defensive* but bewildering all the same.

November 2015's blowout — not the beano type — confirmed two things: Fury has composure and Klitschko has fear. Klitschko was laid bare in that fight, made to look too human — his jab impotent, hanging in the wind. The low hands of Fury unsettled him. He felt all the more foolish for *not* taking advantage of such a reckless guard.

Hats off to Fury. Yet it was not a good fight. It was, in fact, an extremely subdued fight — the punches last time out like Milk Duds falling from their box. Neither boxer was pulverised. Neither boxer "shook up the world." We were surprised — yes. But not astounded. Surprised that Wladimir lost with so little resistance.

"I chose to lose," he has said in the intervening months. For a man whose father died in all likelihood as a result of cleaning up Chernobyl, such words sound incredibly rakish. Klitschko, in interviews, has regrettably come across like a smiling PR man — the very essence of the robotic human he claims not to be. He is clearly uncomfortable in Fury's 'wind it up and go' world, but even on his own it is as if the first fight has taken the last vestiges of who he is.

Klitschko's trainer, Johnathon Banks in a rather excited pitch back in January, stated: "This is my Thrilla in Manila — my Rumble in the Jungle." Fury-Klitschko II — new date all but confirmed of 29th October 2016 — will be many things but it is unlikely to imbue the onslaught of Ali-Frazier III (1975) or the intensity of Ali-Foreman (1974). The month is the same — October — but the pedigree questionable.

There won't be any of the unnatural exhaustion that comes with fighting in the Philippines or Zaire (now the Democratic Republic of Congo). Fury-Klitschko II comes from the moderate autumn climate of Manchester, England thank god. But what evidence have we to suggest it will be a rip-roaring affair, a gallant encounter? That "great 12th round"? That tangled foray which upped the tempo ever-so-slightly from the nothingness of the first 33 minutes?

Klitschko's proud record hasn't disintegrated because of that impecunious circus act (the taming of an invisible lion) back in November, but it has suffered. Fans know that with Wladimir it has always been caution first. He is not a stuntman. He is not a front-foot assassin. He is methodical — all arms, reaching out, gauging the power of the Venus flytrap opponent before him.

Against Fury, something went horribly wrong though. His usual panache was reduced to cinder. In the ring with him was perhaps "sloppiness" as Klitschko later described Fury, but sloppiness has rights also. It isn't just black box algorithms and smoothness that win out. Ugliness is entitled to its day. And if Fury is ugly, if his tactics are deemed unworthy of this professional sport, then tough. Wladimir just has to suck it up.

Behind the Englishman's words and apparent insouciance lie a canny trainer. Peter Fury doesn't like bad language. He is respectful, referring to Klitschko as "an elite champion." He has "worked tirelessly [with his nephew] over the years perfecting tactics." In him one senses a necessary guiding light in contrast to Tyson's craggy bravado. When he says "I want Tyson to wipe through the division…I want him to go down as a great heavyweight" you know he recognizes that the *real work* has just begun.

This is laudable. It is grounded. By his own admittance, he can't control what Tyson says — nor would he want to. But at least the girders are in place. The previously mocked Frankenstein's monster — loved and loathed in equal measure — is beginning to make a little headway.

There are plenty that see this second fight as relatively straightforward now. None more so than fellow 'gypsy warrior' Billy Joe Saunders: "Tyson will meet [Klitschko] in the middle of the ring and take him out — clean and cold!" The shift to Fury's corner from neutrals in the game was noted in June's *Boxing Monthly* — what was 16-15 in favor of Wladimir for Fight One getting doused by a hose still struggling to understand the tentative, trembling Klitschko before us.

Only the rich boxing names of Tommy Gilmour and Barry Hearn have stayed loyal to Klitschko for this fight in a 29-2 voting avalanche for Fury. Maybe that hints at an inner fickleness on the part of Adam Booth, Carl Frampton, Liam Smith, Barry McGuigan and Brendan Ingle to name just a few, but there is also the possibility that they recognize aging when they see it.

"Klitschko seemed to age massively during those 36 minutes in Düsseldorf. I couldn't believe he was such a different, lesser animal to the one who smashed [Kubrat] Pulev and schooled Bryant Jennings. But these things can happen in boxing when you're 39. He appears to have gone over the top of the mountain. He's had his day."

Banks disputes this (even with Klitschko since turning 40). Such a change would be noticeable in the gym when training, he claims. Hearn also sees it another way: "I'm on Klitschko again! Reason being, he can't possibly be as bad as he was over in Germany when he threw about five punches the entire fight. It's possible that he's finished, but it's equally possible, as I believe, that he just had a bad day at the office. While I've the utmost respect for both, Wladimir has far more ability, and if he boxes to the standard of which he's capable, he's an easy winner."

Can a boxer's career wind down so ignominiously, however? Can the feared become the fearful? If we were talking about James Toney after he met Roy Jones Jr. in 1994 then one could understand it. And thirty years before that there was the small matter of Liston-Clay ("The champion, seemingly oblivious to the remarks calculated to make him angry, calmly attempts to neutralize the challenger's screaming by a simple raising of two fingers...indicating to the press the number of rounds he intends to allow Clay [Ali] to function in a standing position.")

But Klitschko-Fury? Was Klitschko universally feared before stepping in to the Esprit Arena eight months ago? The flat answer is 'No' yet despite the lack of menace and mouth Klitschko has orchestrated a modest reign of terror. He has been a dutiful champion. His demolition of Pulev whilst ungainly at times (holding and pushing) displayed to the public Dr. Steelhammer's devastating left hook which, if utilized again, could fell Fury in a moment.

Is he the same fighter though? Or has something crucial and critical drained from him? Now his cover has been blown to a degree one can't help but picture Klitschko in a bar brawl. Would he know what to do or would he sit neatly on his stool and take the taunting? "Let your hands go. Let your hands go, Wlad," his friends would cry. If only to save *them*. *Their* dignity. *Their* reputation.

This is perhaps what Wladimir has to imagine in October. There cannot be another Wild West without the bullets. There cannot be an ineffectual and inept repeat performance. If Klitschko pictures himself on a date instead of inside a ring, then he has to know that not talking is like not hitting. And mute engagement brings only one thing: failure.

Don't drive home without kissing her, Wlad! Don't drive home without landing a few on those chops and that lipsticked mouth! You've gotta roll the dice. You've gotta dance and see it out properly. If you don't, there will be no spoils — only self-reproach. And the maddening sense that you let the lumbering chal get to you again.

"If Wladimir doesn't let his hands go in the rematch, then he's going to wind up getting clowned by Fury a second time," the tireless sportswriter Scott Gilfoid commented back in June. "Clowned" is a good piece of imagery. It does not flatter Fury, but it certainly counsels Klitschko on the task at hand. If it's a war and he loses, fine. But if it's a bore-fest, a teensy-weensy picayune with white-painted faces, then for Klitschko it is over. No Joshua. No Ortiz. And no Wilder. He would be encouraged to leave the arena in Floyd Patterson false whiskers and moustache.

What of Fury though? What can we expect from the 6'9" switch-hitter? "He's flying at the minute. He can hit, and his speed, timing, distance and coordination are fantastic. And now he'll have a new confidence that'll make him even better. This time, Fury's got every chance of stopping him," Ingle asserts.

Peter Fury is more circumspect: "[Fight One] was his first step on the top of the mountain. He has a long way to go. He has to defend and be a great champion — like all the other past great champions. It's too early to tell. You don't know what tomorrow brings. This is a very serious fight with Klitschko. It's by no means a foregone conclusion. This is a genuine 50-50 fight as far as I can see, but I do believe Tyson will come through it because he is a special kind of character and very underrated box-fighter."

Stronger statements do exist from Uncle Peter ("When you get in front of Tyson Fury in that ring he's your worst nightmare in the world because he is rangy, he is tall and he is quick...I said years ago to his dad: 'Look at his legs — he's like a racehorse.'") but it is the solemn and restrained ordinary lines which make you think that behind Tyson Fury is indeed a sobering influence. And talk of "character" does hit the mark — not via the bombast and bluster of the Gypsy King, but through his physical constitution; something in the lineal heavyweight champion is unfazed, steady and unshakeable.

Boxing purists will always question this and return to the comprehensible topic of natural talent. They're not expecting a pre-1952 Sugar Ray Robinson in terms of craft and dedication ("I was in training 10 months, 11 months of every year...say go to sleep about eight thirty, nine o'clock, you run five miles a day, you...do the boxing exercises...bags, ropes, skipping, all these calisthenics") but they at least want a little artistry.

The Fury archive, so far, isn't easy on the eyes in this respect. And what they see or hear outside the ring means squat. "Without me, boxing becomes boring again; back to the old days of [Klitschko]. I put on a show. This is show business for me. Everybody comes...to see my antics," goes the Fury patter. What about substance though?

"Tyson Fury has to be the man because he's the man that beat the man that beat the man," Lennox Lewis reassures us. There can be no disputing this. But in what manner? lovers of pugilism cry. Has the fine crockery of boxing been replaced by paper plates? Has big beast engagement been substituted for a perplexing shift of limbs?

What do we want from Fury as he matures? A Bowe jab? An Ali shuffle? The devastation of Foreman? The closest we get to a little roughhouse action with Fury in recent times is in his slow pounding of Dereck Chisora (Nov 2014). Not a great fight, but a technical one; the straight rights when in southpaw stance, the deft feints, the little rotation of the shoulder — all appreciated much more in the cold light of day as opposed to during the immediacy of the fight.

Aren't there better burgers to flip though, as we think of Fury-Klitschko II, as we examine the boxing calendar? Crawford-Postol (23 July). Santa Cruz-Frampton (30 July). Golovkin-Brook (10 Sept). Canelo-Smith (17 Sept). Joshua-Parker (Nov-Dec). Kovalev-Ward (19 Nov). Even Haye-Briggs (30 Dec). Why stay up for what could be a second shocker (the unacceptable type)?

Because we need to know if Klitschko really is mentally weak. We need to know if Fury can get up off the canvas — as he has always done before — should Dr. Steelhammer connect. We need to know, most importantly, whether the fighter we all wrote off is here to stay — gods, **luck** and aptitude by his side.

David Haye – Temporary Road-Sweeper

Boxing.com, 1 June 2016

In the final chapter of Elliot Worsell's 2011 biography on David D. Haye there is a telling quote from the Hayemaker's father, Deron: "We've always told David that he should aspire to be the best he can possibly be, but we have never steered him in a particular direction. If he wanted to be the best road-sweeper in the world, that would have been fine with us, so long as he put maximum effort into achieving that."

I would suggest that through Mark de Mori — his comeback fight after a three and a half year absence — and Arnold Gjergjaj, he *has* been road-sweeping. Such defenseless ring action is not immediately recognizable as the sweet science. The Dominator and The Cobra, despite their growls and dark looks — the latter the beneficiary of one of the quickest towels in boxing history in his last bout against Marino Goles — are not at the required technical level to be considered boxers per se.

Beating them has been, in large part, like removing chewing gum and cigarette butts from the sidewalk — inconvenient, but ultimately straightforward. No great shot variety has been required (particularly against Gjergjaj) — just clubbing rights and persistence.

That is not to say that Haye has been fraudulent, gimmicky or amenable to specious bouts. Just that his opponents have ridden in from different universes with no perceivable middle-ranking records.

Take de Mori with his September 2008 'fight' against the 294-pounder Robert Kooser (9-7-0); Kooser, a 1st-round victim specialist with the look of an aging biker, falls like an overdosed Hells Angel.

Ten months later de Mori 'toughs it out' with New Zealander Kevin Karusa (1-1-0). So slight is the Kiwi's boxing record (he retires — quits the sport — after going five rounds with de Mori) that he is not even afforded the dignity of a Wikipedia entry.

The **July 2009 clash** is humble testament to boxing's constant nadirs. When you see de Mori shadow boxing on the cheap floor of Perth's WA Italian Club and then walking through the bar area before finally being greeted in the 'wedding room' by the cheering, inebriated locals, you begin to understand the dimly-lit scraps which take place off the radar.

Karusa, de Mori's 19th opponent, however, should not be in the ring. He weighs a staggering 346 lbs. His age is not recorded on BoxRec, but he looks to be in his mid-forties. The way he walks onto and then tries to shake off de Mori's straight rights in the early part of the fight hints at a man who has woefully accepted that his reactions and timing will never return (if they ever existed). When he oscillates his head as if to regain consciousness, you wonder what has reduced him to such plodding necessity; in short, what has brought him here.

There's something wrong with the world today, I don't know what it is, Something's wrong with our eyes, **Aerosmith's lyrics** thrum to the de Mori / Karusa 'highlights'. The original video complete with tartan-skirted, roller-skating girls, hockey sticks and smashed car bumper lights has been replaced by de Mori's backwater swagger, his stiff hooks and Karusa's smudged face. It is harmony of a kind — an apt shift from the street to the ring; not the greatest musical choreography, but six minutes of insight nonetheless on Haye's January 2016 opponent.

If de Mori's arms are hockey sticks, goes the logic, then Haye's must be high-tech, Pentagon graphene. Gjergjaj's, if we extend the metaphor, must be sponge.

This, to some, is the corrupt banality of modern showmanship. Haye, quite simply, has fought two bums. He has indulged in celebrity opportunism.

But has he? And what could he have reasonably been expected to do before 2017 that wasn't too high-risk given his forced sabbatical from the game?

Haye remains the best British heavyweight since Lennox Lewis. Putting aside risible journalism which suggests that Tyson Fury has now taken such a slot, boxing purists *know* that Haye has the necessary dynamism and fire to climb the rankings once more.

It will be as a *different* fighter though — a 16-stone (224 lbs.) heavyweight as opposed to one a stone less; 210 lbs. the shape he settled into against Audley Harrison, Wladimir Klitschko and Dereck Chisora between November 2010 and July 2012.

With such timber naturally comes concern. Has movement been sacrificed? What about speed? Is he still a quick thinker? Is he able to go twelve rounds as he has done only three times in his career (vs.

Ismail Abdoul, Nikolai Valuev and Klitschko)? Or does a new, stamina-diluted game-plan exist, a heavy-thudding, short-term in and out?

That will only take him so far. It will likely nudge him past boxing's grandfather and knockout specialist Shannon 'The Cannon' Briggs in the autumn. But when the real gunslingers start to appear — Deontay Wilder, Luis Ortiz (a Cuban Riddick Bowe) and Anthony Joshua — will it be enough?

Haye's playground breeze against Arnold Gjergjaj hasn't helped his stock price. Such easy marauding was a clear sign of regression rather than the step-up hoped for. Wise words speak of "an abomination", Haye — despite the early win — looking "lackluster", "heavy-legged" and "slow of hand." The leap onto the ropes to salute his fans following the 'less than 2.0' Richter scale performance merely cements the belief, in some quarters, that the Hayemaker has fallen into a kind of parallel reality.

"I suspect that David Haye will see more opposition and more movement from the heavy bags in the gym" the Dave TV commentator wryly observed in the immediate aftermath of the Gjergjaj fight. It was, in all honesty, like witnessing someone busting up Lego. If we're fair to Haye for a moment though, didn't Gjergjaj have a high guard for much of this bout? He did, but then came the left-jab knockdown from Haye early in the 2nd round which undermined the rudimentary ability and thus *credibility* of the opponent before him.

This is what Haye Mk.2 does to fighting fans. One minute you believe in him, the next you question how authentic his current skills really are.

On the plus side, it is easy to buy into the theory that the Bermondsey man is now a *proper* heavyweight. Footage of him bouncing off Klitschko in 2011 supports this. He has always needed the extra packaging, the extra circumference, it seems in order to truly stand opposite boxing behemoths. The slower-striding man we now see isn't necessarily a bad thing therefore.

The negative side is very much the unknown. Can Haye outthink a Fury? Will age and weight combine to produce gusto or garbage? Can he dance with a Bermane Stiverne for eight or more rounds? Can he clean out a ring of up-and-coming talents like Joseph Parker?

The latter two are probably perfect opponents at this moment in time — them or a Kubrat Pulev. Whether Haye is thinking along these lines is debatable though. One suspects that he could quite easily jump the queue and find himself in a questionable IBF eliminator with another bum or vagrant. In him is that boy still craving speed, expedience and rapid attention.

Rewinding the clock a full eight minutes before the bell in the Gjergjaj fight helps us understood Haye. It matters much more than the four and a half minutes of comfortless destruction.

During that pre-fight jamboree — Haye exiting his dressing room and indulging in a cat walk rather than a ring walk (pointless platform included) — we see the childish smiles interspersed with pseudo-seriousness. To Haye the whole thing really *is* a game, a Hollywood script, and the iPhone suckers in the audience who have no concept of experience, *real experience*, in full bloom merely reinforce this; vanity dotted around...in the trunks of the former WBA heavyweight champion...in the preening of vacuous blondes.

This taints Haye the boxer. I would much prefer menace, a walk to the ring, hood up, and then a fight — nothing more; a cloaked warrior here to carry out business, a strand of enigma remaining, punishment imminent.

Haye's grins ill befit such a trade. They partly mock less skillful opponents — some of whom resemble pigeons on a washing line.

Will he park up the dustcart and get serious? I hope so. Both in fighting terms and manners. Haye can be so incredibly gracious post-fight — once the pressure is off — that it seems a shame to blemish such care, considerateness and articulacy with the wanton games of self-absorption.

Time now for the bigger stuff and a half-decent opponent, boxing critics cry. Indeed. Providing he clambers over Briggs.

Nowhere to Hide: Saúl 'Canelo' Álvarez vs. Amir 'King' Khan

Boxing.com, 6 May 2016

Who has the best deal here — the stalker or the technician? Neither boxer will be entirely comfortable.

Amir Khan, despite the puffery, cannot run like WBA super welterweight champion, Erislandy Lara. He cannot sweep the ring like a pencil in a compass. Nor is he as sturdy.

Canelo, the tough Mexican with the uncompromising uppercuts and straight rights, risks being remembered as a "limited slugger" with few places to go if the paint from this bout dries unevenly.

Why has this left-field fight even come about? Business. "Let's be honest, it's a business fight, not a real fight," asserts Barry Hearn, which tempers any serious kind of analysis. Analyse we must though as Canelo-Khan (yes — in that order) promises excitement or at least a mismatch of monumental proportions.

"Khan is brave or plain crazy," *Boxing Monthly*'s Terry Dooley vents on behalf of quizzical fans. Possibly both, I would venture or in possession of a dangerous ego unable to discern the difference between good and great.

Khan has fought some impressive fights — against Andriy Kotelnik, Marcos Maidana and Devon Alexander. He has displayed to the boxing community and wider world his hand speed, hunger, slickness and application. When you watch him engage, it is — in part — a flashback to the Colosseum. But does he possess the requisite giant heart and technique that separate fine fighters from eminent ones? And can he legitimately avoid the Mexican boulder that will undoubtedly roll towards him from the first round on Saturday, 7th May inside Las Vegas's T-Mobile Arena?

"Yes," WBO middleweight champion, Billy Joe Saunders thinks. "Canelo [is] pretty flat-footed, and if Khan uses his feet to get in and out, lands just two or three shots rather than blitzes, he could win. What he can't do is get greedy if he starts having success."

This raises the question: Will Virgil Hunter have trimmed sufficient live wire from Khan's DNA before the Nevada spectacular? Because Canelo is not a boxer, so the saying goes — he is a down and dirty "spiteful puncher," a street fighter from Jalisco. If Khan, even for a second, thinks he can trade with him then it will be night-night.

What of the bigger picture though? What exactly is relevant to this clash? Industry. Form. Weight. Speed. Power. And durability. Little else.

Fighters become 'unknowns' through inactivity and Khan's CV — four fights in three years — is as lean as it gets. Hunting for the glamour tie, the big celebrity showdown, has not helped the Bolton man. Legacies are not borne from palatial encounters, from Mayweather and Pacquiao crumbs, but from doing the business with those immediately around you.

Avoiding Kell Brook — the slayer of Shawn Porter — is quite unforgivable, particularly when such a potential prize would have hauled Khan back shoulder to shoulder with champions, Keith Thurman and Danny Garcia. After that he needn't have unified the titles. Fair-minded fans would have graciously accepted his step up to super-welterweight, but this Disneyland jump *two* weights — into the back yard of Eubank Jr., Saunders, Jacobs, Álvarez and...wait for it...Golovkin — is insane.

For a man that weighed 142 lbs. against Julio Diaz just three years ago and was tagged with a left hook in the fourth round, the catchweight of 155 with Canelo seems like an awfully big leap. No matter what the sound bites from each camp over ring weight though, there is incongruity here.

"I know the fight is at a catchweight. I have never fought at 155 before but I walk around at probably 160-plus so it will be me fighting at my natural weight. Come fight night I will probably be about 165 as well. I can see Álvarez maybe being a little heavier than that, maybe going into the ring at 170, but we know what we need to do," Khan reassured Sky Sports.

Is this bluff? Do Carrs pasties or between-fight luxuries count as 'natural' weight? Shall we let Khan jump another two weights after the Canelo fight and go catchweight with Sergey Kovalev at 169?! Oliver Hardy's natural load was 300 lbs. but that did not make him a heavyweight. It concerns me when fighters get a little lax, a little free and easy with their expression. It worries me more so when they come from my home town.

Here are the perilous facts: Canelo has fought 50% more fights over that three-year period and all around the 155 mark. His opponents have been Austin Trout, Floyd Mayweather Jr., Alfredo Angulo, Erislandy Lara, James Kirkland and Miguel Cotto. No mugs there. While criticized, especially over his performances against Mayweather and Lara, Canelo still *belonged.*

If you do as I did and watch the *other* Cotto-Canelo fight from May 2010, you refreshingly see Jose Miguel holding the center of the ring, walking Canelo down. The Mexican for the first three rounds still appears to be sat at the breakfast table such is the threat from the 32-year-old Puerto Rican.

But then Canelo is 19 years of age, still learning, taking clubbing left hooks from the old pro. At times he is slow, clumsy even. Chuck in the odd middle round siesta and there are plenty of holes in the Saúl Álvarez armor to pick up on.

Have the Khan camp been watching this, deceiving themselves over the vulnerability of the pound-for-pound player with an amateur record of 44-2? I would suggest so. Even back then though — a full six years ago — there were glimpses, coup d'œil, moments to behold: fierce trademark right uppercuts; a right glove at 90 degrees flat in the opponent's face; accuracy when he could be bothered; general sledgehammer shots.

Some of this was stored up for James Kirkland — unleashed on a *real* adult stage during that barbaric 'quarter' fight one year ago. Khan won't do what Kirkland did. He won't be ragged — certainly not for the first three rounds. He won't walk onto power shots and delude himself that he can somehow dominate. He won't have gangly, loose arms flailing around. But what if Canelo smells blood? What if Khan makes an honest mistake?

Watch Kirkland on the HBO replay as he briefly looks up at Canelo from the seat of his pants after taking a straight right with 1min 17secs of the first round remaining. It is as if he has seen God — witnessed for the first time actual wrath. In the Mandingo Warrior's gaze is absolute respect. Fighters like Saúl Álvarez generally don't pass by Austin, Texas.

Canelo is not without his demons. The fog of the Mayweather encounter still rankles. He knows as a fighter that he is not fleet of foot.

He *can* be pedestrian. Style often troubles him. And his 70½" reach is far from ideal (Mayweather 72", Lara 74", Khan 71"). But does he get busted?

The Mayweather fight was an aberration, an anomaly. His last fight against Miguel Cotto — a man with an improbable center of gravity — was criticized in some quarters, but it is useful remembering that Junito has only been properly knocked down by Manny Pacquiao throughout his 45 fights and 15-year career.

Khan, I would dearly like to say, has some of the qualities of a Cotto, a Mayweather or a Lara. Plenty in the game push his wares:

Steve Collins — "He's no fool, a superb athlete, very slick and skilful, far better than he's given credit for. Obviously he'll need to show respect, stay on his bike and box at his absolute best, but I see Khan stealing it in a similar manner to how Sugar Ray Leonard outfoxed Marvin Hagler."

Anthony Crolla — "The speed Amir carries is freakish. There's no one out there quicker and we've seen before that Canelo struggles with movers."

Derry Mathews — "Speed is everything in this game, and no one is faster than Khan. I see him nicking the early rounds, surviving the middle rounds, then running away with it down the straight."

Terry Flanagan — "He just needs to use his speed and boxing, stay clever and not get involved. Canelo is class, but if Khan stays sharp, and uses his timing, he won't get hit. And if he don't get hit, he don't get beat…"

Chris Sanigar — "Amir has the experience and mobility to go back foot, constantly change direction and fiddle Álvarez out of it. Canelo has a lovely straight lead uppercut, but he's pretty pedestrian. The wisdom of Virgil Hunter will be instrumental if Amir is to be successful."

…but then I read the epitaphs and stridently think NO WAY CAN KHAN BRIDGE SUCH A GAP:

Colin Hart — "Khan might prove [to be] too fast for a few rounds, but not for 12. Once Canelo cuts the space, he'll prove far too big and powerful."

David Price — "The plan has to be to get through 12 rounds without getting caught flush. It's a big ask."

Enzo Maccarinelli — "There'll be close to a 21 lbs. difference in weight inside the ring on fight night, because of the day-before weigh in. Eventually Álvarez will catch up with him and stop him."

Dominic Ingle — "Khan has the footwork and ability to avoid danger and possibly get through to the finish if he really concentrates, but he lacks the power to trouble Canelo. Therefore, it's not possible for him to actually win. If Amir risks loading up, he'll fade early and get stopped."

Junior Witter — "Khan's fast, but he can't keep the speed up for 12 rounds, and as soon as he gets caught Canelo will put the finish on him."

Jamie Cox — "I've sparred both of them within the last two years, and I don't see any possibility of Amir winning. Amir's very, very quick and I really admire his balls [for taking this fight], but Canelo hits too hard and is too powerful. Álvarez is a very clever and astute counter puncher. He'll only need one clean shot. And he's got 12 rounds to land it."

It is the last quote which is the most damning. Too hard. Too powerful. One clean shot. And worryingly, Khan is ring rusty — one year out of the game. Even his former amateur coach, Mick Jelley recognizes this: "If you're a professional boxer, you should be fighting three or four times a year. If you're only fighting once every 18 months, your timing will be out, it's only natural.

"You can do as much sparring as you want, but in the ring, competitive, it's completely different."

This, to many, will be Khan's first superfight. Can he herald a new dawn? Can he finally fulfill the potential long talked about? Is he quick enough to have Álvarez merely tickle him when briefly backed up against the ropes (as Lara did so effectively)?

Some say Álvarez is only a dynamic fighter when allowed to be, when the garden gate is left open. The chief problem for Khan though is that Mexicans often do not know broken pride. Khan will unquestionably prove awkward at times, but Álvarez will slowly march on with little fear given his granite chin. He may even play a little rope-a-dope from time to time with that beautiful counterpunch at the ready.

The one chance Khan has — and it is slim — is if weight-cutting has decisively caught up with Álvarez. The naturally big man will be 26 in July and close to 180 lbs. on Saturday evening as there is **no rehydration clause**. The thickness of him when he removes his gown before the bell will be alarming but deep down he may be severely weakened.

It is fair to state that Álvarez probably has more chips on the table in this fight. It is — all said and done — an inordinate gamble. I just think durability when I see Khan, however — a lack of it. As much as I want him to succeed, there are the inevitable shortcomings. A good fighter, not a great fighter — and that will prove the difference.

Klitschko/Fury – Skill and Power vs. Zig-Zags and The Almighty

Boxing.com, 23 November 2015

The boxing fraternity loses its mind at times. Four-to-one underdogs suddenly become credible challengers. What should be wise words from people on the inside morph into dopey algae.

Tyson Fury, first and foremost, has the printing men to thank for his time in the limelight; his brief, blessed tenure. The boards and posters look OK: *Collision Course — Wladimir Klitschko vs. Tyson Fury*. You can almost get drawn in — begin to believe that astute tactics will win out and that these master fighters will offer a veritable feast.

Except, let-downs come thick and fast in this business. Faces and hype are like medicine men of old.

Jack Johnson vs. James Jeffries (1910). Joe Louis vs. Max Schmeling II (1938). Sonny Liston vs. Floyd Patterson (1962). All promised a war of sorts, fireworks, a battle supreme, but left bits of potato chip on the living room floor, sour expressions and, collectively, half a century of one-sided folly.

Tyson Fury isn't as rotten as he was. Some of his sentences do actually make sense — charm the listener in part: "To be the heavyweight champion is the greatest prize in sport…The way to beat a perfectionist is through unpredictability."

The trouble is he can't possibly execute such a plan. Unpredictability is many things — caprice, impulse, whim, uncertainty, a random primordial surge — but when unharnessed it amounts to floundering, jumping around in an imprecise fashion.

Fury, the 6'9" breeze block, the southpaw switcher, has the words of Emanuel Steward tingling in his ear: "I said to Wladimir in training, I said you see that guy, he is going to be the next super dominant heavyweight after you, he said yeah?! I said yeah. I've had Lennox on a nine year run, I'm gonna have you looks like nine years and that's gonna be my next super heavyweight." He also has the depression that pulled him down in 2011 — enough, in other words, to inspire the cavalry of blood inside him. But if you don't have the tools, pretty soon you are scrambling around for advice and enlightenment, hoping for serendipity.

When he steps in the ring with Klitschko on Saturday, November 28, at the ESPRIT Arena in Düsseldorf there will be no miniature overhead bombs or tiny windmills coming his way (as with Steve Cunningham) but instead simple, plain punishment — probing rights from the Ukrainian, nose-breaking jabs and the type of left hook that viciously clubbed Kubrat Pulev ("separating Pulev from his own will").

If Fury believes he has been in with the equivalent of a Klitschko during his career to date then he is in for a shock. Dr Steelhammer — despite the three defeats in 1998, 2003 and 2004 — is formidable. He is a physical specimen to behold. When Fury was queuing up for his paunch, Wlad was in a different line entirely swinging dumbbells from his little finger.

There *are* ways in. It would be foolish to think of Klitschko as impenetrable. But earning the right to such a door is beyond most. The negative clamor that followed his last fight against Bryant Jennings was from fans and analysts not fully compos mentis or able to see the bigger picture. "Keep working," was the bombast or padding from Jennings' corner, but did he really threaten? Do rabbit punches to the ribs and ducking low constitute that these days?

Klitschko is a reluctant trader — at least until the final 30 seconds of each round. He is cautious and circumspect. He does not dive in or submerge himself in a fight unless there is a real need to do so. Let's not forget those other Cs which are central to his boxing wares though. To quote Brendan Ingle, "There's no substitute for class and cleverness."

Even when listening to his now trainer of three years, Johnathon Banks, it is noticeable that Wlad does not nod or readily acknowledge what has been said. He just processes what he needs to do with that large PhD brain and gets off his stool with a chess mentality.

There *have* been problems — particularly with the 225-226-pound brigade (Corrie Sanders and Lamon Brewster) — but *who* slowly wears down opponents in the manner of Klitschko? Who has a long jab and rocket-like right hand like Klitschko? (Both burrowing their way through tight, gloved defenses.)

Talk of Fury unseating Klitschko is misguided at best, certifiable at worst. *Where* is the evidence? Soft fights since February 2014 against Joey Abell, Dereck Chisora and lastly, Christian Hammer? Charitable words from the now sadly departed 'Manny' Steward? Even Manny got it wrong at times. He also predicted that Liverpool's David Price would be heavyweight champion. Unfortunately, not every boxer with a bit of Kronk inside them (directly or indirectly) can be a champ.

"Tyson Fury hasn't faced a real heavyweight, and I'm more than sure that I need just one single punch to his body or his head, and that will show him the reality," Wlad commented in October's *Boxing Monthly*. "I actually prefer to fight the guys who are undefeated because they don't know the other side, they don't know where it's going to get difficult. How are they going to react? The fear of the unknown, that's what makes Tyson Fury actually a little paranoid and a little nervous. The way he acts, it shows that he's insecure inside."

Indeed. And while the prospect of overturning Joe Louis' title reign of 11 years and 8 months (25 consecutive defenses) remains unimaginable, Klitschko would certainly step down with pride were he to equal Larry Holmes' 20 defenses (and middleweight Bernard Hopkins') by taking out Fury and one more opponent. That would be a whole new school, a whole new legacy.

Admiring Wladimir Klitschko is admittedly a slow burn. He is not a gung-ho performer. Neither is he a maniacal fruit cake. The steady bursts serenade you. There are few over-the-top missiles or uppercuts. Risk is kept to a minimum. But what a fine architect because of it: calmly deconstructing faces, subtly carving through the resolve of the man opposite.

Fury calls this "boring". And in a fit of oxymoronic poetry refers to himself as "Tyson Fury — entertainer." The Wilmslow man mistakes outside-the-ring regalement with *inside*-the-ring harshness, however. For now, counting down to the fight, he is a strange kind of equal to Klitschko. They sit on the same chairs. They court the same press. They share the same posters. Fury is making the most of his Andy Warhol fifteen minutes of fame.

Once inside the ring, stripped down to boots and shorts, and aware of the red/orange-attired 'astronauts,' 'F1 pit men' and 'Guantanamo Bay' jumpsuits in Klitschko's corner, Fury might start to feel a little different. If not, the distinctive red shorts of the Ukrainian will posit nineteen years of know-how, nineteen years of greeting onrushing bulls and fantasists with slick armory.

Even Klitschko's cutman, one observes, works the petroleum jelly better than his rivals. Rubbing it between his fingers *before* applying it, Jacob "Stitch" Duran understands the contours of the face, the need for blows to slip across the surface of the skin. After round six of the Jennings fight, there was no kerfuffle from Team Klitschko. Examining the corner was like looking in on a seminar, a hushed library meeting — everyone focused and just Banks speaking, offering guidance courtesy of his slow, Detroit drawl.

Uncle Peter (Fury), in the other corner, is no mug but there is only so much he can do with the piece of clay that is his nephew. Tyson Fury has arguably improved. His movement and footwork have risen above the nadir of his early fights. He now jabs while in the correct stance. But punching power? Flair? "I hope there are going to be no excuses," Klitschko told *Boxing News*. "He's trying to improve his punching power and either you have it or you don't. You can't learn suddenly."

Fury is apparently steeped in faith and awkwardness though — power and flair of a different kind. "I have a personal relationship with the Almighty…Whatever is conventional, I am the opposite. If you want to walk in a straight line, I am going to walk in zig-zags. If you want to throw a one-two, I'll throw a two-one. I don't want to be an ordinary person. Because if you are ordinary, you do ordinary things."

This recent verbiage from the "Gypsy King" recorded by the *Mail*'s chief sports writer, Oliver Holt suggests — as many have indicated — that a strange fusion of bluster and personal doctrine have gripped Fury. He has always had mouth and bravado, but this latest set of dogma dangerously separates Fury from the mammoth task ahead. And such a blueprint cannot possibly transfer itself into the ring.

"A man who does evil things and worships an evil one, how can he win over a man who wants to do good things and preach good stuff?…God will not let him defeat me, not at all." It is not too clear which bastion of greatness is central to Fury's character particularly given his non-scripture like belligerence, but a re-enactment of Cassius Clay's rushing to the edge of the ring in 1964 after victory over mob fighter Sonny Liston ("Eat your words!" he exclaimed to the press) is unlikely.

Clay (Muhammad Ali) was genuinely funny: "After I beat him I'm going to donate him to the zoo," he said of Liston before their first fight.

Wit and sharpness oozed from every pore. The creation of Clay/Ali —
as fighter and man — was clearly uncomfortable for much of the press
at the time. Fury, by contrast, emanates from a poorly-written script that
got wet in the rain. His discourse is a blancmange which hasn't set right.
He is a pseudo-pioneer, a bunkum fraud up to this point.

Will he shake up the world? A mass of voices seems to think so:
Clinton Woods; Carl Froch; Robin Reid; Derry Mathews; Enzo
Maccarinelli; Anthony Crolla; Joe Gallagher; Terry Flanagan; Scott
Welch; Billy Joe Saunders; Mickey Vann; Lee Selby; Jimmy Tibbs;
Steve Collins; Richie Woodhall. The talk is of Fury being young, big,
strong, tall, powerful, skillful and confident. Also, smart, intelligent,
hungry, in the best shape of his life, unorthodox, great hand speed, a
talker and taunter, "the fastest heavyweight around," full of heart,
strategic and with "the tools to beat anybody."

Couple this with Klitschko aging, holding his hands low at times,
being a little ponderous and not the enforcer that people crave, and you
perhaps have an unforeseen jolt in the thesis. And don't forget the
gloves: "Wlad let the cat out of the bag completely today," Fury
commented a few weeks back. "I got my fight gloves through. Pure
shite, they're the biggest gloves in boxing, a non-puncher's glove.
Every other fight he's had, he has Grant gloves. With me, he's taken
the easier option by picking gloves that you can barely close your fists
in.

"If he's this great puncher going against a non-puncher, then why
go for defensive gloves? I know he's mentally weak. I can tell you the
type of mentality a person has got just by looking at them for two
minutes."

Fury, to his credit, analyses most things and is occasionally incisive
in what he says. The problem is that scrappers and bit part poets are no
match for phenomenal skill and boxing guile. Words only have a certain
shelf life when not backed up through implementation. The theory that
Fury can win this fight is from the safety of the gym because his
pedigree to date in public rings suggests he is not ready for such a
challenge.

Back in November 2012 — just over a fortnight after Manny's death
— it was odd to witness the undefeated (and doped up) Mariusz Wach
having his hair scrunched up between rounds as if preparing for the

catwalk. Wach was the taller man just like Fury will be three years on and yet Klitschko picked him off in sublime fashion, outpointing him comfortably, unloading his jab with ease.

The knockdown never came but then drugs and hypnosis similarly kid the brain. We know that Fury will be clean. He is well aware of the putrescent damage that pills, powders and liquids do to the body long-term. God, at least, has steered him sensibly in *some* areas. But is he a sleek heavyweight? Should he even be in the same ring as Klitschko? Is he perhaps another Alex Leapai (pre-fight seductiveness included) destined to be outclassed? And what will it take between rounds to get him going?

In stark terms, this is Frankie Dettori saddled up against Frankie Howerd; one with a titanic record in his chosen sport, the other told he has been entered for the Epsom Derby after a few donkey rides on Blackpool beach (ironically the Las Vegas of England). If Fury stayed quiet once in a while such metaphors would not be required. Instead, he has chosen to cover himself in vulgar tinsel.

Seeing him jogging on the front at Morecambe (Lancashire) with a small crowd around him, one is briefly reminded of Ali running a mile and a half with Norman Mailer whilst preparing for his heavyweight showdown with George Foreman in 1974. *Briefly*. Before the facile and fatuous lines return and sting one's mind.

"You're in pretty good shape, Norm," Ali said half a mile in. This is the thing. Ali, despite his rumbustious soundings, could be engaging, gentle, honest and vulnerable. The "big man" in him took the odd break. If Fury wants to *be* Ali so badly (at least in his head) or compare himself to such a genius, he needs to understand this and ease off the gas marked 'Balderdash.'

"Ali served as a guide, pointing to holes in the ground, sudden dips, and slippery spots where hoses had watered the grass too long…Wherever possible, Ali ran on the turf."

Fury, alas, continues to stamp on the concrete. The bias and support shown by Froch, Crolla, Saunders and Collins going into this fight is laudable. Unfortunately, the lens is smudged for many — even great fighters. If Froch is "bored with the Klitschkos [*sic*]…They've dominated for too long" then he needs to tout a plausible alternative. Anthony Joshua *might* be that and his fight with Dillian Whyte on 12th

December at the O2 promises to offer more of an insight as to the state of the heavyweight scene.

But *Fury*? Where is this great archive of bouts which prompts Saunders to drool, "People will be surprised how comfortable Tyson beats him...he'll dance round him all night"? Fury's physical rendezvous have lacked fluidity, entertainment *and* that spellbinding morsel which transforms fights. When he says he is not ordinary what he means is that he dreams of the big lights. When he issues sclerotic statements, it is a sign that he is still checking a number of ideological boxes behind the scenes.

Stunned amazement will greet Fury if he pulls it off in Germany. Fanfare and brouhaha will lift the roof. But if he turns up as Peter Parker or Clark Kent or Bruce Wayne — as is expected — then the usual roll of film will have the audience reaching for the pretzels.

"I will take care of business," Klitschko says, simply and without embellishment. And you have no reason to disbelieve him. For Fury, solace will come in the form of German-stretched canvas, Rod Stewart and $5.5 million. Flat on his back, he might even lose God and find himself.

Amir Khan – Lancashire Bomber

Boxing.com, 28 April 2014

Manchester, that large English city, Bolton is not. It is the provinces – a 15-minute train ride away; New Jersey rather than New York. Some say the people have six fingers. Others say they are richer, not drowned by polluting city air (carcinogens hiking up their nostrils) or too much sophistication.

Amir Khan was born here in December 1986. I only *really* became aware of him on his 21st birthday in what was his second defense of the Commonwealth Lightweight title against Graham Earl.

Earl (25-1) had crossed my path before. He was a gutsy fighter I just happened to tune into one Saturday night ten months earlier slugging it out with Australia's Michael Katsidis (21-0). He seemed to be a jack-in-the-box performer regularly cranked from the depths of defeat.

"Look for some solace in the middle of the ring," the commentator Duke McKenzie had desperately urged with eighteen seconds of the fifth (and ultimately final) round remaining.

I winced a little. I was watching a 2007 WBO lightweight title fight which was not just full of fortitude but represented something arcanely affluent. It appeared to be a bludgeoning master class. Not a great lesson in defense from Earl, but a rare, stinging battle which craved respect and approbation. Such was the raw ferocity in parts of this tussle that Earl's corner threw the towel into the ring in the second round, only for it to be thrown out again by referee, Mickey Vann.

Earl lost – retired by his corner. And he would not win again with the exception of his last, somewhat ignominious, scrap against Karl "Plug" Taylor (16-125-7) at the Liquid Envy nightclub in his home town of Luton; a promising career over at the age of 30.

When he found himself in the ring with Amir Khan (14-0), the Bolton speed merchant, it was arguably only the latter's second significant test since turning pro; the brave Glaswegian, Willie Limond being the other.

It took the silver-trunked Khan a mere 73 seconds to dispatch Earl. Looking at them side by side, you understood the physical threat of the Boltonian – his stature casting an almost Dracula-like shadow over the Luton man; Earl never great with his reach, but muffled, silenced and quelled – made to look like a circus midget.

And so Khan's boxing road trip truly began – sixty years after Pakistan's independence and decades after his paternal grandfather, Lal moved to England following his discharge from the Pakistan Army (formerly part of the British Indian Army).

Bolton – its motto *Supera Moras* ("overcome difficulties") – was a mill town, a moor town, with no shortage of famous individuals: Samuel Crompton – inventor of the mule-jenny and pioneer of the cotton spinning industry; William Lassell – the astronomer who discovered Triton, Neptune's largest moon; William Lever – soap monopoly king.

The sprawling Lancashire town was thus able to dress you, wash you and tell you about the night sky.

Into this heady industrial area – in the 1950s – came hundreds of workers from the Indian subcontinent. The textile industry was soon to fade though and by the 1980s was dead.

With an estimated 10,000 Pakistanis in Britain in 1951 and nearly 500,000 by 1991, the ensuing need for new professions became evident. Always more than the caricatured takeaway owners, taxi drivers and fabric shop proprietors, British Pakistanis began to further penetrate the 'higher' sectors of health care, accounting and computing. Khan, after strolling into a local gym at the age of eight, dismissed such dutiful avenues and chose the never-never land of boxing. His precocious skills were immediately evident to those around him. In many ways it was a subtle shift from the school playground and street corners to the thankfully padded floor of the ring.

The amateur highs we know about: 2003 AAU Junior Olympic Gold Medalist; 2004 European Student and World Junior Gold Medalist; 2004 Olympic Lightweight Silver Medalist; 2005 – revenge over his Olympic foe, Mario Kindelán.

Then came the 18-year-old pro – his first few fights (Bailey [3-4], Carey [9-13-3], Gethin [9-18-2], Thorpe [19-44-2], Martynau [10-1], Williams [12-3]) like a warden rounding up stray poodles; the usual fare of stiffs and inflated stats.

Khan's lightning-rod jab was almost unnatural at this weight, his thudding rights deceptively hard. Such ability pushed him handsomely up the next rung of boxing's evolutionary ladder past Komjáthi (24-10-1), Bain (9-1-1), Barrett (12-2-1), Drilzane (10-3), Medjadji (17-3) and

Bull (24-4-1); pee-wee fights but valuable ring time – the Hungarian, Komjáthi his first respectable opponent.

Boxers enter arenas to surprising and unforeseen music at times. Khan's choice of **Amarillo** at his half-dozen fight point on 25th February 2006 perhaps lightened the mood, perhaps mitigated some of the pressure and expectation building.

"There's a church bell ringing
Hear the song of joy that it's singing
For the sweet Maria and the guy who's coming to see her
Just beyond the highway, there's an open plain
And it keeps me going through the wind and rain"

Five days later Khan felled a man outside the ring – Geoffrey Hatton – breaking his right leg on a *Bolton* highway while in his BMW. It was an incident with dire echoes of Chris Eubank (Feb. 1992) and Naseem Hamed (May 2005) and one which the 19-year-old was ill-equipped to handle.

Perfunctory remorse offers nothing to a family – it deepens the wounds more than silence. Khan's inadvertent interview with The Wall Street Journal's infotainment "reporter" Lee Hawkins on the matter was commensurate with inviting Beelzebub to afternoon tea. Goaded by Hawkins's delinquent merriness and talk of fast cars, Khan's words fell from his lips with the plentiful naivety of Candide.

I suppose a strange, moneyed language can seep into the best of us – its bruising necessity harnessing a man's tongue, but churning over the subjects of death and the pitiful scrapings of one's brand (however coerced) in the same moment is careless…quite unforgivable.

Perhaps we shouldn't dig this particular hole though. Khan's art is his boxing and it brims with superlatives cultivated by his hands. Watching him is a "thrill ride of the first order," to quote Robert Ecksel. The great Flaubert, as Julian Barnes recently wrote in the *London Review of Books*, once said "…in reply to a journalistic inquiry about his life, 'I have no biography.' The art is everything; its creator nothing."

Fight number 13 with those artistic hands for the Commonwealth Lightweight title meant running into William Wallace or rather the 5'7" Scot, Willie Limond (28-1). Not likely to give up his entrails easily, Limond showed us in the sixth round what we weren't supposed to see so soon, if ever: that Khan is partially made of glass – a human decanter when on certain sideboards.

Limond's hooks were a prelude to fights 19 and 29 against Breidis Prescott (19-0) and Danny Garcia (23-0) – the Prescott clash more startling due to its similarity with Tyson/Berbick (Nov. 1986); the same bewildered expression dancing across Khan's face as with Berbick's. Not quite the "Child in a play pen" (Reg Gutteridge epitaph) from Khan but nonetheless a staggering, wobbling Moet Champagne guzzler and wreck of a man.

Notice Khan's mother in the seventh and eighth rounds against Limond – praying, short of breath, anxious, up and down; her whole being contorted and afraid. Seeing that makes you understand the wider implications of this sport – those that are affected, those that travel with the boxer into the deep caverns and gristle-laden areas of this dark trade.

"You're trying too hard," Khan's trainer, Oliver Harrison had told him. He was. Indulging in rucks. Getting involved in a street fight with the steadfast Scot. The gnarled expression of Frank Warren's face alone (in its usual ringside seat) was sufficient to inform us that Khan's tactics were wrong, defective, counterpointed by Limond's steel and willingness to hunt down a wounded opponent.

But for the broken jaw (Limond retired at the end of the eighth) this could have been a savage introduction to 12-rounders for Khan. As it was, he became a boxer for real, largely dishing it out even though worryingly vulnerable.

"You've still got the L-plates on," was the rhetorical assertion from the happy-go-lucky sports presenter, Jim Rosenthal. And he was right. What could not be softened, however, were the twisted faces in the crowd – aghast at the spectacle they had just borne witness to. Somehow they had seen too much. Boxing had crossed the line between entertaining warfare and a form of thuggery.

It kills me to watch and re-watch all of a fighter's fights – the endless mismatches, the pre-bell bullshit, parts of the crowd like babies having their first diaper changed, but I plough on. I do it because a man's essence is often found. Usually near the end, usually in a split second sat on their stool or when off-balance clutching for God. Never during an interview. Never when posturing.

Khan was Bruno-esque after the Limond encounter – his words interspersed with the aching cypher "You know what I mean…you know what I mean." But then he was still only 20 years old. Learning. Seeing things. Pounding the granite flesh put before him. The "lethargic legs" amply noticed by Barry McGuigan were rueful almost – yes. What we cannot expunge from his efforts though is the disquieting sense that here is a fighter who wishes to trade and overpower people.

Scott Lawton (20-3-1), Stoke's answer to Elvis, came next. It was brief. Flurry, flurry and out in the fourth. Earl (25-2) – we know what happened there.

Then Gairy St Clair (39-5-2), the experienced Australian; Khan, now 21 – a man needing the longevity fighters, wishing to distil their staying power. It was a coming of age for the Bolton man, his first 36-minute walk. Very much part of a slow-mo fight, Khan filled the ring with feigns, flicking left jabs and daunting hooks. It was an assured night of graft and endeavor.

Seventeen (Kristjansen 19-1-3), eighteen (Gomez 35-8-0) – Khan progressed. He was guilty of dropping his left guard against the Dane and not cleverly picking his shots, but the Irishman he simply walked through in retaliation for damaging a rib in the fourth.

In between these bouts, trainer Oliver Harrison – with Khan since the start of his pro career – was sacked. His replacement, the Cuban Jorge Rubio lasted just two fights; the disastrous pairing up with rangy Prescott (19-0, 17 KOs with a 72" reach) hastening his downfall.

Enter Freddie Roach (Oct. 2008) who would ironically put Khan on a par with his own 26-1 record after seeing off Fagan (22-5), Barrera (65-6), Kotelnik (31-2-1), Salita (30-0-1), Malignaggi (27-3), Maidana (29-1), McCloskey (22-0) and Judah (41-6) in a bit of 8-ball pool.

Roach's 1982 tormentor on a split decision (or UD depending on the source) was Pawtucket, Rhode Island resident, Rafael Lopez. Nearly thirty years later via his proxy, Khan he was 'defeated' again (SD) – Washington man, Lamont Peterson (29-1-1) the fortunate recipient of dubious refereeing by Virginia's Joseph Cooper and glad eyed judging from Philadelphia's George Hill and North Carolina's Valerie Dorsett.

If history is anything to go by, Khan has two more wins in him before a Louis Burke blocks his path. He once claimed to love the smell of blood and sweat. Whether that applies to his own is doubtful.

Misadventure has tailed him in the manner of Prescott (Sept. 2008) and Garcia (July 2012); Garcia's signature left hook having more lather than the political creed of Tony Blair and François Mitterrand.

In and around this time, growing into his mid-twenties, he has polished off the doleful and enervated Malignaggi (May 2010), got lucky against Maidana (Dec 2010) – running away in the last three rounds (Glenn Trowbridge calling it correctly at 113-112 nonetheless) – and staggered to victory over Julio Diaz (40-7-1 Apr 2013).

His performance versus Carlos Molina (Dec. 2012) was an encouraging show – the words of new trainer Virgil Hunter guiding him. But the gaps between fights have become too large. He is, in part, now an unknown finding a new style in his twilight years. He has never struck me as needing an apoplectic trainer of the other Hunter variety (Barry), yet perhaps those words from the opposite corner two days after his 25th birthday (Dec. 2011) are needed now:

"He's just a man. He's not a fighter. You understand? This is **! This is your home!....We worked too hard, son. We've come a long ass way to get here and not put mass on the game. *Tomorrow* we are hurt. *Tomorrow* we are pain. But right now ain't none of that. Let's go to work…This is **, man. There'll be no partying on our floor tonight. How bad do you want this, man? How bad do you want this, son?"

Lamont Peterson's possibly drug-induced 'win' was Khan's blip. Danny Garcia's ascent was Khan's fall. Now, it is Luis Collazo (35-5) and Khan's chance to get up – at least onto one knee from where he can realistically survey the welterweight division.

Collazo, the Brooklyn southpaw is most surely a step down from both Maidana and Garcia. He is a low-level, prosaic fighter. If this rendezvous is not a formality for Khan, then he needs to gracefully retire, learn about the masters that came before him, jockey a different world hopefully not full of weasels like Hawkins.

There just remain the questions over *who* to fight, *how* to fight and *why* to fight if he returns from the MGM Grand on May 3, 2014 with a fragment of restored kudos.

Who

Khan needs Keith Thurman, Devon Alexander, Adrien Broner or even Timothy Bradley. Victory over any one of these will save the flickering candle that is his career.

How

The much underused hooks to the body are an essential part of Khan's raids and incursions. If he can somehow replicate his first round demolition of Maidana and sustain it in waves then he may well finally ripen as a fighter.

Why

Khan may not know about 1889 when Bolton was granted County Borough status, independent of Lancashire or 1974 when such independence was abolished and Bolton became part of the new county, Greater Manchester. Forty years on the locals still refuse to write 'Greater Manchester' on their postal envelopes – preferring instead the de facto grandness of 'Lancashire.'

If Khan can for a second imagine the importance of this and throw each punch as if he is defending the old county lines, then Bolton may once more become a town much talked about – not simply full of comedians.

Disquiet over Big Club Radcliffe 'Saving' Minnows Ladybridge from Relegation

TableTennis365.com, 11 April 2016

Premier Division (final week 11th vs 5th & 12th vs 10th): Ladybridge 'A' 9 Radcliffe 0; Ramsbottom 'C' 1 Burning Desire 8

'What are your thoughts on table tennis teams fielding severely weakened sides on the last match of the season?' I asked with no undue bias or specifics. The question was purposely texted to players *outside* the Premier Division with no obvious connections to the events that unfolded on Monday, 4th April.

What came back ranged from diplomacy and comicalness, to disillusionment and outrage.

Kirit Chauhan (Harper Brass): "Sometimes situations are beyond our control."

Dave Jones Snr (Heaton): "I would object strongly to it unless they were playing us."

John Barker (Hilton): "I think that'd be pretty low."

Mark Greenhalgh (Heaton): "It's against the spirit of sport. Sport is about giving your all against your opponents no matter what level you are at. It's skulduggery!"

John Hutchinson (Farnworth SC): "My view is that the season should end the last week of March. Asking for trouble going in to April."

Paul Tatlock (Little Lever): "Negative, rude, selfish, complacent, insulting. Most players would be mortified if they realised how their actions can be construed. Adopting a 'couldn't care less' approach in the final week is a special kind of mystery because it runs counter to the 'strain every sinew' ethos of sport."

Ray Isherwood (Harper Brass): "They can do as they wish. It's their team."

Dave Wyatt (Farnworth SC): "I have no problem with that at all UNLESS the outcome of the match has some sort of impact on relegation or promotion."

Dave Mottershead (Bolton TTC): "Depends why. Could be tough on other teams with promotion or relegation interests."

Roy Alty (Hilton): "We have four players and try the best we can to rotate. We want a good game of TT with a bit of a laugh and if we win…ace, if not bring on the next game. After all, it's the Bolton League, not world domination."

Mike Brierley (Harper Brass): "Don't agree with it if it's a match that can affect promotion or relegation. Nothing worse than being in the bottom two and playing somebody's best team and finding out that the other team have had a match against somebody's second string."

Mel Brooks (Heaton): "This type of thing goes on at *all times* of the season and does seem to be on the increase. The league needs to manage better all the elements of team behaviour."

The theme running through the responses seems to be one of 'If it affects promotion and relegation then it's not on. It's injudicious. It's wrong-headed.' The astute words of Brooks further the argument into matches that take place "at all times of the season" – less conspicuous evenings, but equally as important when it comes to the final tallying of points.

So what exactly occurred here? The normally proud and indomitable side, Radcliffe would appear – on first inspection – to have 'taken a dive' against lesser opposition, leading to the unexpected relegation of Burning Desire.

Radcliffe over the last four seasons have finished a very respectable 3rd (2014/15), 3rd (2013/14), 5th (2012/13) and 6th (2011/12). It is evident that they have got stronger and are recognised in the game as a top five club – firmly up there with Little Lever 'A' and Wharton but outside the stratosphere which houses Flixton 'A' and Ramsbottom 'A'.

Radcliffe's squad consists of highly-able players: Robert Hall (68%), Zak Cantor (54%), captain Jim Chadwick (75% before Monday, 4th April) and highly-unpredictable 'weapons' Gabriel Wilding (46%)

and Michael Dore (29%). Opposition teams know that they are in for a fight, as demonstrated just last month when Radcliffe bludgeoned Little Lever 'A' 6-3 (a Hall treble, Cantor brace and single for Dore).

How, then, can such might lose to perennial Premier strugglers, Ladybridge? And by a hefty 9-0?

There are a number of strands to this – some statistically evident, some based on opinion and some which plumb the depths of history. We should start with the hard statistics.

In 2013/14 – Jim Chadwick's last full season – the Radcliffe captain 'took care of' recent Ladybridge opposition (Andrew Evans, Stephen Barber & David Bolton) like Giant Haystacks throwing a mischievous child out of a wrestling ring. The results were magnificently one-sided, delicious, suggestive of a heavyweight boxer in with a few featherweights:

9.9.2013

WIN versus Andrew Evans: 11-5, 11-5, 11-1

WIN versus Stephen Barber: 11-9, 11-6, 11-9

WIN versus David Bolton: 12-10, 11-4, 6-11, 11-7

6.1.2014

WIN versus David Bolton: 11-9, 11-6, 11-8

WIN versus Stephen Barber: 8-11, 11-5, 11-6, 11-9

WIN versus Andrew Evans: 11-7, 11-5, 11-8

There was the minor inconvenience of a dropped game to Bolton in September 2013 and one to Barber in January 2014 (like a child jumping on the back of an adult), but otherwise the results are quite striking when it comes to the litmus test of 'Who do you fancy having on your team?' Chadwick. Chadwick, without a doubt.

Fast forward to the present and we see the core of the controversy:

4.4.2016

Barber vs. Chadwick: 11-7, 11-7, 11-4

Evans vs. Chadwick: 11-5, 11-7, 14-12

Bolton vs. Chadwick: 11-2, 8-11, 11-8, 11-9

Are Ladybridge the table tennis equivalent of footballing Leicester in 2015/16? No. Their inflated stats following Monday's 'giant-killing' still stand at modest levels: Barber (38%), Bolton (30%), Evans (39%). Does this result sit right? Again – you would have to plump for a firm 'No'. What about the other Radcliffe players on the night? Well, they didn't show up. From a rich squad of five, four players (Hall, Cantor, Wilding & Dore) were either "injured [or] working" according to their captain. So what happened? There was a 'Forfeit' (three easy points to Ladybridge) and a 'Step-up player' (the hiring of a player from a lower division).

That loanee was Derek Watmough – an able 70% man from Division One, but kind of like taking your aunty to an action movie. He is good, but alas not of the required Premier pedigree. His win percentage when last in the top flight (2014/15) was 17% and he lost five out of his six matches to Ladybridge that season. There'd no doubt be a big box of popcorn for those lucky enough to be in his company, but as for critiquing the movie, stronger candidates exist.

"With every agreed deal, there's always a loser" so the maxim goes. Did something untoward go down either inside or outside the historic Racecourse (originally formed in 1885) before the night of 4th April? We cannot assert such a thing. But it is safe to say that the last time Radcliffe conceded three points before bats had even been picked up was against Wharton on 14th September 2015; their first home match of the season.

Present that evening were Chadwick and Dore. The latter, in the words of Burning Desire captain, Ben Armstrong "would play on one leg if asked to" such is his dedication to the sport. It is quite feasible that Dore – a driving instructor – *was* working, however, as is common in such a profession or in fact injured.

When initially asked for specifics regarding "all four absentees", no elaboration was forthcoming from Radcliffe's captain other than: "I cannot add any more about our players being unavailable. Can I add it's only a game of local league table tennis. We have had certain players this season swearing at our players…It's not nice to listen to. I think that's a story – why the league does nothing to stop it!"

It would be easy to digress at this point – climb into a hornets' nest of recriminations and list the faults of the league in their entirety – but such manoeuvring would not help unbundle the initial steer of this article: Fielding severely weakened sides – can it be excused?

We all have our 'band of merry men' – those we align with depending on their opinions and level of vehemence. In this instance, I am firmly behind John Barker, Mark Greenhalgh, Paul Tatlock and Mel Brooks. It is good not to shirk our responsibilities, hence speak out over perceived injustices. When players use the words "only local league" or "not world domination" I have to confess to finding that inherently irksome. No matter what the level, you have a duty to compete with a sense of fairness; "Strain every sinew", as Tatlock demands.

I have met Jim Chadwick. It was in January 2014 during a Warburton Cup 'last 16' match (Radcliffe vs. lower division 'upstarts' Boyzone). "Jim is a pleasant chap, a perfect ambassador for this great sport," I unashamedly wrote. He struck me as humorous, affable and warm-hearted. We even went for a beer in the famous Radcliffe clubhouse after the match; Jim making me feel welcome on my first visit and playing the role of perfect host.

If there is to be disclosure of any kind in the writing of this then it is that evening over two years ago. A much more significant date, however, is *August* 2014: the month that Jim Chadwick (Radcliffe captain) resigned or was dislodged – depending on your source – from his place of employment…a company run by Ben Armstrong (Burning Desire captain). Their relationship of 14 years – as both friends and work colleagues – perhaps became more fractious after that point.

It would be imprudent to suggest that Chadwick had the foresight or cunning credentials or mathematical genius to light a fuse 20 months ago which would ultimately detonate a small stick of dynamite on Monday, 4th April 2016 (Burning Desire & Ladybridge both finishing on 69pts but the former relegated due to fewer matches won) – thus sending his former boss to the gallows – but such a pattern of events does intrigue the mind.

https://tabletennis365.com/bolton/Tables/Winter_2015-2016/Premier

The intricacies of the Chadwick / Armstrong relationship are not what this article is about and stray into sensitive, legal territory; facts more akin to *Private Eye*. From a table tennis perspective though, a complaint has been made to the Bolton & District Table Tennis League committee which will, in due course (following their 18th April meeting), be referred to the Lancashire Table Tennis Association.

What comes back – in an advisory capacity only, it should be noted – may set an enormous precedent in terms of "team behaviour". This is a story that will rumble on and have backers in both corners, but one cannot help but conjure up the image of a Frenchman ripping the shirt off his 'Mr. Burns'-type boss, whilst feeling perhaps indignant and undervalued.

It would be difficult to find a team across the entire league that is beyond reproach over the last five years. Incidents happen all the time – as is life – but do we excuse politics (if that is proven) fandango-ing with sport?

Examining things on the other side of the fence, we see the single, serendipitous beneficiary in relation to this episode – namely Ladybridge 'A'. Their captain, Dave Bolton when asked what his vibes and thoughts were on the critical '9-0' evening was understandably circumspect:

"You are probably aware that I am on the committee of the [Bolton] league and therefore don't think it appropriate to air thoughts. As a player you turn up and can only play who is in front of you! Any potential side issues regarding other players is for others to discuss. Obviously this was the last game of the season, however if scores are to be scrutinised I feel you have to look at all the season's games where similar events have happened which all have a bearing on the final table."

Indeed. And something echoed by neutral, Brooks. But what of those four Radcliffe 'alibis' from Hall, Cantor, Wilding and Dore which I have been unable to glean? Is it a case of one alibi too many? Was there a party of some description in Radcliffe on the evening of Monday, 4th April which attracted them all much to the dissatisfaction of Burning Desire?

We will have to wait and see what the B&DTTL committee and the LTTA dig up.

Time Table Tennis Took Its Rightful Place

TableTennis365.com, 13 January 2016

The upbeat jingle expected in this paper must sometimes pave the way for the hard reality of obligatory debate.

It is the assertion of many that table tennis continues to be marginalised – in schools, by the media, at local council level and in clubs – and that such a state is inequitable given its fanbase and participation rates around the globe.

A rough Google search ranks the sport 6th in terms of worldwide participation and 7th in terms of fanbase numbers ("900 million," the statisticians gloat); well below football and cricket, and distorted by populous China, but high nonetheless.

Your Sport (Grassroots) – a now three-year experiment – appears complicit in sidelining this great sport; apt to demote it (perhaps unwittingly) to the margins, the periphery by coating the journalism in a different shade of paint.

Column inches, in other words, at the *rear* of the paper – the traditional *hard liquor* section of any self-respecting media outlet – are mainly given over to football, cricket, racing, rugby and athletics. Grassroots, the brave, new Tuesday 'product' of *The Bolton News,* has thus created a class divide, a caste system from which worthy sports coverage cannot escape.

The question that needs answering in 2016 therefore is: What exactly is *Your Sport*? A kids' memento? Lighter journalism? Amateur sport?

It should be said that John Hilton – Flixton's old guard – did not win the 1980 European Table Tennis Championship in order to play second fiddle to other sports. His titanic efforts were meant to showcase the sport's magnificence, its guile and skill, the underdog with a splash of Hai Karate.

Why then does table tennis coverage feel like the B-side of a record within the pages of our foremost local paper?

The Bolton News has admirable sections (Monday's *The Wanderer*, Wednesday's Mark Halsey, Friday's *Views in Brief*, Saturday's *Inside Wanderers*) but Mark Iles, its chief football writer, must feel like a privileged pub landlord with exclusive access to the whisky. Where are the sportswriters nipping at his heels, permitted delicious, lengthy subjects and the mutual challenge of competing articles?

Modern table tennis is dismissed by many as unwatchable – even its own players. Marty Reisman referred to "Imperceptible flicks of the wrist rather than athleticism". The International Table Tennis Federation (ITTF), however, remains the largest sports body in the world (affiliated with 222 countries).

Surely this fact alone makes it eligible for the back pages.

This article was withdrawn for intended publication in The Bolton News *after their Head of Sport wished to write an opposing piece but also have editing rights over Weston's piece.*

Super Dave Holden

The Bolton News, 24 November 2015

Division Two: Harper Brass 'B' 1 Meadow Ben 'A' 8

If Meadow Ben's Dave Holden does not turn you over in a legitimate manner, there is the distinct possibility that he might strangle you with his gargantuan hands and forge the scorecard.

His wedding ring alone resembles a section of copper pipe and his tumbling hair – which has the habit of falling into a centre parting – has that look of severe graft about it.

He is a big fella. And whilst the table tennis hall does not exactly shake upon him taking his position in front of the five feet wide Cornilleau table, Richter-like rumbles are heard once he begins to throw himself around.

Decked out in black Joola top and shorts with Puma socks and Stiga trainers, Holden is either a sponsor's dream or the man sat in reception each day eyeing up a potential deal. The stats are there to warrant maybe a minuscule business association (2012/13 50% Div1, 2013/14 67% Div1, 2014/15 70% Div2), but what is particularly noticeable is Holden's low attendance on the Bolton circuit.

Not over-extending himself – generally making seven match-night appearances each season – he does what many do by juggling larger Bury commitments across the border. The Carlton Club, former Nomads' and now Meadow Ben player exudes a rare confidence no matter which region he is performing in. Of redoubtable stock, Holden stalks his opponents as if auditioning for David Attenborough's *The Hunt*.

This was a strange evening in that Harper's no.1, Dave Jones was away in Geneva and no.3, Dave Brookes not picking up and so an experimental three was hastily assembled: Roger Bertrand vacuumed out of retirement; Jim Bolton making his expectant debut; Jeff Weston attempting to correct a torrid season.

The reality, however, in league terms was 10th versus 2nd; Division Two newbies against adroit 'members of the bar'. Meadow's tall, Kangol-wearing Peter Cooper was mauled a little – losing to Bertrand

15-13, 9-11, 11-9, 7-11, 8-11 and scraping through against Bolton and Weston (each in four games) – but otherwise the night went with the form book; James Bollard, in particular – tattoos beaming from his forearms – making a statement via his three short wins.

Jim Bolton, Harper's secret weapon from Wigan, battled with the perspicacity of a foreign spy but the shot variation of Holden and muscle of Bollard proved too much. Even for Bolton's lucky 'Sunday roast' socks.

The Shrewd Signing of Johnny Scowcroft

The Bolton News, 20 October 2015

Division Two: Heaton 'C' 7 Harper Brass 'B' 2

Not reported in the wider press over the summer was the transfer of John Henry Scowcroft from Heaton 'B' to 'Heaton 'C'. Although seen in many quarters as a final acknowledgement that his 79-year-old body could no longer handle the rigours of life in Division One, the real story was somewhat different.

The largest clubs – Hilton, Heaton and Harper Brass – during the close season rejigged their teams and went from a combined 22 league teams (out of 60) to a lower figure of 20 (out of 59). Now representing 33.9% of the entire league these behemoths have had to cope with an economic downturn, injuries and in the case of Harper, a small mutiny.

Three key figures emerge from this – club functionaries in charge of combing through the squads and holding at least one annual meeting. Brian Young of Hilton, Paul Mort of Heaton and Kaushik Makwana of Harper Brass are effectively the dons of the Bolton table tennis scene. It is 'Morty' though who is central to this story.

When Johnny Scowcroft did not get the usual call before the start of the 2015/16 season, he began to wonder where his white and blue Stiga trainers would be squeaking come September. A familiar face on the circuit, Scowcroft – his barrel frame always decked out in green, Mizuno polo shirt and blue 'velvet' shorts – is not one to opt for muesli and rocking chair. His stats indicate a 4-5% decline each season, yet he is ever capable.

Behind the scenes Morty was talking to Division Three promoted captain, Mark Greenhalgh and it was this together with a hip injury to relegated Division One fellow, Bill Fairhurst that led to the cull of one team. A natural joining of players in Two was considered (to the detriment of sacrificial lamb, Greenhalgh) the best, but controversial way forward.

"Morty and myself had the conversation in late August. I knew Scowcroft was what we needed," Greenhalgh generously conceded.

And so Scowcroft was unleashed in Division Two for the first time since 2012/13. His win percentage before this match was 83.33%. A satisfactory evening against my Harper strugglers only slightly dampened that: Versus Jeff Weston 8-11, 11-8, 12-10, 11-8; versus Matthew Brown 6-11, 11-9, 11-3, 11-9; but defeat to Dave Jones 6-11, 7-11, 8-11.

The consensus is: You cannot train someone up to *be* Johnny Scowcroft. He is unique and probably fell from the sky in a pod.

"You Wouldn't Have Won if We'd Beaten You"

The Bolton News, 13 October 2015

The passing of the Major League Baseball star, Yogi Berra (aged 90) late last month is a reminder that daftness will always have a place at the heart of sport. The feared clutch hitter famed for his Yogi-isms was said to have a homely face and a talent "routinely underestimated". Some of his quotes are like gold dust: "If you see a fork in the road, take it"; "Half this game is 90% mental"; "It's so crowded, nobody goes there any more"; and surely the best of the lot, "You wouldn't have won if we'd beaten you".

The final quote is a ridiculous, yet hilarious taunt to the opposition at the end of a match – any match, be it football, table tennis, cricket or that American stuff. Berra, the son of Italian immigrants, liked to speak his mind even if mocked and derided. And in this ludicrous age of squareness and grim pontificating, he is a fine example of not being bound by the narrative of the day.

Ten World Series rings with the Yankees is testament to his greatness, but more than this he was one of America's best-loved stars; "small and squat" but he made people smile.

Looking through the early tables of the Bolton League is in some quarters eerily familiar: Flixton 'A' and Ramsbottom 'A' battling it out for the Premier crown; Heaton 'D' (they've had a few letters along the way) tucked in nicely near the top of Division Three; Meadow Hill 'A' and their annual see-saw between Three and Four (often assisted by a benevolent committee).

Behind these team names and others are Yogis of our own, however: Roy Caswell – rarely seen not wearing beige pants; Roger Bertrand – the man with the plastic bags (one for his bananas, one for his bottle of cordial that resembles cleaning fluid and two more for good luck); Alan Lansdale, known for his acerbic yet sardonic lines ("You can't use them serves against an old man"); Ray Isherwood, zipping through the divisions faster than anyone (an ode to his skills on the side of his carpet van, "For Quality, at Affordable Prices"); Paul Brandwood, perhaps loosely attributed with "He's only got a backhand and that's poor".

This is shaping up to be an interesting season both on and off the tables. May the wry words of Boltonians and those coddled and adopted in this north-west heartland long continue.

Longworth Stock Surges

The Bolton News, 22 September 2015

Division Two: Harper Brass 'C' 6 Ladybridge 'B' 3

The real hero tonight was not the winning team, Harper Brass C. Nor was it the players inside it – captain Faizan Bhura, Kirit Chauhan and treble terminator John Nuttall. It was instead Ladybridge's stand-in player from Division Three, Ellis Longworth.

The 15-year-old lad with the wedge haircut and lanky legs lost all three of his matches, but one must look inside that raw number just as a humanist studies the bereft GDP figure that is an economist's Holy Grail.

Versus Bhura: 11-5, 7-11, 8-11, 11-7, 9-11 (46 points to 45 but still the loser). Against Nuttall: 8-11, 11-13, 11-6, 9-11 (savage). When entertaining Chauhan: 4-11, 8-11, 4-11 (head understandably gone).

You play twelve games, you usually deserve something. You rock Nuttall 11-6, people sit up. To look at Longworth, you do not initially spot the majestic player. There are the private pet talks muttered serenely: 'Come on, Ellis' (like a whining call to the gods). There are the occasional, soft-trickled shots into the net.

He could be a six-foot rake in the corner of a garage, a *Pale Rider* but what he probably is is Keir Hardie walking into Parliament as an MP for the first time in August 1892; unperturbed, courageous, a fighting man not dragooned by protocol and reputations.

How ironic that hours before this exalted performance Longworth was grounded from school for wearing "unacceptable" shoes. The world of table tennis has no such piffy rules – merely that playing shirts and shorts are "of a uniform colour other than white".

Given that Longworth had to borrow a bat for this clash (his preferred blade locked in the house of his usual teammate) and was of course 'playing up', his exploits were remarkable. Ask Xu Xin to use the bat of Ma Long. There would be a look of disgust, the clear recognition that one's normal game would be compromised.

Longworth did not tangibly assist his temporary teammates, Brian Greenhalgh and John Cole in their annual quest for survival, but his hard-hitting, accurate forays surprised many. Greenhalgh's range of expressions on the court and self-criticism ("Fingers…Oh, you plonker…Frilly underwear") – despite his double – could be said to embody this. And Cole's renewed impetus was arguably due to the gee-up of the younger competitor and colleague.

As for Harper Brass – this was a good win, but they must start talking between games. Bhura's two losses could have been avoided with a canny word or two from his elders.

Spinners and Steel Benefit from Top Teams' Exodus

The Bolton News, 15 September 2015

A perfect 60 teams in the Bolton Table Tennis League was never going to last. Scurryings down the road to Bury, retirements and the odd AWOL during a summer of madness were always going to unhinge things slightly. The consequent pain has fallen on Division Two in that following all the shuffling around the middle division has been left with only 11 teams; two scrubbed fixtures from the normal list or "open dates" as the committee like to say.

Table tennis widows will rejoice such an outcome – plan that extra line dancing class or add grim tasks to the infamous 'jobs list'. But it is the peculiarity of having at least half a dozen teams in Division Three that could legitimately turn over their higher rivals that now piques. Rarely have so many teams been promoted from lower down the league – the traditional two per division swelled to four and five including fragmented sides.

The scars are evident and there will be some cup 'shocks' as a result. A point in case is the group of teams that finished fourth to seventh in 2014/15: Harper Brass B (112 points); Farnworth Social Circle C (110); Hilton J (108); Boyzone (107). A mere five points separated this cluster of teams, yet only Harper Brass B have been given a golden ticket to the Division Two funfair. Perhaps shamed into anonymity they have subsequently changed their name to Top Spinners. Are they the luckiest team in the world?

'I found it strange that the Heaton team that finished bottom of Two were relegated while the team that finished fourth in Three were promoted. Maybe the Heaton team had had enough,' a player who wished to remain anonymous commented.

There is a reason for this and it comes straight from the General Secretary, Roy Caswell's lips via a bit of paraphrasing: The committee felt that those teams which were so far away from the pack that it would have been absurd to keep them afloat in the same division were relegated. Given that Heaton were 61 points from the official safety line this seems credible.

As for the charmed and blessed a fleeting examination of Division Four's final table shows Irlam Steel massively off the pace in third – a full 45 points – behind the kids and Poles of Harper Brass D and Polonia but waved through.

No solution is ideal in these circumstances but suffice to say Bolton will unfortunately be a weaker league in 2015/16.

Tim Vaughan: The Five-Set Man

The Bolton News, 18 August 2015

'Truth is going out of fashion,' Nomad's Tim Vaughan tells me. I had phoned him to ask if he had any ideas as to why his table tennis matches last longer than anyone else's, why he has an extraordinary amount of five-setters under his belt and before I knew it he was talking about pianos, community painting and self-education.

I don't mind a bit of discursiveness, a few Woody Allen non sequiturs, but sometimes I need the facts fast – quotes to shape a story, relevant background information and insights.

This was meant to be a simple pick up – a collection of words from a player which I could massage into a short article. Match Secretary, Brett Haslam had warned me beforehand, however: 'I think if your two brains come together there'll be some sort of Hadron event.'

Vaughan was going to be difficult – like talking to a *Mastermind* contestant or a Frenchman. Nothing was for free. Being on the phone for less than 20 minutes was incomprehensible to him; five minutes a mere pulling out of the station, 10 minutes a slow unscrewing of the flask top. Hang on tight for the journey!

Vaughan is a rarity among table tennis players. He is a multi-layered man – one of only two I have met that like to sit around the camp fire and mull over life. The record for wordy responses is currently 2,400 held by Flixton's Paul Cicchelli following an interview with him. After much to-ing and fro-ing, Vaughan claimed to be sat on a stash of 5,000 words prompted by twenty questions I had put to him. He had apparently doubled the ante.

Why did I want answers and riffs from this Ashton resident (Liverpool born in 1963)? Why did I seek critical facts underpinning his game? Because his stats were staggering. Normally a player is lucky to reach 25 per cent in terms of five-set matches participated in throughout the league season. This Division One player was off the scale at 42 per cent. A bounteous 24 of his 57 matches in 2014/15 were sweat-inducing marathon sessions.

It was uncanny – almost as if Vaughan wanted or needed plentiful ding-dongs, as if the whole thing was staged. But who in their right mind prolongs things?

Perhaps it is not within him to be merciless. But then fellow players applaud his technique: 'He reads people's games, plays close to the table with a good natural style, attacks very quickly on both flanks and takes spin easily.'

The 5000-word haul never arrived. Maybe it is Vaughan's attempt to indemnify the truth. Maybe a larger piece on him will follow.

The Return of John Nuttall

The Bolton News, 28 July 2015

Special signings are rare. They reinvigorate a club. They act as polish to the existing ranks.

The news that The Lostock Lasher, John Nuttall is considering a return to table tennis after temporarily retiring in March 2014 is significant indeed. There are not many with his thirst, his drive, his sublime, unorthodox technique.

Past reports have lauded him – taken note of his ability to constantly win ("No Stops Yet for Nuttall Steam Train"). In 2012/13 he did the impossible – he won all 57 of his league matches and joined a select group, the '100% Club'.

So where will the 24-year-old play? What contracts and promises have been texted, verbalised and emailed to this still young man with the settled mind of a 35-year-old sage?

Discussions have been had with Meadow Hill, Harper Brass and Heaton to date. When a conqueror hits the market, there is no shortage of takers, no feigning disinterest or stroking one's chin.

Who will land him? There are sticking points to a deal with each club. Meadow Hill, captained by league general secretary, Roy Caswell finished the 2014/15 season in 11th place in Division Three – one of the relegation spots. Should their logical fate play out then a Division Four birth will not be attractive to a player that has gone unbeaten in the league's bottom division and has actually achieved 96% in Division Three.

Harper Brass offer a natural route forward having been promoted to Division Two, but team loyalties – still beating in some quarters of the UK – will prevent such a transfer…for now. Their squad is full and ripe and very few teams desire a dressing room of five players when only three walk the table. A perfect fit it would have been, but its time may come again in 2016/17 with an anticipated restructuring of the Harper stable.

Heaton then – that little cricket club on the hill which offers great bar facilities, limited parking and alternative sports. The irony here is that Nuttall's last tormentor, Dave Jones Snr plays for them. The

16th January 2014 remains etched in both players' heads. Could the old enemy merge, join forces? It is more than likely. Dave Jones Jnr, of the same club, is a long-time admirer of Nuttall and understands Heaton's deficiencies following relegation from Two to Three.

Concerning the man himself though – Nuttall's words say a lot: 'The main thing I want to do is play with people I like and know.'

A simple wish, but the wish of a force, a table tennis whirlwind.

When Losing Becomes a Habit

The Bolton News, 23 June 2015

On possibly two of their twenty-two evenings there was hope: the opening Division Two fixture on 4th September 2014 when captain, Dave Jones Jnr wrestled the night's first match away from Krishna Hooton (12-10, 11-9, 10-12, 11-3) and then again on 12th December 2014 when they salvaged a hat-trick of wins against a weakened Hilton H.

But in between and *after* the beatings came; hard and heavy – six evenings in October/November with a meagre return of 2/54 points and a horrible February/March racking up that same sombre total.

Heaton 'D' (formerly 'E'), a mere six months before, were considered giants in Division Three – runaway promotion kings with 110 points and the experienced hands of Dave Jones Snr, Philip Beales and the aforementioned Jones Jnr. Journalistic notes on them from their heyday read (respectively): footwork of a ballerina; rangy and lethal; affable but deadly.

This ageing crew, however, has fallen foul of the cursed middle division. Plenty have trod this path and failed – immediately understood the dedication or innate ability required in order to flourish. You cannot, it seems, just stride into the table tennis halls at this level and cement a result or sneak numerous points on your serve. Division Two has that ominous combination of "long established players and young guns being coached", Beales mourns. In other words, there are no safe matches.

Finishing with a season low of 19 points (Jones Jnr 9, Jones Snr 4, Beales 2 and part-timer, Martin Hulton 4), Heaton have well and truly gone from punching the air in March 2014 to "desperately looking for inspiration from each other" in 2014/15. "By the end we had little belief in our own ability and looked forward to the end of the season and a chance to regroup", Jones Jnr opines.

The really disappointing aspect was that they'd "somehow underperformed" though – "too many easy points given away…poor reading of serves…too hesitant to attack".

After a wonderful beginning (75% after his first four matches), Jones Snr won only once more (1/47) – a Christmas present from Jean

Smart who was 'playing up' anyway. Such habitual play can torment a man. Noises begin to mess with one's psyche. 'Will I ever be the same again?' is the voice – 'Even on my return to Division Three.'

Heaton will be grateful for their experience once September arrives. They are too good to implode. Until then, there will be a ghost over each shoulder, a slight nervousness with the bat and renewed belief slowly baking in the background.

Faizan Bhura: The Diminutive Warrior

The Bolton News, 12 May 2015

The names of the Nobel Prize nominees are not revealed until 50 years after the event. This adds a certain fascination to the awards given out. Who did the eventual winner beat? Was he or she up against the cream?

Away from the bookies' chalk and inside the Swedish Academy papers are passed around and eyebrows arched enquiringly. The initial list is cumbersome – it includes around 200 potential laureates selected by professors, society presidents, previous winners and academy members. This is whittled down to a 'long list' of 15-20 *preliminary* candidates in April and then a 'short list' of five *final* candidates in May.

Much rigour and due process takes place and that is *before* the three months of reading and assessment which occurs in order to prepare reports and discuss the merits of each candidate.

It would be nice to think that similar levels of deliberation and brooding happened prior to and on Friday, 27th March at the pre-Finals committee meeting. Present were officers Alan Bradshaw, John and Margaret Scowcroft, George Berry, Jean Smart and head honchos Roy Caswell and Brett Haslam.

On these shoulders rested the fates of the season's big-name players – most challengingly *who* was to be engraved on The Albert Howcroft Trophy for Most Improved Player. Not an easy thing to decide. An algorithm can only churn out an unloved number. It does not factor in personal circumstances, the general feeling amongst your peers and the inevitable politics that prevail.

'It's a bit like politics and statistics. Which way do you jump?' General Secretary Caswell admitted with redoubtable insight into the workings of the loyal few that give up their Fridays. Which way indeed when the list is so strong, so full of games revamped?

Six candidates shone across the five Bolton divisions: Robert Shaw (Div4, from 8 to 42%); Keane Mills (74 to 100%); Nathan Rhodes (29 to 70%); Christopher Boys (Div4, 80% to Div3, 51%); Faizan Bhura (Div4, 72% to Div3, 58%); Ray Isherwood (Div2, 27 to 68%). It was Bhura, however, who impressed the old guard. 'In the end we all just looked at each other and went for Faizan.'

Science perhaps left at the door, but then in the 4' 11" Bhura they have made a genuine discovery. 'I always do rubbish in the [pre-match warm-ups]. I make them think my technique is not good at all and then when the match is ready I pull my socks up and turn my brain into gear. That's what I do.'

'A proper kidder,' to quote Scott Brown. Too dry to read at times, but there with his secret weapon – his consistent forehand.

You can get a thousand sentences from Bhura on the game and how he has tracked its idiosyncrasies from the age of 12 – charming, colloquial passages that reach out and shatter any sense of smoothness. All that matters though is his devotion to table tennis, his 1994 Bolton-born (Indian mother/Zambian father) bones that have lifted this trophy once held by Andrea Holt.

'Mild' Max Brooks

The Bolton News, 5 May 2015

Max Brooks knows very little about Rocky Balboa yet skips five times a week – outside, near the back gate. Such rhythmic poise augments his low centre of gravity and remarkable balance. He claims to stand 5' 6" tall although one suspects that underneath the slicked-back, mountainous hair he is actually 5' 5.

The grandson of treasured Lancashire cricketer Harry Pilling (himself a dynamic 5' 3") and professional ice skater Yvonne Rayner, Max has a blood line that almost forcibly places a sporting implement in his hand. After first picking up a table tennis bat at the age of ten, however, he soon lost interest.

Smooth trajectories rarely chart a player's career. Most of the time it is a rugged path forward – a Snakes and Ladders board – full of pitfalls, hard dice and the odd bit of luck. Max's serendipity came in the form of Sport England visiting his Tottington school two years later, informing him that he "had some talent for the game". This neutral observation acted as a stimulus, a catalyst to where he is now.

Awarded the Ralph Palmer Memorial Trophy in early April as Bolton's 'Most Promising Junior of the Season', Master Brooks – still just 15-years-old – took 44 scalps out of 45 in Division Three; his one blemish losing to the Austrian, Bernd Dumpelnik two weeks before Christmas when gifts are traditionally wrapped up in readiness for handing out.

Such an ascent into the annals of Bolton's history (and indeed Bury's if you consider his 49/57 win record with Seedfield in its equivalent division) has largely come about not as a result of any fortunate DNA, but rather through the guidance of surviving *paternal* grandfather, Mel Brooks (now 73). 'Grampa Mel started me off at Heaton CC. Both grampas have been role models in helping me achieve my goals.'

Max's approach to the game is surprisingly serene. There is none of the 'mad' or mercurial synonymous with such a christening. 'Mental toughness and never, never give up – play for every point,' he casually elucidates. Intensity doesn't ride with the words but instead an internal grit and indomitable belief. It is the same when discussing education (refusing to fuss and be drawn on his favourite maths discipline): '*All* maths I enjoy. It will be what I need when I start work.'

The pragmatic side of him is startling in part – perhaps too clean or manufactured. But then, as Grampa Mel – chief mentor and disciple of Cliff Booth – tells me, returning to the main subject: 'We spend time discussing strategy and the mental side of the game. He is like a sponge for taking in information, though being his own man he sometimes tries other things.'

Holding the Ralph Palmer trophy is like a ten-year pass to beautiful things – a soft guarantee of climbing the divisions. Big names have gone before Max including England's Andrew Rushton (1996/97) – had their names inscribed on the silver plate.

A 'B-game' is what is required now. 'He needs to dig short and develop an aggressive backhand block and kill,' coach Brooks asserts. As for the skipping ($3{\times}40$) – that will continue.

Keane Mills: The 100% Kid

The Bolton News, 28 April 2015

He has the hard jaw of youth – an almost inert face that gives very little away. After speaking to him, you do not get the sense that he has won anything, but rather lost. There is a bit of the dour Scot in him – a solemn, behind-the-eyes weighing up of events. And yet he is a Boltonian, a successful English lad who has walked through his home town's 4th division untrammeled and unbeaten.

Keane Mills, 15-years-old and 5'9" tall – a product of the Harper Brass stable (along with team mates Ellis Longworth and Nathan Rhodes) – has done something only two other people have done in recent years: he has gone through a full season without losing. Two extremes of the table tennis circuit seem to cosset such triumph – the Premier Division and Division Four; Michael Moir and John Nuttall earlier beneficiaries of the grandeur.

Mills is a special case though. The title was confirmed on April Fools' Day when he was still 14 – *eight* years ahead of 22-year-old Nuttall's startling achievement in 2012/13. 'No matter what age you are, you can still match the best,' he believes and asserts in equal measure – the candour not exactly pouring from him, but offering a rare glimpse of his conviction. 'I show everyone respect and expect it back and I don't show my anger as I believe it is a weakness. If you lose your head, you lose the game.'

It is this maturity and precocious flowering which has seemingly led him to where he is now: the recipient of a 'Double' in only his second league season (Harper Brass 'D' securing the Ron Hindle Trophy days after their title win). Indeed, he claims to have picked up a bat for the first time a mere "two and a half years ago while on holiday" – his exceptional hand/eye coordination obvious to all.

Fellow players around the clubs beat the Mills' drum. In describing 'the 100% kid' a consistent array of words passes their lips: steady; good temperament; right attitude; attacking; patient; level-headed; lots of potential; great serves; focused. These qualities alone cannot have built such a force, an emerging warlord when at the table. They perhaps complement the evident desire and ministrations that exude from him, however.

Necessary, critical voices that stray from the consensus point to the young man's middle game, his unforced errors and also the fact that his mobility seems to be, at times, like a granny reaching for the sweet tray. "He only moves a bit," one source commented. But what if he only *needs* to move a bit thus regularly returns to his upright stance whilst flogging the opposition.

Keane is uncompromising: 'I'm guessing I didn't move much against this one person.' The stats bear this out – just two of his 66 conquests have gone to five sets and they were in September. More impressively, he cares. When the title was briefly in the hands of rivals Polonia at 9.30pm on 31st March, he could not bear it: 'My heart was in my mouth. I thought we had lost it and I was very frustrated.'

Bowing Out

The Bolton News, 9 September 2014

Winston Churchill once referred to Clement Attlee as "A sheep in sheep's clothing." As I grow weary, old, fast approaching 45, more and more sheep seem to cross my path – mostly in the world of financial services but in other areas too.

We all have small dreams. Mine from the age of 23 – sat in a New York hotel room listening to the blaring taxis down below – was to write a novel. A work about 'the street'; society if you will. Despite my best efforts – five of them in fact – I ultimately failed.

And so began the drift – into table tennis reports after a 'knock' with friends. Into radio plays, children's story poems, interviews with who I deemed to be the more interesting colleagues or pariahs at my place of work and short stories. Anything and everything: a lovely excuse to write and feel good, worthy even.

I recall approaching The Bolton News's Neil Bonnar on 1st April 2013. I padded the email proposal with talk of New Journalism which unofficially began in 1962: Tom Wolfe picking up a copy of *Esquire* and reading a piece on Joe Louis, written by Gay Talese.

The article was mesmerising, intimate – a form of literary or 'short story' journalism. It was a turning point indeed, but such art was to be hounded out of fashion by 1981; fashion – that villainous word.

A few notable voices still held the torch aloft – the irreverent and mighty, Hugh McIlvanney on this side of the Atlantic for one; his prose allowing you to swim across the ably-depicted sporting scenes as if you were God. When you read McIlvanney's work, you are forced to stop, gasp, replay the word combinations over and over in your head such is their allure.

My comparatively feeble samples – nine of them written between 2007 and 2008 – were included in the email to Bonnar in an attempt to 'firm up' negotiations and show him my wares, my 'Del Boy' goods. I had a habit of getting home after matches, taking a shower and then staying up 'til about midnight dissecting what had unfolded.

I invented boyish nicknames for my friends, my opponents: Bazooka, Hustler, Alamo, Raider, The Destroyer, The Reverend;

simple alliteration usually behind the grand title as if I imagined us walking out to lights and music.

Bonnar phoned me up one evening not too long after. The deal was cut. I was to follow in the footsteps of fine predecessors, Alan Calvert and Ian Wheeldon.

"Just try to be less flamboyant," he advised me, referring to the work I had sent in (www.thesportswriter1.com).

I understood this. I didn't entirely rail against it. Papers have codes to follow. Crossing the line into the semi-fantastical was unnecessary – it risked reputational damage.

Now, after writing a total of sixty-seven pieces for the paper – quite an apt number – I feel it is time to step down. The joy in sitting alongside players from the Premier Division through to Division Four has been a true privilege. Letting me into their modest venues has been kind and not always trumpeted in the manner it should have been.

New projects await me including the better nurturing of my family. I hope there is someone to pass the baton to in this rich, sporting garden.

Pathway to Quantity

The Bolton News, 2 September 2014

People do good things. Help the blind across the road. Pick up change for old ladies. Hold doors open out of courtesy rather than coincidence.

Some volunteer. Give ten or twenty years of their life to causes they believe in. And occasionally, just occasionally, recognition shows up at the door.

Through luck, perception or merit people are handed certificates, badges, scrolls and chances to further their philanthropy.

Karen Edwards OBE is a case in point. Chief Executive of the Bolton Lads and Girls Club (BL&GC) and part of the Queen's Birthday Honours list in 2012, she has put in a long shift, been imaginative, dogged and tenacious since the 1990s.

Spearheading a team (more recently) in control of a circa £3m budget, Ms Edwards has mostly looked after the coffers well – built relationships, developed her soft language skills with particular emphasis on words such as 'opportunity', 'pathways' and 'evaluation'.

Her efforts overall should be furiously applauded.

But there is a gaping hole; a hole which only started to appear towards the middle of August. And the table tennis community is at a loss to explain it.

When the list of teams was compiled and sorted into five divisions for the forthcoming season, one noticeable absence was evident: BL&GC – the oldest club in the league.

Why? Digging has begun in earnest in an attempt to get a satisfactory answer yet words hung together collectively in the form of responses can be an ugly business – they turn into racketeers, miscreants, contortionists, any number of twisting and bending creations.

The general take thus far is this: There are two RBs at the Lads & Girls Club – Rachel Burke (Sport Development Manager) and Roger Bertrand (their only qualified table tennis coach). Ms Burke, a glance at on-line archives reveals, has been photographed in celebratory pose alongside Ms Edwards on numerous occasions. Mr Bertrand has not.

Ms Burke, being a member of the Senior Management Team, has the ear of Ms Edwards. Mr Bertrand does not.

The recent decision at the club therefore to replace competitive league table tennis with a 'Try Train' model and somewhat insular youth club versus youth club scheme must be put down to blinkeredness at the top and wilful neglect of those 'in the know'.

Whilst this summary is not entirely without sporting bias or conjecture, it does hold water.

The grand myth concerning Cassius Clay's fourth round knockdown at the hands of Henry Cooper in 1963 is that Clay (later known as Muhammad Ali) glanced over at Elizabeth Taylor, who was sitting at ringside.

Such a story, whether true or not, is marvellous. In a similar vein, it can only be assumed that Ms Edwards in August of this year – whilst in a high-level meeting – glanced over at a spectre and was sufficiently overcome that she acceded to a proposal – perhaps from her Sport Development Manager or her Youth Club Manager – that would deny at least four young players league table tennis.

The BL&GC's new schemes may have their place but when marinated in the disillusionment of players about to break through in what would have been a key season (Jack Daniels 2012/13 [35%], 2013/14 [65%]) such plans can only be recorded under the heading 'Folly'.

They may even result in the wholesale abandonment of half a generation of players unless designed or mapped out more clearly.

Cold, Cold War

The Bolton News, 26 August 2014

What happens if we're all bluffing, living half a life, churning out an existence which bows to the demands of politics and business?

Philip Larkin said "the eyes clear with age". He was right. As a consequence, we begin to shut out the noise, no longer chase the pointless – steer clear of bogus thrills.

Table tennis remedies some of the hurt, acts as a part-time panacea, transports the mind to a better place. In its rhythm is joy, health, a beautiful nothingness, a disappearing act.

People play the game with wit accompanying them, the occasional growl and the odd bit of controversy. A night is rarely complete or perfect – just riddled with more good than bad if driving home with a smile.

It is 'controversy' which fascinates me the most.

Sport can be a truly dazzling thing capable of mending relations as in the case of the Sino-American thaw in 1971; Cold War tensions eased by the friendship between table tennis players, Zhuang Zedong and Glenn Cowan.

It can also muddy itself, exampled in 1969 by the Marylebone Cricket Club's refusal to allow the mixed-race player, Basil D'Oliveira play for England against South Africa thus indirectly condoning the apartheid regime.

Boxing, of course, is not without its demons – unbeaten US fighter, Joe Louis (24-0) defeated by Germany's Max Schmeling in 1936; Schmeling lauded by the Nazi Party as a symbol of Aryan supremacy.

American writer, Langston Hughes echoed part of his nation's mood at the time: "I walked down Seventh Avenue and saw grown men weeping like children, and women sitting on the curbs with their head in their hands. All across the country that night when the news came out that Joe was knocked out, people cried."

Such magnitude and meaning I have yet to witness in the table tennis halls of Bolton, however it prompts bigger questions over politics and rights within sport. On the outside, sport has embraced physical disabilities and differences. At a local level I regularly play against Asians, whites, blacks, people with Alzheimer's, Parkinson's and autism. It is the norm – nothing unusual, nothing new, something that arouses only bigots.

But start talking politics, start getting *inside* a person, and it often ends in a rumble. Some people confuse reasoned arguments (or dialectics) with feuds. Some are hard-wired not to listen at all – see between the black and the white, or the numerous religious scriptures.

Little known is that Schmeling actually had a Jewish American manager (Joe Jacobs) but was trapped by the ideology of the day. Muhammad Ali, not all hero, was so consumed by the Nation of Islam that he chose not to mourn the assassination of the reformed Malcolm X in 1965. Two years later, a maturer Ali refused to be drafted for the Vietnam War, laudably costing him his freedom.

This week's column was meant to be about a left-wing table tennis player who I happened to meet earlier this year. I then realised – and he concurred – that by printing his name and espousing his thoughts it might compromise his position of employment.

The default 21st century political position is not yet common sense and kindliness it would appear, but something still aligned to the interests of the day – a never-ending track to nowhere.

Perhaps one day change will come after the remaining dogs are driven out. Perhaps.

Duncan, The Diamond and The Lip

The Bolton News, 19 August 2014

The stand out, plum fixture of the table tennis calendar's opening week is Hilton 'E' versus Hilton 'D'. The latter, captained by Andrew Morey, cleaned up Division Two last season yet worries now permeate the camp that ex-player Craig Duncan's new team will make a mockery of the Hilton ranking system.

Win percentages mostly do not lie. Minh Le (73%), Stephen Hunt (48%) and Morey (81%) can expect the usual dilution of their stats now they are a division higher, however more worrisome is the imminent match on September 3rd versus Division One foes Wilson Parker (93%), Duncan (87%) and Josh Sandford (50%).

If Sandford raises his game and shouts a little less (or more), then this first fixture could be discomfiting for Hilton 'D' – a psychological hammerblow just days into the 2014/15 winter season.

Hilton 'E' is a team whose combined personalities have not tread the circuit for some time. Rich in horseplay, humour, intensity and steel, its three amigos ask you to indulge them, stand back while the fireworks go off – respect not their antics but the grounded sorcery which they bring to the table.

Duncan, a southpaw, schooled in the French sassiness of Lads' Club import and coach, Roger Bertrand believes the time is right for an assault. His fleeting appearances in the league – a mere nine in 2011/12, zero in 2012/13 and 15 in 2013/14 – conceal a wider truth. Although not 'match fit', he is hungry, slavering in anticipation of a full season.

The record book shows that his pithy efforts for the soon-to-be enemy were timely and repartee-like. Dispatching Division Two's finest, Alan Lansdale, Krishna Chauhan and new compatriot, Wilson Parker, Duncan's form was almost too impressive, 'rigged' and ridiculous (symptomatic of a secret training camp). The only black marks were against Ramsbottom ringer, Neil Booth and Meadow Ben's hard-hitting bull, Philip Calvert.

Duncan last played Morey, Le and Hunt competitively on 10th February 2012 – beating Hunt only. Two and a half years on, his awkward style is expected to pick off all three players – avenging two four-set defeats in the process.

Parker, the youngest member of Hilton 'E' at seventeen, yet probably their most serious player is a fine example of how to fast-track a rough diamond. With only two seasons under his belt, his stats are incomparable in the middle divisions: 96% (Div3: 2012/13); 93% (Div2: 2013/14). Ready now to climb even further, Parker is the face, the consequence of good coaching.

And then there is Sandford – the third wheel in the operation. He reminds you a little of Cassius Clay, the Louisville Lip pre-Sonny Liston half a century ago. He talks a big game, disses the opposition, yet the more you witness such behaviour, the more you realise it is an act of affection.

Sandford cannot for one second drop his guard, his facial gizmos, his play-acting. Even at work you get the feeling his horsing around keeps him sane. He is centre stage – Hamlet, King Lear, Macbeth – yet a different clock ticks inside him when alone.

In his mind he is writing his next wacky script. Sure – most of his words are arbitrary, off the cuff, impromptu, but the core are constructed. *He* is constructed. Like a clown inside the big top; a painted sneer instead of a smile.

Will he guide Hilton 'E' to glory? If the bat is working – yes.

El Borrachos

The Bolton News, 12 August 2014

If there was to be a raid on the table tennis community – bats stolen, an *Italian Job* of sorts – then it would be here, outside The Crown (1 Chorley New Road). Or a mile up the road (B6226) at the Bank Top Brewery Ale House (36 Church Street).

Both public houses are frequented by the cream of Bolton's table tennis world. Both offer sustenance to weary players intent on forgetting the more rueful moments of their drills and practice sessions.

Notable patrons – be they politicians, artists or sportsmen – have congregated in certain spots since time immemorial. Public officials wag their tongues in The Red Lion, the Marquis of Granby and the Commons Strangers' Bar in and around Westminster. Writers latch on to the faded footprints of the literary masters whose regular haunts included Kennedy's in Dublin, the Vesuvio Café in San Francisco and Les Deux Magots in Paris.

Inside Horwich's modest watering holes sit two motley crews – paddles thrown in the boots of their cars or lovingly placed in the glove compartments, sweat temporarily masked by the deodorant from a selection of canisters.

The Alan Ingerson crew generally comprises Dave Scowcroft, Steve Hathaway and occasional invitee Steve Barber. Promotion and relegation in the ranks this season has meant a swapping of status for the players; Barber giving up his Premier Division mantle – allowing the Hilton 'B' gents a shot at survival in 2014/15. For Ingerson, banditing his way around Division Three in 2012/13 after a long lay-off, it is a minor miracle.

Opposite the Parish Church of Holy Trinity they convene – on the chairs, stools and red-chequered banquette of the Ale House, elbows shifting in order to raise their pints. Formerly the Brown Cow, this new-found table tennis haven and resting place is a curious modern phenomenon, a refurbishment gamble left to the locals to judge.

It borrows some of its grandeur from the Francis Octavius Bedford gothic-designed Holy Trinity across the road, yet there are still small touches which clamour for your attention: the beautifully curved bar, the simple chalk boards (*Today's Real Cider/Summertime Specials*), the square lamp shades and the twenty-three white light switches on a single brass plate. Also, the Sterling & Noble clock with Roman numerals – tilted slightly to the right, but beguilingly so.

Away from here, from the ash and sycamore that greet you as you exit, it is a roll downhill, then onto the flat before arriving at The Crown. Motion never quite leaves you if sat at the front of this establishment in the bay window – the old Wigan B5238 sign on the grass roundabout outside directing drivers new to the parish.

A fir tree is plonked on this spot awaiting Christmas decorations that will brighten up the area. For now, however, Brett Haslam and his seven *borrachos* (Dennis Collier, John Bradbury, Dave Smith, Jim Chadwick, Mick Dore, Phil Riley and Steve Barber) provide the necessary exuberance.

This isn't a fancy pub. In many ways it is trepidatious – the sign on the wall next to the huge sash windows stating PLEASE DO NOT CLOSE THE CURTAIN. The tables, separated like planets, orbit the bar. Candelabras hang from the ceiling. Flashing fruit machines beckon victims. Willow-pattern plates snuggle up next to Horwich Harriers.

Walk in late on a Thursday and you witness history: table tennis's Ernest Hemingway gabbing away.

Barry Walsh – The Inverse Buccaneer

The Bolton News, 5 August 2014

To look at him now is to miss the man he was. Perhaps in the small, wrinkled canyons which line his face, it is possible to see a sliver of the past, a glimpse of the famous de Havilland Aircraft Company – his former employer – but mainly he is as unrecognisable as the large field and forest that Horwich once was.

Barry Walsh, born in June 1942 – six months after Pearl Harbour – loves three things: history; football; and table tennis. His living room is lined with books about the Second World War – fights at sea, land battles and the prodigious personalities that dominated the era.

He reels off, in a slightly stuttered fashion, a quote from Franklin D. Roosevelt following the destruction of USS Kearny by a German U-boat: "…history has recorded who fired the first shot. In the long run, however, all that will matter is who fired the last shot."

Such feeling, such inspiration, matters to Walsh. Powerful radio broadcasts, before he even travelled the womb, somehow capture what he represents – what he stands for and looks to uphold.

A former committee member at the Hilton Table Tennis Centre and one of six official key holders, Walsh only recently stepped down. Seven years of 'letting people in' was enough. The man always seen on Sundays, Tuesdays, Wednesdays and Fridays was reducing his outings to just one thus finally retiring in legitimate fashion.

Recent years on the table tennis circuit have led to this moment – his number of matches declining from 72 (2011/12), to 21 (2012/13) to a mere six (2013/14); his last victory a season-ending barnstormer against John Lawrence on 6th April 2012 (11-8, 11-8, 11-6). Lawrence twice bowed to the might of Walsh that season, as did Eric Shaw and Bob Waller.

Those days cease to hold much significance for Walsh though. Despite being one half of the uproarious Summer League outfit, the Coffin Dodgers and noted for wearing a fine collection of bob hats and T-shirts at the club, it is the 1950s and 60s that still have him entranced.

Re-awakening memories of his first few years of employment in the engineering sector and his initial rejection by de Havilland, he recalls:

"Listen to this. This is what people can do. My brother Clive knew an upstairs guy – one of the bosses. He got me in. Those eight or nine years made me. It was proper engineering. Horwich was a massive place."

Given the nickname 'Chert' from his footballing days, Walsh understood the importance of working for a grand and reputable British aviation manufacturer – its premises built in Horwich in 1937; "part of a group of 'shadow' factories constructed in Lancashire, away from the main bombing zone in the south."

The Mosquito (1940), the Vampire (1943) and the Comet (1949) still fly through the mind of Walsh. They provide succour and compound his great thoughts of Church Road "bomber command" teacher, Mr Worrell.

Aware of his pupil's eyesight deficiency and the need to wear glasses, Worrell produced the classic words: "Walsh – you'll have to play at left back."

From left back to engineering to table tennis, Walsh's size 7 ½ feet now stand at the crest of a small mountain having been made an Honorary Lifetime Member of the Hilton Centre. For the inverse buccaneer, it is another beginning.

BLGC Seek Next Generation

The Bolton News, 29 July 2014

Empires fall. Bit by bit they disintegrate – marry their mortar with the dust and dirt on the ground. The Ottomans, the Romans, the Persians, the Mongols – all had their era, their might, a trail of subjects and slaves; hubristic legacies now largely forgotten, yet represented by potent dents in the minds of historians and archaeologists.

The Bolton Lads' Club began life in 1889 as the Children's Bolton Club. It was the same year that gave birth to the Eiffel Tower, Adolf Hitler and Vincent Van Gogh's *The Starry Night*.

Founded by two church leaders and three industrialists, acutely aware of the plight of young, cotton mill children and their need, initially, just to be "able to wash, eat and sleep in peace away from their looms", it served a distinguished role as a hostel.

Less than a decade later, the stampede began: "They came in their hundreds, for of all animals, lads are perhaps the most gregarious. They came to meet their fellows under conditions somewhat more comfortable and convenient than their natural meeting place, the street. They initially came for amusement and for games and for nothing else, and if we had told them it was our intention to improve them they would certainly not have come.

"But it is interesting how quickly their attitude to the club has changed, it is no longer our club, it is theirs, and we merely manage it for them. It is no longer a mere place of amusement, but is a place which plays a real part in their lives. It is a place for honour and for success."

In 1947 table tennis entered the Lads' Club's doors. Bark Street – the old location – welcomed the fevered game, entered its recruits into the Bolton League. And so, the beautiful sport was inaugurated, two decades after the first World Championships in London and the year the International Table Tennis Federation or ITTF was formed (1926).

This led to a crossover point in 1952 – Japan's World Champion, Hiroji Satoh signalling the end of the hard bat / pimpled rubber era and the rise of the sponge bat. From wiff-waff, to ping-pong, to table tennis sophisticates, the game developed – reducing the net height from 6 ¾" to 6", introducing US celluloid balls and embracing technology on an unprecedented scale.

The Lads' Club evolved by introducing girls into its ranks. In 2002, Team BLGC moved to its new £5million premises on Spa Road – the rear of the building resting impressively on White Lion Brow.

Inside, *Tomorrows Citizens* roam. Sports and games are played – basketball, pool, Xbox, football, boxing, gym. Underneath the Harrison Burton Climbing Wall, however, is a pitiful sight: two TT tables. (There used to be five permanently unfolded.) Numbers are short. Coach Roger Bertrand and volunteer Ian Monk have just three 12-18 year olds for the forthcoming September-April season. They are, in many ways, the Blackpool FC of the table tennis league.

What has gone wrong? How can they resurrect the glory days (2012/13) when their 'A' team finished a credible 6th in Division Four?

By its very nature, a youth club loses players. Suddenly, there is nothing to replenish the squad though. The feeder club's diet is now a mirage.

Bold/passionate, empire-saving youngsters required: Mondays 5-7pm & Thursdays 6-9pm. Bertrand is waiting.

A Tale of Two Dogs

The Bolton News, 22 July 2014

Summer League Final:

Ivory Toasters   12

Hilton C   10

In the panoramic slide of action inside the Hilton Centre, it is as if a rainbow has fallen. The coloured tops are many, the mannerisms assorted, the styles like a succession of rival comedians.

On the top wall are pinned seven notices: IMPORTANT REMINDER ABOUT SHOES; PLEASE REMEMBER – TURN ON ALL FANS; etc. One imagines they were last read many years ago. One imagines that even if they were waved around by an air stewardess pre-match, the players would still be singularly focused – not bidden by the flat charms of instructive words.

The summer league final is an important marker of talent. It defines a limited field of entrants, affords them the chance of playing against loftier or dubious opposition. And yet the winners are neither recorded in the annual handbook nor engraved on a panel out of reach of sticky hands.

They should be – if only to attract a deeper body of competitors.

No matter. The finalists are of good calibre. Representing the Ivory Toasters are Krishna Chauhan and Wilson Parker – combined age 33; players pulled from a whippersnapper enclave. Hilton C – Chris Naylor and Annie Hudson – are veterans by comparison (73), although mostly loaded up with Naylor's fifty years, keen reptilian eyes and quick-talking mien.

He kneels and chats beforehand with Division One foe, Mark Speakman, toys with a bottle of water, thinks not of the matches about to unfold but of something more serene.

Hudson, his playing partner, pretty feet bound up in green-trimmed socks and purple Nike, has an air of cross-legged relaxation about her. The kids opposite are nothing she has not seen before.

'Are you ready?' comes the prompt from Parker, his hair quiffed to the side, looking dandy – surely washed less than two hours ago.

He steps up. Opposite is Hudson, the tormentor, the British League doyenne – not to be fazed, not to be out-swaggered by the pumped-up game of Parker.

Except, Parker leads 11-9, 6-0. Hudson appears ragged – hitting too many long; a slight look of disgust permeating her face. Composure rarely leaves her, troops out of town, yet she seems wounded by the Parker artillery – unsettled and faint.

A nick of the table reduces matters to 6-2, Parker 'net and off' 7-5, a trademark Hudson positional shot: 10-8. Then comes the Hudson resilience, the know-how: four straight points – Parker tossing away the second set (10-12) as if on an agitated horse.

Naylor calls a tactical break – has a word with his recovering lioness. We then see the new Annie, the old Annie – whichever makes this game look so easy. Barely moving, it is as if every ball TomToms to her blade. Parker falls, loses sets three and four 10-12, 9-11.

'I just choked – whole game went down the drain.' A glimmer of honesty beneath the often tart mouth – a player's fortune reversed within minutes. This is not football, or cricket or any of those 'long' games. It is table tennis – judge, jury and executioner; the swing of a bat critical and unforgiving.

Parker "The Rottweiler" is fortunate to have the calm, southpaw Chauhan in his camp. Apoplectic tirades suggest otherwise during their doubles loss (2-3), but Chauhan "The Labrador" – two singles wins (3-2 versus Naylor *and* Hudson) – is instrumental despite reigning champ, Parker's timely skinning of Naylor (3-0).

Keep on Runnin'

The Bolton News, 15 July 2014

"The dread of getting old is a universal, if intermittent preoccupation. 'As I give thought to the matter,' said Cicero, 'I find four causes for the apparent misery of old age: first, it withdraws us from active accomplishment; second, it renders the body less powerful; third, it deprives us of almost all forms of enjoyment; fourth, it stands not far from death.'"

2014 will not come around again – neither in number, nor in its sweeping assailment of great names. Football has mourned the imperious Alfredo Di Stéfano (aged 88), the exquisite Tom Finney (91) and the explosive Eusébio (71). Politics/journalism has lost the ameliorative Bob Crow (52), the messianic Tony Benn (88) and the outspoken Joe McGinniss (71).

One could compare the year – if ballsy enough – with 2005 when literature lamented the departure of Arthur Miller (89), Hunter S. Thompson (67) and Saul Bellow (89) – men whose perception of that around them astounded and left in wonderment the reader and listener.

Squeezed into this life are naivety, easy optimism, flair, fear and the wisdom of knowing that we know nothing. Beyond the pallor and impoverishment of old age, however, are those ready to defy Cicero's first cause; players and sportsmen for whom creaking knees and ravaged minds are modest hindrances.

Across eight table tennis clubs, the septuagenarians stretch – the two octogenarians in the league, Brian Hall and Colin Roberts respectively ruminating over the "continued challenge...obsession" and the perhaps unmatched feat of winning "seven Ron Hindle trophies".

	Player	2014/15	Club	Born
1	Brian Hall	Div 2	Hilton	May 1933
2	Colin Roberts	Div 4	Heaton	Jun 1933
3	Alan Lansdale	Div 2	Little Lever	May 1935
4	Johnny Scowcroft	Div 1	Heaton	Feb 1936
5	Alan Bradshaw	Div 2	Hilton	Mar 1936
6	Keith Phillips	Div 4	St Paul's Peel	1936
7	Jackie Smith	Div 4	Meadow Hill	Apr 1938
8	Neville Singh	Div 4	Irlam Steel	Sep 1938
9	Ian Wheeldon	Div 2	Meadow Ben	Feb 1939
10	Alan Hibbert	Div 4	Meadow Ben	Aug 1939
11	Brian Young	Div 3	Hilton	Feb 1940
12	Geoff Rushton	Div 2	Farnworth SC	Sep 1940
13	Mel Brooks	Div 3	Heaton	Oct 1941
14	Barry Walsh	Div 2	Hilton	Jun 1942
15	Dave Waite	Div 4	St Paul's Peel	1942
16	Dave Jones Snr	Div 2	Heaton	Oct 1942
17	Richard Reading	Div 3	Hilton	Apr 1943
18	Dave Parker	Div 4	Hilton	Aug 1944

The bug that is table tennis surpasses the doom-like proclamations of hardy philosophers ("Wrinkles are harbingers of a slide to nothingness, not marks of a transcendence to come.") It casts a wand over leaden feet and comfy chairs. The tales of the 'oldies', of the players that keep on running are but specks in a whirling universe, yet they must be heard:

Alan Bradshaw – "I did my 2-years national service from 1954 to 1956 [during which time] I won a lot of regimental table tennis contests. After winning thirteen competitions in the NAAFI canteen, I was advised not to enter any more."

Neville Singh – "I used to play on a rolling and pitching ship in the Atlantic Ocean."

Ian Wheeldon – "There was a room under the local church where we could practise at any time…collecting the key from the vicarage."

Geoff Rushton – "Coached my son, Andrew to the Commonwealth Games silver medal (2006)."

Richard Reading – "First played table tennis at Bovington (Army) Camp in 1960. It led me to becoming an international athlete."

The birth certificate of Dave Parker will be scrutinised next month. He will be the newest member of the clan, of the 70+ brigade and to Brian Hall a mere pup.

Unassailable

The Bolton News, 1 July 2014

"He'll know." The words of Flixton's John Hilton were not exactly suppliant. John doesn't do suppliant, beggarly or any of that scraping around. He had simply nodded in my direction, somehow recalled my face from four months earlier, and assumed that I had lodged in my brain the November 2013 match score from his first encounter with Hilton A's Mark Gibson.

I had a few things left in my tin head but that was not one of them. John Hilton, 1980 European Champion, had endured a five-set marathon on that chilly autumn night yet had managed – as with all wily champs – to plunder over the line (6-11, 11-7, 11-7, 8-11, 11-9).

Gibson's Achilles' heel was too much respect and a game not finely tuned after each point in the manner of Hilton. Their second foray in March 2014 was a straight-sets disaster for him (9-11, 9-11, 10-12) – fine margins but still…a beating, a whipping, a crucifying exposé. Only delusional players think 'What if…?'

Hilton had been complimentary before the latter smash and grab – psychologically dressing Gibson's mind, attuning it to a quiet satisfaction borne from 'a close match' rather than victory. As such, Gibson walked away – amiable handshake and all – not knowing that he'd been pickpocketed.

People meet, say things, interact and are either impressive or tolerated. It happens in table tennis halls, business, within families, almost everywhere. Had I remembered that they had shared 92 points in that initial ding dong, casually enunciated each set to Hilton like Magnus Magnusson then perhaps other things would have transpired.

Perhaps we would have chatted about the Frenchman, Bruno Parietti – his 1st round conquest (21-13, 21-19, 21-15) back in 1980. Or the Danish player, Bjarne Grimstrup – his victim in the next round (21-17, 21-9, 21-13). The German, Wilfried Lieck had been the first man to take a set off Hilton but John had dug in (14-21, 21-14, 21-13, 21-9).

A bruising match with Hungarian, Tibor Kreisz (18-21, 21-13, 21-18, 21-18) put Hilton in sight of glory, with the small matter of him needing to knock the reigning European Champion, Gábor Gergely –

another Hungarian – out in the Quarter Final in order to reach the last four.

If you look at the twenty-two minute footage of Hilton's exploits on YouTube you are transported to another time. The surroundings look quaint. It appears to be a tight arena. To the left of the table is an early advert for Betamax – just black letters on a white background. The picture of Gergely reminds you of Harry Enfield in *The Scousers* such is the enormity of his moustache and hair.

Hilton got through the harrowing match as you would have deduced. 18-21, 18-21, 21-19, 21-16, 21-19 tends to build character in a man – that or the belief that luck and the gods are with you.

Fast forward thirty three years: had Gibson known acutely that Hilton had seen it, done it, been on the rack – really *studied* the fortitude in those 1980 numbers – then maybe he would have conceded…grabbed his coat earlier. Statistics generally do two things to a player: have them leaning in for the scalp, or fearful, knowing that the conveyor belt is coming for them.

When Hilton smiles into the camera before the Final with Josef Dvořáček (Cze), having turned over Jacques Secrétin (Fra) – the 1976 champion – in the Semis, you know, you just know that he is relaxed. Insurmountable. Unassailable. Ready for action.

Cart Before the Horse

The Bolton News, 24 June 2014

"When I was a boy of fourteen, my father was so ignorant I could hardly stand to have him around. But when I got to be twenty-one, I was astonished at how much he had learned in seven years."

AGMs are *generally* less humorous than Mark Twain, full of froth, bequeathed ground to pensioners and those seeking a 'day out'. They can be troublesome affairs as in the case of G4S at the Excel Centre recently, but in the main they are paper-waving, acquiescent spectacles void of excitement or lustre.

The Bolton Table Tennis League AGM on 9th June promised an array of proposals – most of them modest, a few contentious and one so overwhelming in its ambition that the league set up as we know it was in danger of being ruptured permanently.

Forty seats excluding the big three traversed this cavern at the Hilton Centre, Horwich. Early arrivals had the choice of green or orange plastic, and brown or orange leather. Strangely enough, most wanted a head-on view of the proceedings and so the leather furnishings running down the left wall were largely neglected until seconds before the booming croak of General Secretary, Roy Caswell got matters underway.

Either side of the top man were Match Secretary, Brett Haslam wearing a grey T-shirt and candid face, and Treasurer, Roger Bertrand staring out like Mole in *The Wind in the Willows*. If you wanted an explanation, a mini-ruck or tussle you went to Haslam who would willingly afford you his non-metered time.

Late entrants were Ian Lansdale in hooded top, Steve Barber catwalking coolly and 'The Roadie' Dennis Collier.

Proposal 1 – "...rule 5 should be amended as shown: The annual team subscription fee shall be paid upon application for entry in the League. All team subscriptions shall be paid as a condition of entry in the official handbook and are non-refundable. For a team consisting entirely of juniors, the team fee shall be ~~one fifth of the normal team fee~~ waived."

It was an effort in securing the future of this splendid game. Many still perceive table tennis to be a game for relics with less cachet than athletics, martial arts or football. Kids, unfortunately, buy into grandness, stardom and money.

My ten-year-old son, Matthew tells it as it is: "None of my friends are into table tennis. They think it's an old man's game." And yet the pride on his face when he umpired three summer league matches this month was, to me, worth more than England winning the World Cup.

Beneath the yawn fest of a typical AGM are things that matter. Despite the oxygen being different and the small rectangular windows being boarded up for fear of escapees, proposals come out of the woodwork which settle often year-long gripes.

Proposal 12 – "That Ramsbottom teams and players should no longer be in the Bolton & District League. That Flixton CC and players should no longer be in the Bolton & District League…"

You have to read this twice – perhaps more for it to sink in. To Derek Watmough it embodies the "nitty natty of league bosses". To Geoff Rushton "suspensions [are] required".

For many years now, Ramsbottom'A' and Flixton have remonstrated when not victorious (ineligible players, fixtures questionably shifted etc.). The "end of season ritual…had become annoying". Fortunately, for the health of the league, the motion was withdrawn.

Scott Brown – Struggler Extraordinaire

The Bolton News, 17 June 2014

Something in his game reminds you of the divorced man getting married again. There is a kind of amnesia, a joyful, bright-eyed expectation. It is loaded up, stricken with naivety, however.

Scott Brown, Harper Brass's Division Four no-hoper has the soft, bristled face of a baby gorilla and quite a decamped expression if things aren't going right. His hands appear to be made out of putty. They are squidgy, nail-bitten affairs – part sausage factory, part heavy duty maulers.

The shots – mostly high-crested loopers – sail in on the other side of the table too gracefully at times, unarmed and full of conciliation. He would rather rally than send someone packing – or so it looks. For a big man, he exudes an extraordinarily high level of politeness in his play.

There is a hint of Neville Chamberlain – a willingness almost to share the points. Whether this 'Sudetenland' strategy is tactical, beneath the radar of mortal men, is not clear. Tennis players have been known to adopt similar 'easing off the gas' pacing. They have bought themselves valuable time in which to re-energise and really *breathe*.

The trouble is Brown is a struggler. During his Lads' Club days in 2011/12 it took four whole months to win just four matches – a miserly 8% win record (4 out of 48); those early conquests – Nikul Ajwani, Kishan Patel, Connor Sutcliffe and Waqas Ali – inscribed in his mind to this day.

Hope comes in many forms though. Strugglers FC Moda, an Ottoman Empire football team founded in 1908 by Istanbul Greeks, finished runners-up in the 1909-1910 season. They were second only to Galatasaray. Sporting blood is in the Brown family – his grandad playing in goal for Lancashire Rebels FC in the 1980s.

Brown too has donned the green goalkeeping jersey whilst at secondary school. Was he good? "I was OK," comes the unboastful mantra. Getting him to elaborate on *anything* is difficult. Not because he lacks the wherewithal, but because he is genuinely unassuming – one of the most straightforward and laid back people I have ever met.

Now, 24-years-old, signed by Harper comptroller, Kaushik Makwana in 2012 after 'outgrowing' the Lads' Club, Brown – one senses – is gazing out over a sun-drenched, flower-filled field that no one else can see. His mellow disposition has managed to detach itself from the harshness of those table tennis numbers by which we are all judged: 17% (2011/12), 24% (2012/13), 29% (2013/14).

He *is* improving. The Scott Brown performance chart without a labelled Y-axis looks half decent. To a private establishment bent on efficiency and big returns, however, his contract would not be renewed.

What of the future? "Been playing penhold since March [2014], but I'm getting little bits sorted then I'll be pro at penhold lol."

Such a table tennis grip is traditionally Chinese – difficult to master for most westerners who prefer the 'shakehand' style. The wrist moves more freely. The player no longer has a crossover point. Given the shorter reach, players tend to stay closer to the table needing faster footwork and good stamina.

I recall Brown playing quite deep which makes such a move rather odd. Perhaps it's those flowers again. And another marriage.

Step into the Barber's Chair

The Bolton News, 10 June 2014

If you hang around the corridors at Harper Green Leisure Centre long enough on a Tuesday night, you will stumble across a man who claims that Steve Barber is the best table tennis player in England. No medication has yet been found on the said individual, but suffice to say the numbers do not back up such an assertion.

A quick examination of the ETTA's website reveals that it is German-based, Liam Pitchford – with 4370 ranking points – who currently holds the coveted crown; regular matches for TTF Liebherr Ochsenhausen against the likes of Zwischenstand Düsseldorf's Timo Boll typifying his week's work.

Barber, on the other hand – a Bolton TTL Premier player – routinely plies his trade against relative unknowns including Frederic Turban. And his stats over the last three seasons read as follows: 35% (2011/12); 28% (2012/13); 35% (2013/14). One could say Barber is back where he was two years ago but that would be to define him incorrectly.

Rarely seen with a grimace on his face, Barber is representative of everything good about the game. Approachable, allowed out "four nights a week" by his "understanding wife" in order to pursue his mini-dreams and guzzle the odd beer, and firmly appreciative of the nourishment that the Bolton League provides, Barber views life simply yet keenly.

He is symbolic of a certain caste of men who stopped ageing at 29. The wisdom increases and the body continues its inevitable slide, but the boyish longings of yesteryear remain: a beautiful partner; meeting up with friends; a damn good TT session with the occasional clubbing shot.

Upon first meeting Barber, you wonder, you stew momentarily, you question whether anyone, *anyone* can be so buoyant yet sincere. There is no religious zeal about the man, no upbeat fakery – just an upturned smile; a signal to all that laughs are expected, that humorous observations need to be made.

A Ladybridge regular, one of only six men to play all 66 matches in the Premier Division this season, Barber's proud *Scarlet Letter*-like scalps have included Radcliffe's Michael Dore (44%), Little Lever's

Ron Durose (58%), Radcliffe's no.2, Robert Hall (60%) and Hilton's Jordan Brookes (62%).

Asked how he managed to turn over such an array of superior talent, Barber's modesty rolled before me: "Me and Mick always have a great game. To beat Mick I have to work hard. Rob is a very good player but can easily get frustrated with his own game which he did against me. I beat Ronnie at Ladybridge away from his comfort zone of Little Lever and their table. Jordan's mind was somewhere else that night (I think)."

After the grit and grind of the Winter League (September–April) comes the somewhat gentler Summer League (May–July) which manages to harness man's goodwill in a manner which would be inconceivable in the preceding months. A cascading ding-dong of sorts, Barber perfectly captures the essence of two of its entrants: "My old teammate, Johnny Scowcroft after every winter season finishes phones me and tells me I am playing in the summer league with him."

No switching tracks for Barber (best not mention Heaton). No letting pals down. Just grounded loyalty. A rare man he is indeed. Perhaps the Harper Green fellow was right all along.

The Bandit Hits Town

The Bolton News, 3 June 2014

Bandits, hustlers and ringers all descend from the same family line. Generally speaking they have had parts in old Westerns (mixing it up with Clint Eastwood), have hung around pool rooms waiting for the notes to stack up or have stood on the first tee at golf clubs with concealed smiles (their better scorecards destroyed before the hearth).

Raymond Isherwood, table tennis's 94% man from Division Four and bit-part 27% man from Division Two must have perfected the position of his holster for he regularly slays summer league opposition courtesy of his blazing '8' handicap.

Controversial and unwieldy such a buffer appears to be – at least to the players that stand ten or eleven feet in front of him; the number impaling their senses given its preposterousness.

Isherwood himself is only semi-contrite: "Yeah – it's wrong, but I'm not moaning."

A somewhat stocky player, not obviously skilful or threatening, Isherwood serves the ball as if making bread. His hands belie the archetypal clumsiness of the 'big man', turning the ball into a spinning piece of dough, floured up and ready to bake.

The results so far – assisted by his mesmeric serve – have been methodical if slightly tainted by the furore which surrounds this particular competition each year: 11-7, 9-11, 10-12, 11-9, 11-5 versus Paul Brandwood; 8-11, 11-7, 11-9, 11-2 versus Bob Bent; 6-11, 11-6, 11-2, 11-6 versus Krishna Chauhan; 10-12, 11-9, 9-11, 11-6, 10-12 versus Wilson Parker; 11-4, 12-10, 11-7 versus John Biggins; 11-7, 12-10, 11-2 versus David Holden.

Apart from the Parker reverse (at one stage prompting the titanic cry of "He's five-nil up!" just a point into the set), the Isherwood cruise ship has ploughed through big name after big name. And it is this leisurely ice-breaking which has led to calls for a further revamp of the handicap system.

How can this man be ranked alongside Division Four's 29% player, Scott Brown the critics demand when he is three times more successful? How can he be three shelves lower than the Ladybridge duo of Brian Greenhalgh (handicap 5) and John Cole (5) when he recently sent them stumbling to relegation courtesy of three and four set victories in the winter league?

Born in July 1991 and a carpet fitter by trade, Isherwood – one could say – has been given the opportunity of smothering his opponents with underlay before the play has even begun. Invited into the 'last man standing' wonderland of unburdensome competition, he has taken full advantage of this bountiful scheme like an otter discovering a fish bar.

Apolitical, yet with the teeth of Tony Blair, Isherwood when not playing 'the bandit' is actually an astute player. Coached diligently by Billy Russell and a regular attendee of Hilton's (unofficial) "Pro night" each Thursday, his game in the medium term is expected to be that of a Division One player.

"Lower working class" beginnings have not halted the man from Gilnow. They have merely instilled greater tenacity and fight. And such is the commitment of Isherwood – another product of the Bolton Lads' and Girls' Club – that his notorious pre-match meal of burger and coke has been replaced with steamed chicken and water (and a splash of Thai boxing).

Asked if he has any heroes, he replies "No" but then thinks again: "My dad due to his determination."

The Man from Congo-Brazzaville

The Bolton News, 20 May 2014

I first met Malcolm Ngouala, the man from Congo-Brazzaville on 22nd September 2011. He ambled across the car park which was flush diagonal with the back of McDonald's and offered his hand as if he had known me for twenty years.

Such was the welcome and 'Vitalite' smile that I looked around momentarily wondering if they were aimed at me. "Jeeefff." He had the warm, African drawl of a man who had seen much yet had somehow managed to retain his dignity.

We drove to the Lads' Club around the corner – half the team in my car, the other half in his. It was to be my first taste of league table tennis, amongst the cacophonous din of an Under 21s home venue.

I watched my exotically-named teammates – Nigerian Hank Fahm, Zambian Chone Chumalusu and Ethiopian Abdiwali Ali – outflank their younger competitors, Chris Rawlinson, Robert Masters and Haroon Khan 8-1 and so gain crucial points after a drubbing to title favourites, Heaton the previous week.

It was after that reverse that I had phoned BRASS's secretary, Malcolm and enquired about the possibility of playing. He duly invited me along and before I knew it I was umpiring matches and soaking in the exhilarating air on my inaugural evening.

After that initial outing to the Lads' Club it transpired that Hank had teaching commitments in the form of evening classes and so my opportunity came earlier than I imagined. It wasn't so much the thrill of getting wins on the board which was satisfying but the conversations I had with Chone and Abdiwali.

Chone, it turned out, had similar passions in life: chess and Leeds United. We talked about the great Ghanaian Tony Yeboah and George Graham's parochial ditching of him for the 'minor' offence of throwing his shirt in Graham's direction after being substituted.

With Abdi, it was more political: Haiti and what a great country it had once been, and the intellectual riffs of the hugely erudite, Noam Chomsky.

Beyond all of this though, it was clear that the relatively quiet man, Malcolm Ngouala from the former French coastal colony, Congo had the most interesting story to tell. Born in the Republic – its capital, Brazzaville uniquely to the north of the Congo River, while neighbouring DR Congo's capital, Kinshasa lies to the south – Ngouala is the product of a simple, yet war-torn upbringing.

Ranked 142 out of 187 countries in the 2013 Human Development Index (DR Congo is 186th), Congo was ravaged by a civil war between June 1997 and December 1999 and this wrecked any sense of having a normal future there.

After a four year journey that puts into sharp perspective modern Western concerns over which wallpaper to choose or which blouse to wear, Malcolm finally reached the UK. Now a Bachelor of the Arts and a Postgraduate Certificate holder, he has one special sporting memory:

"Ali versus Foreman – Kinshasa, 1974…I remember I saw this fabulous fight. Ali Bomaye! That's how we shouted during the fight [watching it] on black and white TV. It was a massive event. My uncles travelled to Kinshasa to watch it. They took a ferry two days before. It's about ten minutes' journey across the Congo River. They stayed at their friends' house and made their way to the stadium hours before it started. Kinshasa is a very big city, so it took about three hours to reach. There were thousands of people outside the stadium. They couldn't get inside."

Sandford the Sandman

The Bolton News, 13 May 2014

There can be fewer noisier players on the table tennis circuit than Hilton's latest recruit, Josh Sandford.

Set alongside the league's current controversy overlords, Paul 'Mad Dog' McCormick, Mark 'Clubber Lang' Martin and the heaving tension which resides between Premier rivals Ramsbottom 'A' and Flixton, Sandford would appear to revel in his new-found acting role.

The purveyor of sarcastic witticisms and verbal musings, Sandford will undoubtedly be misunderstood in many quarters. His occasional bombastic ravings will be met by a peeping through the dividing curtain and admonishment from his fellow amateurs.

Escaping or evading the Bolton Table Tennis League's iron clad rules is beyond most and Sandford, it is predicted, will come a cropper at some point in the near future if without restraint.

A cursory glance at the Code of Conduct suggests the potential shackling of even the land's least volatile personages (Postman Pat and *The Beano*'s Walter Brown, be warned!):

"All players must show respect for their opponents, umpires and spectators by conducting themselves in a sporting manner. Gratuitous swearing, intimidation or misuse of equipment must not take place at any time on the premises of any match under the control of the League."

Born in September 1993 and introduced to the game under the stewardship of unorthodox Frenchman and bearded wonder, Roger Bertrand, it was for Sandford – as with many unfocused teenagers – a revelatory moment, a trip to the table tennis orphanage or rather the Bolton Lads' & Girls' Club.

"I started going to the Lads' Club when I was about 14 to stop me being on the streets causing trouble. I didn't start playing TT 'til I was 15 and I loved it from day one."

After the 'orphanage' or feeder club via the steady duo of ex-Ladies no.1, Andrea Holt and Division One flamethrower, Graham Clayborough, Sandford donned his frame with the red and black training gear of Farnworth TTC.

Taught the technical aspects of the game by the five-times National Champion, his game developed well. In the 2011/12 season, he played across two divisions and ended with the respectable win percentages of 50 (Division 2) and 84 (Division 3).

For an 18-year-old, it wasn't explosive or likely to augur a rush of scouts, but it was noticeably decent in what was only his second full season.

The real flash pan stuff came the season before in what was a temporary cloaking into musketeers of the apprentices and the master – Craig Duncan, Sandford and Bertrand scooping the 2011 Warburton Cup under the guise of Hilton F.

Benjamin Disraeli once said: "Youth is a blunder; manhood a struggle; old age a regret." Sandford, in 2014, may just be on the cusp of something truly good in order to escape such a fate.

Humour still drives him (understandably so). He has the obligatory youthful passport of a large tattoo and often speaks above 65 decibels, yet his planned 2014/15 Division One team including Wilson Parker and Craig Duncan promises to be a Hadron Collider of sorts.

Either that or a derailed train. With 'The Sandman', you never quite know.

Brandwood Finally Shows his Mettle

The Bolton News, 6 May 2014

The week after the Winter League season ends, Hilton Table Tennis Centre plays host to the Divisional and Warburton Cup finals. Days later, a different kind of show comes to town.

Call it the Oscars. Call it a 'plumped up cushion' of an evening. The Closed Championships are – to many – the highlight of the season; a bountiful gathering of kith and kin.

It is the one night when you see a solitary table basking in the centre of the hall – plastic chairs, not seen in an aeon, prized out of the storeroom to accommodate the merry and expectant crowd.

There are no tuxedos or ball gowns on display, no paparazzi (with the exception of the odd graceless snap from a mobile phone), but rather a sea of faces awaiting the multitude of talent.

Six finals offer solace and comfort to those in attendance – table tennis bats occasionally fluttering through the air like the webbed wings of their namesake.

In the growing crowd, you see the familiar faces of Dave Parker (flat cap and white tash), Malcolm Rose (blue-lined coat and glasses), James Young (mysterious girl in tow) and Barry Walsh (bob hat and a smile that refuses to retire).

Practising beforehand is the Stiga-clad 10-year-old, Amirul Hussain in readiness for his Junior Singles final with 16-year-old, Wilson Parker. It is reminiscent of when the gifted Danni Taylor used to entertain the crowd before the night got under way.

Except, Amirul is the ETTA's 7th-ranked 'Under 13 Boy'; he thus addresses the table with the composure of a starship commander. Parker – his name familiar to aficionados of the Bolton game – is quarrelsome at times, intolerant of his own deficiencies. Hussain, the shorter player by about a foot, whistles through this encounter (11-5, 11-9, 11-3) with panache.

Parker need not despair though. A Handicap Singles finalist also, retribution may be his against 'Le Roadie', Dennis Collier. Collier, famous for his defensive meanderings, loses the first set 11-9 – the

Parker +3 handicap proving invaluable. After that something cracks in the Collier game and Parker rolls home 11-5, 11-5.

There is a conflated hush and buzz about the place this evening – a sense that the matches before us are part of a wider whirlwind. And we are in the vortex of its shifting swirl.

Next is the Handicap Doubles – the grey-haired, Keith Dale and Lancashire belle, Annie Hudson versus Steve Hathaway and Dave Scowcroft. It is the only four-setter of the night: 11-4, 11-13, 11-8, 16-14; plenty of nerve from the grinning assassins, Dale and Hudson.

Interspersed between these matches is Paul Brandwood. I had a duty in storing up his results, in lingering with the hard statistics of this man. Why? Because despite his modest Premier win percentage (52%) and the gulf between himself and the elite (85%+ men), he can turn it on if he chooses.

On the way to his three finals Brandwood weaved his way past some of the lesser names, but he did it in the manner of a seal swimming through a kelp forest. It was, on occasion, like witnessing a re-signing of the Magna Carta.

I cannot say any more.

Results

Veterans (40+): Brandwood beats Collier 11-8, 10-12, 11-5, 3-11, 12-10

Level Doubles: Brandwood/Mick Dore beat Collier/Steve Barber 9-11, 11-9, 4-11, 11-8, 11-8

Level Singles: Brandwood beats Barry Elliott 11-5, 11-4, 12-10

Dark Rumours and The Great Escape

The Bolton News, 22 April 2014

Division Two*

Ladybridge B   3

Harper Brass A   6

It was on Tuesday, 25th March that a fellow player mentioned the "dark rumours" concerning Harper Brass A's meteoric bounce from the depths of certain relegation. Suspicions were aroused after the debut of Mike Brierley on 5th February and the team's subsequent haul of 33pts over five matches with just two evenings remaining.

Jan 2014		Played	Points
7.	Meadow Ben A	13	58
8.	Hilton G	13	50
9.	Ladybridge B	13	44
10.	Bolton Univ B	13	36
11.	Harper Brass A	13	34

As with most things, such a statement was missing crucial context. It was easy to intimate that Brierley was a ringer brought in to save the day, but the story of my beloved Harper Brass went much deeper than this. I was happy to enlighten the player – who shall remain unnamed – however, a more substantial rebuff via this column was necessary I felt.

The summer or close season had not been kind to Harper Brass A (formerly BRASS). Having climbed the divisions rapidly from Four to Two in the blink of an eye, its lustre disappeared following the news that Alan Ingerson was leaving to join Division One side, Hilton B.

In that moment on 4th June 2013, I knew I had to act, get reinforcements in, strengthen what had become a ragged ship with just Roger Bertrand (98%), myself (47%), Dave Brookes (36%) and Abdiwali Ali (33%) left. If I didn't then the bright lights of our new home, Division Two would be too strong, too bewildering. We would be pummeled and slaughtered each week – pushed to the back of the points queue like an ignominious runt.

The beauty of the Bolton League is its comprehensive data pool courtesy of www.tabletennis365.com/Bolton. This allows captains to scour the divisions for unused talent. Utilising this, I honed in on my first transfer target: Farnworth TTC B's Malcolm Ferrier (89%).

He hadn't played for them since 10th January 2013 and so something wasn't right. Late, Sunday evening – a mere five days after Ingerson's departure – I got an email back: "OK, count me in then…" It was the result of telling an unloved player that he was wanted. If he was the Paul McGrath of the table tennis world (rarely training) it didn't bother me.

The season began in September, but not before the news that Ali had been hospitalised and Ferrier had injured himself. It was back to the bare bones. I let things roll for nearly a month hoping that Bertrand would produce some of his old magic but the results were terrible: 1-8, 1-8, 2-7.

On 30th September, I emailed the league's General Secretary in an effort to get contact details for Meadow Bank's Allan Auxilly (assuming he was French) and Heaton E's underused Mel Brooks (73%). The latter returned my call, politely declined and I was fine with that. Brooks remained Bolton's Roman Emperor to me – a giant sipping his Raki.

Auxilly was a different story. He had suffered a heart attack during the close season and was still out of action. On 5th November, however he made his debut for us in a respectable 4-5 defeat to Little Lever C. Exactly three months later his best pal, Brierley – despite signing on 17th December – made his Harper bow following a gentleman's agreement with Hilton F.

And so fast forward to that grand night on 31.3.2014: Ladybridge versus Harper ('Lady' leading 3-2, needing just one more point to stay up). Enter the rocket men: Brierley (2), Raymondo Isherwood (1) and Auxilly (1). "It's gonna be a long, long time…"

  * Both teams finish on 75pts – Harper stay up courtesy of more wins.

Ramsbottom Crowned Champions after Lightowler Treble

The Bolton News, 8 April 2014

Premier Division

| Ramsbottom | 5 | (Lightowler 3, Moir 2, Jackson 0) |
| Flixton | 4 | (Rosenthal 2, Cicchelli 1, Biggs 1) |

Is there a different kind of pressure on a night like this? I ask the question to Ramsbottom's 100% man, Michael Moir or 'Mick' as he calls himself when struggling, when bludgeoned by a force he's not used to. He hesitates a little. "No. Not really."

I push for more – ask if it still matters…mention the fierce Glasgow-like rivalry between Ramsbottom and Flixton and wonder where it sits in the wider Moir perspective. "Yes. You wanna win…I've only done the British League [remember]."

They are the words of a man either playing down his fine achievements in this sport or enunciation constrained by potentially ribbing teammates. Through the now familiar and strikingly-bristled face, Moir keeps his expression tight, clipped – the opposite of his rangy play.

Ramsbottom need only three points this evening to make it insurmountable for Flixton; three points to regain the title so mercilessly taken from them on 4 April 2013. On that night, Moir produced his usual treble but his team was overwhelmed by Louis Rosenthal, John Hilton and Paul Cicchelli.

The personnel are similar now: Moir, Richard Lightowler (100%) and Andrew Jackson (88%) – Mark Ramsbottom watching – versus Rosenthal (100%), Cicchelli (93%) and Phil Biggs (88%); Hilton -1980 European Champion – never seen in these parts, like a convict fleeing the Crown.

Cicchelli, thrown in first, moans to his captain, Biggs: "I'm still on the motorway. I don't need to go on first!" Biggs is insistent though – calming his player, trying to talk him round. Waiting in the wings is Moir, just keen to get started, keen to show his dominance and fluidity. 11-3, 11-3. Cicchelli's rage heightens: "Got no touch!"

He is a man being bossed by Moir, a man whose job has largely taken over his life; too many motorway miles, too many – by his own admittance – KFC Fiery Bites. You feel like throwing him an iceberg lettuce – *something* to stem the abysmal form. Because on his day, Cicchelli has the most elegant chop in the game – it has a 'baby rocking' motion to it, a perfectly aligned forearm.

6-4 in the third. Moir appears to be coasting, but then Cicchelli finds his gear. In amongst the heavy breathing, the overuse of his white towel and the reddened face, he clutches at something which transforms his play. 6-9: five straight points. 8-9: Moir is not easily felled. 9-11: Cicchelli is back in it.

Moir begins to tighten up. At 2-3 a couple of shots hit the top of the net and then drop back onto his side. 2-5: Cicchelli pulls away. 6-11: We have a five-setter.

Biggs moves in for a tête-à-tête, a final set briefing. Lightowler does the same with Moir. The words from Cicchelli are still damning despite his comeback: "Can't believe…playing this shit and still in it."

If Moir is unsettled, disconcerted by the Cicchelli Jekyll and Hyde act, then it doesn't show. The impeccable Adidas attire (blue top / black shorts / white socks) has the effect of veiling his sweat, disguising how spent he really is.

They make their way to the table. Cicchelli serves. It is a beauty – deep left. Moir twitches. He refuses to lie down (that will come later versus Rosenthal). 2-1: his crumbling game momentarily stops. 3-3: a fierce diagonal backhand from Cicchelli. 5-3: net and in from Moir. It is the heartache point which Cicchelli cannot come back from. 11-4: Moir is respectful but pleased.

Ramsbottom sail away.

Michnowiec Puts Spoke in Flixton Wheel

The Bolton News, 1 April 2014

Premier Division

Flixton	8
Hilton 'A'	1

Hilton's Andrew Michnowiec is a man from a time machine. In his old, yellow Joola T-shirt, Umbro socks, and shorts evidently hired from Nomads' Paul Brandwood, he represents a flashback to a better era – one without polish, without modern gizmos that empty our minds.

The Polish name, perhaps anglicised (formerly with three 'i's), would seem to emanate from the south-eastern corner of that tough region. It is one of many fine, European appellations to bless the league; Maciejewski, Cicchelli, Dobrzanska, Dumpelnik and Szorcz the others.

The first pairing tonight is Flixton's *Paul* Cicchelli and the man himself – Michnowiec. The venue – best car park on the circuit, Tibhar Smash 28/R table, wood climbing the green walls – is ripe for an intoxicating encounter, an Italy versus Poland spectacular and more.

There is a pink sheet of paper on the far wall's tiny, cork noticeboard. It announces: NO SWEARING OR UNSPORTING CONDUCT. Cicchelli will struggle. There will be a few bejesuses that pass his lips before the night is out.

It begins. Michnowiec succumbs to a slender Cicchelli lead (4-3) in the first set at which point Flixton's secretary, Phil Biggs interrupts. "Can you just throw the ball up a bit, Andy?" It is a clear hint regarding the legality of the Hilton player's serves – the minimum '6-inch toss' rule being ignored.

Michnowiec has an old-school serve – a low-swooping, swallow-like trajectory with the grace of a pinball. He addresses the ball hurriedly – catches opponents off guard. Cicchelli is too experienced, too big in the chops, to fall for such a ploy, however. 11-7: It is going to plan.

Watching Cicchelli you come to realise that it is at times like observing a craftsman in his shed, a woodwork maestro using a plane. One can almost see fine shavings from the ball such is his bat's phenomenally thin contact with it.

There is a problem though: his stamina. I count the points before his breathing changes; thirty – at 6-6 in the second. Cicchelli's natural rhythm and bounciness are affected. Despite the whipping forehands, his game becomes littered with mistakes – a grating inability to finish inferior talents off quickly and tellingly.

8-11: Michnowiec sees the disparity. He then manages to turn around a 5-1 deficit in the third, pulling it back to 8-7. Something in Cicchelli snaps. Abound with comment after comment, slating his own play, he becomes the mad Italian at work in the kitchen – saucers and pans crashing to the floor, minions running for their lives. An almost echoing and desperate cry of "Jesus Christ!" helps him take the third set (11-7). And the fourth follows: 12-10.

Phil Bowen steps up. A gold chain dances at the neck of his black, Arbory T-shirt. He is a no-nonsense southpaw celebrating his 61st birthday at home with his Flixton 'family'. Jordan Brookes, navy and white Le Coq Sportif jersey, is the table tennis thief – happy to roll up, take what he can, make a grab at the points and then return to his palace. Not tonight alas. It is a late present for Bowen: 11-8, 11-3, 11-9.

John Hilton finally trots in. His face dons a permanent smile. "Golfing all day. Won it – the doubles." He squeaks past Mark Gibson (11-9, 11-9, 14-12) and demolishes Brookes (11-5, 12-10, 11-7) but then comes Michnowiec, the Polish slugger.

Low, flat, bruising forehands race over the net. 10-12, 9-11. John's panache seems to have disintegrated. At 4-9 down in the third a comedic line bursts from him: "He's not missed any!!!" It is true: a giant, giant scalp for Michnowiec (8-11).

Farnworth on Fire

The Bolton News, 18 February 2014

Little Lever CC 'B' 5 Hilton 'C'   4

Of the 77 points now accumulated by Little Lever, a slight majority (40) have been won on the road. This would suggest that visiting teams take great delight in driving along the aptly-named Victory Road to the Little Lever lair.

Not tonight. Bethany Farnworth is waiting for them like the apoplectic owner of a house about to be burgled. The sleek 15-year-old may appear humble and graceful, yet underneath this deceptive demeanour is a long-limbed warrior, a young ETTA-ranked woman with something to prove each match.

Turning left through the wrought iron gates clasped by the imposing letters 'LLCC', you immediately get the sense that you are entering a club with a great history. Indeed, Sir Garfield Sobers played here – as he did more famously with Radcliffe Cricket Club just up the road.

In the shrouded darkness, filled with heavy rain, the weaving track up to the clubhouse could be leading you anywhere – to a country estate, a regal manor or Count Dracula's castle in the Carpathian Mountains. Lightning doesn't strike, thank god, when home captain, Paul Tatlock finally skids next to the building in his Citroen C4 at 7.29pm.

We struggle to get inside. One of the bolt locks refuses to budge and so the metal grill cannot be lifted to gain access to the door. Tatlock looks genuinely worried. There is an uncanny resemblance to Bob Parr in both his frame and face. Incredible it would be right now to just get this show on the road.

A second Paul arrives with great mastery of the said lock and sure enough, we are in. It feels like a changing room. It *is* a changing room, I am told – two of them joined together courtesy of a retreating divide. A terracotta-tiled floor greets the players, along with the feeling that a crazed interior designer with a penchant for red has been allowed inside.

The first match is Tatlock versus Hilton's impeccably-attired Chris Naylor. The fury of both players is evident: "Oh, no – what's going on? Come on" "Nooooo!!" "So slow" "Greedy" "Move your body". 12-10, 8-11, 11-7, 6-11. Tatlock is breathing heavily. This is uncomfortable territory. His Velvet Underground T-shirt is soaked already. The final set leaves him demoralised: 1-11.

Bethany Farnworth (red top) takes her position against Annie Hudson (blue) next. It is the neutral's showdown with a hint of 'Merseyside derby' about it. Their win percentages are 62% and 90% and such stats account for the early Hudson dominance (11-6, 11-6); trademark forehands swatting and dismissive. I confess to writing off Farnworth's chances at this point. She seems a little disparate, not quite the force I had expected.

"Hit it harder," comes the simple advice from teammate, Richard Simmons. 11-9, 11-5. Instinctive backhand returns, great reach and a quiet steeliness get Farnworth back into it. There is, all of a sudden, a Mediterranean-like poise to this girl. Neither player deserves to lose such is the grand spectacle before us, but it is Farnworth who toils with her deadly forehand to the end: 11-9.

"Flippin' eck!!!!!"

Div One – Top 7	P	W	L	F	A	Pts
Coburg	16	16	0	96	48	96
Hilton C	16	10	6	88	56	88
Standish	15	9	6	85	50	85
Heaton A	16	10	6	81	63	81
Hilton B	14	9	5	80	46	80
Nomads C	16	9	7	78	66	78
Little Lever CC B	16	8	8	77	67	77

George Laks R.I.P.

The Bolton News, 7 January 2014

"Most men lead lives of quiet desperation and go to the grave with the song still in them."

I heard these words for the first time while watching a film with my children over the Christmas period. I suppose they act as an emphatic plea to us all. Henry David Thoreau – author of them and the famous *Walden* (1854) – lived such a short life himself (dying aged 44) yet, as with many of his quotes, observed things in a rich, philosophical manner.

Numerous great minds were inspired and influenced by Thoreau: Leo Tolstoy; George Bernard Shaw; Mahatma Gandhi; John F. Kennedy; Martin Luther King Jr. He lived the life only *he* wished to live and for that should be commended.

George Laks, Bolton's adopted son, followed a similar route it could be said. Of Polish origin, George fled the invading Germans on 1 September 1939 less than a month after his 20th birthday. Biking it with his brother to the Soviet-controlled east, he effectively traded Adolf Hitler for Joseph Stalin. A proud Pole, however, George refused Russian citizenship.

The consequences of this intransigence were harsh. Accused of being a spy in a slightly surreal twist to his already dangerous plight, George found himself sentenced to 12 years hard labour in the gulags (Vladivostok and Magadan among others in Siberia).

Serving 18 months of this before being permitted to join the Polish Army, George then worked in Tashkent and Kirkuk before a London delegation invited him and his compatriots in 1942 to join the Polish Air Force in Britain. Initially stationed in Blackpool, he finally made his way to Bolton via RAF Halton as a burgeoning wireless mechanic.

A stint in Italy (1944-46) and demobilisation from the air force in 1948 left George free to finally pursue a normal, civilian life. Jobs with Metropolitan-Vickers, Marconi and Kendal Milne & Co (now House of Fraser) gave him a taste of electrical engineering British-style, but this son of a prominent Polish engineer knew he had to start something of his own.

Breightmet Electrics was born in the 1950s. Two decades later it had six shops and around thirty employees. Slot TV was the thing and George was one of its early pioneers. Outside of his professional sphere though, George developed a philanthropic streak and it is for this generosity that many remember him today.

George's Wood in Ainsworth (planted with the help of fellow Bolton CHA Rambling Club members) was donated to the Woodland Trust. The swish 'top table' (Cornilleau 740) – Hilton Table Tennis Centre's very first quality table – was a gift from George and is the source of much amusement to this day (Jean Smart misspelling his name on the tiny plaque as George Lax).

I think we can safely say that George's song touched many. He lived 'til 94 – a ripe, old age (just one year younger than Nelson Mandela). There are fewer and fewer of his generation about, but such vitality – playing table tennis right up until the end (for Hilton, Breightmet Electrics, Heaton) – is an example to us all.

Colin Roberts: "George had a table tennis room purpose-built at the back of his shop. I met his wife, Joyce following the Keogh/Ritson merger in 1968. I have enormous respect for him."

Alan Bradshaw: "Johnny Leach [Table Tennis World Champion 1949 & 1951] toured RAF Aerodromes during the war challenging all-comers whilst sat down. He soon got off his chair when George started playing."

Jean Smart: "George would not let me change the plaque. We had many a laugh."

Derek Weston: "He would often keep staff on when not needed and would famously pop in even when retired."

Alan Ingerson: "A very quiet and softly spoken man – a decent defensive player."

George Laks: 2ⁿᵈ August 1919 – 13ᵗʰ December 2013

Desperate and Without the Gods

The Bolton News, 24 December 2013

Division Two: Ramsbottom 'D' 7 Harper Brass 'A' 2

I am sat here tonight in one of the less silky venues – Ramsbottom. Great history (Australia's Michael Clarke played for Ramsbottom Cricket Club in 2002), but the table tennis room within the ground is, for a craftsman, an artist, quite hellish and imposing – in need of lottery funding.

The wooden ram horns mounted on the far wall curse all visitors should they look up at them and the painting (signed 'R.F.') above the umpire's chair seems to be from the Napoleonic era; a hint of war despite the sporting scene.

I hand Josh Sandford his 50p win bonus for turning over Hilton E's Roy Alty the previous week. He looks slightly perplexed, yet I firmly believe such an arbitrary and jocular system helps to galvanize the squad. No additional £1 as Wilson Parker smashed him, but a financially stable week nonetheless.

Ramsbottom are not what we expect. Tim Fields is working and Dominic Siddall studying hard. Their experienced replacements, David Cain and Neil Booth appear iron-like and insouciant next to the chipper face of no.1, Martin Ormsby.

It is Ormsby versus Harper Brass's Allan Auxilly first. Auxilly is like a surgeon, a mechanic – each move thought through; a refined and unruffled match player with a cool head. His backhand topspins arrive from nowhere and are too much for Ormsby (11-6, 11-5, 11-6).

Raymond Isherwood is next – 'playing up' from Division Four against the man with anti-spin rubbers, Cain. Cain's eyes have a luminous quality to them – an optimism that has hung around despite his ageing years. He wears an Oldham Athletic top, has white socks and tanned 'holiday' legs.

Isherwood is a 97% man but such lower league stats mean nothing here. It is like a little boy asking out Marilyn Monroe. Cain ravages and torments him: 11-7, 11-3, 11-4.

2011 Warburton Cup winner, Sandford steps forward. I have every faith in the 20-year-old, Bolton-born looper. His opponent is Ormsby; granite-chinned 'ringer', Booth unfortunately delayed. 11-9.

Sandford's forehand topspin is working. A 5-2 lead in the 2nd suggests an imminent win – the Harper player, when not attacking, having the meticulous push/vision of a man staring through a submarine periscope.

6-5. But, oh no – what is this? Sandford's bat has broken mid-shot having got trapped in the rear curtain – the blade flying over Auxilly in the umpire seat. He borrows a bat, but his soft rubbers are now a distant memory and it is a cruel slide to defeat: 9-11, 13-11, 5-11, 9-11.

Auxilly loses to Booth (9-11, 8-11, 10-12), yet turns over Cain (11-6, 11-9, 11-9). The rest of the evening, however, is a horrible blur, a turkey shoot, a mauling.

I stand in a large puddle returning to the car. It has not been a good night. Bah! Humbug!

Division Two Table	P	W	L	F	A	Pts
Hilton E	11	7	4	67	32	67
Little Lever Cricket Club C	11	11	0	65	34	65
Hilton F	10	9	1	64	26	64
Ramsbottom Town TTC D	11	6	5	59	40	59
Meadow Ben B	11	7	4	56	43	56
Meadow Ben A	11	5	6	51	48	51
Farnworth Social Circle A	11	4	7	41	58	41
Hilton G	11	3	8	40	59	40
Ladybridge B	11	3	8	35	64	35
Bolton University B	11	3	8	32	67	32
Harper Brass A	11	2	9	30	69	30

Very Superstitious

The Bolton News, 10 December 2013

Superstition is defined as "Belief in supernatural causality: one event leading to the cause of another without any natural process linking the two. It contradicts natural science." Opposition to it (omens, astrology, religion, witchcraft) was particularly strengthened during the Age of Enlightenment in the 18th century.

And yet, three hundred years later, it is everywhere: in every game; on every bit of grass; on every track; in every sports hall. We all have at least one little habit, one conscious finger-crossing, 'touch wood', salt over the shoulder moment which, it is believed, will improve our performance or defend against bad luck.

In US stock car racing, shelled peanuts are almost NEVER sold at an event. "According to 1930s racing lore, peanut shells were always found in the smoldering remnants of a badly wrecked car." Beware the driver that eats nuts before a race!

Likewise, in Major League baseball, you "DO NOT talk about pitching a no-hitter!" In other words, you're pitching against the final man with the potential to reduce the opposition team to zero hits across nine innings. Any mention of what COULD happen is anathema, a curse, a total "no-no". It is like leading 8-0 in table tennis, with the final match player warming up with a huge, mocking and complacent grin on his face.

Cricket has its own superstitions especially when you're part of the batting side. Always put the left pad on first like Tendulkar. When there is a great partnership at the wicket, DO NOT move seats. In fact, DO NOT get up!

Nick Faldo – winner of six major golfing championships – only cut his fingernails on a Monday, "so as not to affect the balance of his putting grip". And he certainly DID NOT have lunch with fellow leaders on a Sunday which is common these days.

Table tennis has its peculiarities at local level almost as if Dr Kananga (*Live and Let Die*) were sat on your front bumper on the way to the match.

Graham Clayborough pats his thigh twice before receiving a serve. He refers to it as a "confidence trigger". Tim Fields wears his lucky Santa socks no matter what the season. Roger Bertrand cannot play without eating three bananas during match night. If John Barker sees the slightest gap in the court curtains, he HAS TO fasten them. Personally, I HAVE TO flip the ball into my left hand before serving.

Good luck this Friday. Voltaire will be watching.

Hail King Louis

The Bolton News, 3 December 2013

Premier Division: Hilton A 1 Flixton 8

They stroke the tables at this level – make sure there are no damp spots or rogue bits of dust. I am sat next to the 1980 European Champion, John Hilton now representing Flixton. He is knowledgeable – the Lovejoy of table tennis, his voice a little gruff.

The table is a grand piano to him – its surface, spruce rather than Masonite. This 'twiddler' of the bat and table tennis giant is in good spirits tonight. A range of subjects smatter the air – tax, Chinese players, old foe Ramsbottom's venue.

We begin. I remind Hilton's Mark Gibson that he'll be facing three undefeated players in Flixton's Paul Cicchelli, Louis Rosenthal and John Hilton. "No pressure then," comes the gallant retort.

The first match goes with form: Cicchelli too refined, too canny when pitted against the raw power of Gibson (11-7, 11-7, 12-10). Cicchelli arches his body like a yoga teacher – his wolfman arms twisting and bending, his Killerspin paddle case an early-warning system, a 'DEFCON 3' to the opposition.

Jordan Brookes is next – Hilton's laid back, yet sinewy 15-year-old. Headphones on, music between matches, you sense that he's drifted off at times – is walking a beach in his Hollister joggers. 17-15: a tough, impressive start by Brookes – two game points down versus the hair-lacquered Action Man, Rosenthal but living with his speed.

Rosenthal, 29, Puma top, Butterfly trainers is the perfect embodiment of counterdrives. You think a ball has got past him, but no – the super-fit Flixton man swings an arm from nowhere and mops up the points. 11-6. 11-7. 11-2. The comeback is not unexpected, but still, it resounds with SAS-like flair.

Gibson again. Graham Coupe, Hilton's third man has yet to arrive and so it's up to the Hilton bomber to try to dismantle the game of Flixton spinner, John. Only one black rubber for JH tonight – his preferred two long since outlawed.

11-6: Gibson on top. "I'd say you're playing him too much down his backhand," Cicchelli tells JH. An immediate response from the 1980

Champ: 11-7, 11-7, 8-11, 11-9; faded Athens 2004 T-shirt soaking up the sweat, shot variation colossal.

Brookes stops the rot in a topsy-turvy spectacular with Cicchelli (11-1, 11-8, 6-11, 2-11, 11-6), but after that the dominos fall: Coupe 0-3 Rosenthal; Brookes 0-3 Hilton; Coupe 1-3 Cicchelli; Gibson 0-3 Rosenthal; Coupe 2-3 Hilton.

The Rosenthal aftershave just about lingers through the grind and perspiration.

Farewell Ingerson

The Bolton News, 2 July 2013

The text arrived at 1.14pm on 4 June 2013. 60-year-old Alan Ingerson, rejuvenated through his brief spell with Division Three, BRASS announced to me that he had signed for Ladybridge 'B' in Division One.

Despite BRASS winning the 4th tier title – in large part, of course, due to the heroics of 96% man, Ingerson – he had decided to walk away. There wasn't quite the press coverage of a significant football transfer or the fanfare in Ladybridge to welcome the new player. And certainly no stepping off a plane to be greeted by a marching band (just 3.3 miles separate BRASS's venue, Victoria Hall from the Ladybridge Community Centre). But to the table tennis community – fully aware of their marginalised status – this was a pivotal moment.

Players' careers at local level can last for 70 years. Ingerson had already put in a 46-year stint and the old sparkle had seemed to return. There had been tantrums, heated moments and snarls as with any relationship but also plenty of mirth and camaraderie. Ingerson had been a par excellence signing for BRASS – an 'out of contract' (so to speak) mercurial wonder. His game was different to anything I'd seen before – the south-paw top spin like watching an industrial worker crank a heavy piece of machinery. Returning such balls was little short of impossible given their accentuated kick. Only the canniest of opponents knew how.

Having made his debut on 31 October 2012, he lost two of his initial fifteen matches. To most players returning from a two-season sabbatical such statistics would please them. Ingerson, somewhat traumatised by his 'black November', set out to correct and fine tune certain parts of his game; the result being that in his final thirty-three matches he was unbeaten. 46/48 wins – one for each year of effort since he first picked up a bat in 1967.

I have had the privilege of playing alongside many different nationalities – Ethiopian, Zambian, Iranian, French – and when Ingerson approached BRASS with a view to joining the team, I was expecting a fair-haired Scandinavian giant. Instead, we got a follicly-challenged, affable grumbler – one a joy to be around though.

Backroom transfer deals in table tennis are unlikely to be replaced with a transparent electronic system anytime soon, but I bear no ill will. We have lost our 'Eric Cantona' like Leeds in 1992, but his sublime presence will not be forgotten.

Wilson Parker-Roger Bertrand III

The Bolton News, 25 June 2013

Rivalry can demoralise, panic or excite a table tennis player. To know that there is one specific person out there who is your nemesis can be disheartening or revelatory. The relationship is usually borne out of a lingering stare, a reluctant acknowledgement of your opponent's skills or mutual respect. Wilson Parker/Roger Bertrand, a McEnroe/Borg-type affair, sits between reluctant warfare and ever-so-necessary victory. The match up is many things: The Ashes; Froch/Kessler; Real Madrid vs. Barcelona.

In this instance, it is a precocious and fiery young Englishman versus a proficient and dogged Frenchman; a Wellington/Napoleon re-enactment 200 years later but without the satin breeches. Three points separate them competitively – Bertrand winning in Nov 2012 at Victoria Hall (11-8, 11-5, 11-9) but Parker gaining revenge in May 2013 at the Hilton Centre (11-7, 10-12, 11-7, 13-11).

I ask the black-clad Wilson Parker what strategy he plans to adopt tonight. He looks puzzled for a moment. "Play", he then calmly mutters. It is dismissive and bold – the monosyllabic answer in keeping with his intransigence, yet somehow embodying the essential shrift of a broken intercom (the suggestion being that his body will know what to do – it will throw itself on the battlefield without inhibition and see what transpires).

What happens, what actually transpires is barely recognisable. I write the words 'long', 'net', 'any ammo?' repeatedly in relation to Bertrand's play. His backhand is not functioning. He looks ragged, tired, far from the great, tactical genius I know. It is disappointing. Like watching *Lord of the Rings* without Gandalf. 11-5 (an intense, but futile Bertrand-winning-rally pulling it back to 9-5). 11-2 (a nasty nadir). 11-5 (a brutal ending – more punishment from Parker).

There is a huge, collective intake of air. Can it really be over? Already? A 3-0 whitewash? Sometimes table tennis bludgeons you, refuses to follow the script, the form guide, expectation levels. It cavorts on the horizon and laughs at your game plan, your execution of shots.

Let us not take anything away from Parker though. His chin, at times, was almost down to table height so keen was he to see the opening, thrust the ball back with extra spin on it. Despite the panache, however, I believe the subtler side of Wilson's game is the *real* difference; the elegant nudges over the net; the masked concentration.

Will Bertrand return from this harrowing experience? Undoubtedly so.

The Ultimate Banana Skin

The Bolton News, 11 June 2013

Everybody's got a shot – a good shot. Irlam Steel's Neville Singh included. His looping forehand might surface as often as a sleepy judge striking his sounding block, but it's there. Ready to put you off balance. Ready to demonstrate that nothing is a foregone conclusion in table tennis.

Conscientious players check the form guide before meeting the opposition. They run through their opponents' typical points per game, whether four and five-setters are a common occurrence, whether their strength lies in playing against choppers or attack-minded individuals; lastly, whether they love the big scalps, the big wins – an underdog's paradise.

Singh's Division 3 Win Record reads: 1 out of 45 (2011/12) and 5 out of 40 (2012/13). There *is* progress – 400% one might say – but in many ways he is the ultimate banana skin. Players fear getting caught up in his cycle of carefully sculpted shots, the slowed-down grace of his 'utilising the skills I have'. The psychological damage of losing to Singh can be immense, career-threatening even. Speak to Garvin Yim (his first conquest), Diane Moss and Danni Taylor (his only 'double' – that famous night on 13th September 2012). All have since quit the league, walked away.

And yet, just as Floyd Patterson's defeat to Sonny Liston in 1962 did not make him a loser, so too must the indefatigable Singh not be labelled or tarnished. He may not have had the highs of Patterson but he is an example to us all in perseverance and refusing to let his love of the game be dampened. "I have rarely felt humiliated even though humbled by my scores…I observe the good points of others in style, skill and temperament."

Still keeping fit, "eschewing large meals and regularly walking around [his] village", Neville Singh is not a celebrity. He is much more – a gallant battler, soon to be 75, still standing amidst the wasteland of his match scores. "My victories are indeed few…but I love the game." When he says it, you want to nod your head, put your arm around his shoulders. Singh is a talisman for us all. There is something extraordinary and unassuming in his manner.

From the tropical climate of British Guiana in the 1950s, to the storm-laden Atlantic Ocean in 1963 (courtesy of a rolling and pitching ship), on to bitter Scotland (1986-2007), Singh's table tennis evolution has ended in Bolton. Glory be.

Three Steps to Glory

TableTennis365.com, 20 April 2013

Warburton Cup Final – Thu, 18th April 2013

Heaton 'E' (Dave Bevitt, Mel Brooks, John Hilton Snr) [handicap 37.5]
vs. Hilton 'H' (John Lawrence, Adele Spibey, Jean Smart)
Venue: Hilton Centre, 7.30pm

Red. A deep red. Like the Ali Sami Yen stadium. The walls of the Hilton Centre can disturb a player, wash his or her mind with hell-like images. IS THAT A PLAYER OPPOSITE OR BEELZEBUB? I'M SURE I SAW A HORN. Above sit forty two strip lights – a 6 x 7 gaze up at the Gods, the stars, or times tables with the kids.

I look around, peer at the players already here. Bevitt – beach shorts, brown work socks and ghetto trainers – warms up with Brooks (red top, grey/white hair, suitcase-carrying hands). I expected Mark Greenhalgh tonight, Heaton's regular player but they have opted for the wise head and formidable past of Brooks who has 30% more in the locker. Sensible. Very sensible.

Their revised no.3, John Hilton now enters the court. He has the calm deportment of a doctor; this a casual trip out, away from the wards, crying patients and enquiring nurses. He is resplendent in tank top, grey t-shirt, belted jeans and Steve Martin trainers. Someone shouts YOU'RE NOT WEARING THOSE JEANS?! to which the Doctor just shrugs, smiles, as if unable to find his kit but not concerned. He has whiter hair than Brooks – some accolade – yet still retains a certain disco fever with large gold watch and ring.

We are nearing 'dawn' for this showdown. The opposition enters. Lawrence – like an assassin all in black. Spibey – centre parting, squaw-like, demure, a red-band keeping her hair tied back. Smart – standard red top, black joggers, nerves seeping through a little. A female SAS to some, with Lawrence as Wing Commander.

We know the order of play (1×2, 3×1, 2×3, 3×2, 1×3, 2×1, 3×3, 2×2, 1×1) and so Bevitt and Spibey enter the fold. The former has kept away from this league fixture (season 2012/13), is therefore relatively unknown, potentially dangerous, without a genetic print. Spibey shows an initial wariness through that famously skittish expression of hers (something that should have been purged eighteen months ago given her win percentage). She is fidgety, not used to the modest crowd – the blush and flush of youth strangling a large portion of her natural game.

Bevitt starts. A couple of low, flat, cagey serves. 2-0 up. Effective. Riding high. He then handles the first Spibey serve. 3-0. Like a dream. Beauty and the Beast with the Detroit Tigers man (check out that faded, dapper t-shirt!) proudly roaming the table tennis jungle. Spibey crouches down, does her trademark hand-close-to-the-table multiple bounce with the ball, the 40mm celluloid pop – whatever you want to call this cataclysmic sporting invention (its white matte and 0.9 coefficient as significant as Edison's light bulb). The ball streaks across. Bevitt fluffs it. "Ahhh, rubbish," comes the soft lambasting, but Adele has her first point of the evening. Necessary. Urgent. Now for that belief!

11-7. 11-9. Spibey's backhand flicks are still not delivering. She looks rusty, out of sorts and Bevitt is a worthy early leader with some phenomenal angled drives. Time to enter the 3rd game with a different tactical head. Less gung-ho from Spibey, more circumspect – lengthening the rallies, choosing her shots. The Assassin, Lawrence looks at her. No words, but she knows she has to turn it around. Christ – nothing miraculous, but she storms into a 6-0 lead. 10-0. Now she's playing with flair, gunning Bevitt down with her fly-swatting forehand. 11-1. Relief.

Sweat appears on Bevitt's head like a man stood under a leaking gutter. He wipes himself down – towel to hand, Murrayesque, aware of the need for grip, good vision and aerodynamics. Keen to make amends after the disgrace of the 3rd, he starts impressively. 5-0. A mirror image of the last. Then 5-1 after a well-executed angled chop from the young woman opposite. 7-2. Still in pole position. Spibey bounces the ball on the floor, thinking, thinking HOW HAS THIS COME ABOUT? A net cord drops in to force it back to 8-6. She's skating again, motoring, but too late. Bevitt pulls into the driveway with a firm 11-7. Thirty-four points each but Heaton's handicap gives them a net lead of four. Bevitt is congratulated by his team mates. Spibey continues the demonstrative gestures: hiding her face behind her bat; head in hands; spinning round as if in search of her game; two fists up to her chin; biting her bat. She is annoyed. Generally annoyed. Too many misses. And she's yet to settle.

The Doctor takes his place. Hilton vs. Lawrence next up. There are slight, limbering jumps from the Assassin. He feels good, confident against the unassuming man before him. A deadly first serve down the right with extra spin and cut reinforces this. 4-1 if you turned away. Hilton seems fearful, his game shaky – far too hesitant in his shot selection. The technical simplicity of Lawrence is undoing him. 11-7. Over. Hilton is cheating himself. I have seen the graceful deceptiveness of his shots in Victoria Hall and this is not him tonight.

A pet talk from Brooks – his Roman-emperor face trying to assert some quiet authority. Hilton listens then meanders over to the table. A tentative start, but 1-0. He quickly loses his way though. 5-2 down. And then a slow slump to another 11-7. Brooks nods at him. HANG IN THERE. USE A DIFFERENT WEAPON.

It just isn't happening. A looper from nowhere though deep into the 3rd game, his arm suddenly recognising the stage. Game point (10-9). A chink of light for Hilton. Bang. Bang. Bang. The Assassin was never a kindly gent. 12-10 to Lawrence.

There is certainly not the magic of Bevitt/Spibey to this match. It feels more like a holiday friendly in the forests of the old Yugoslavia. Something unreal about it, too carefully sculpted. Guarded shots, malfunctions in the wrist. Perhaps Cup Final night has shredded them a little, sapped them of energy. 7-3. Beautiful forehand from Hilton. 8-6. Placement shots letting him down. Damn it. I feel for the man. I can't look. Don't throw it away. ****. ****. ****. 11-9. Safely home. The Doctor salvages a game.

Brooks vs. Smart. A tester. Brooks – post-shoulder op', eyes on the wane, ex-Division One so I hear. Just back from his holiday home in Turkey (although I'd swear he flip-flops through Florida). Smart – a subtle effervescence to her, watchful, with dark piercing eyes. A careful chopping game gets Brooks on his way. 6-1 before we've settled into our plastic chairs. The Smart forehand is slack, not its usual self. 8-3. 10-6. The first 'let' of the night due to a menacing but wayward ball from the Brian Gittins Cup final on the adjacent court; hard for the eyes not to wander in times of drought. Smart hits four consecutive points. Brooks wobbles a little (10-10). Shell shocked (10-11). The pressure, the intensity, the cool head see him through though. 13-11. Ooohhh.

Thoughts of the trophy, the importance of the evening, perhaps start to fill Smart's mind. Her footwork is slightly amiss despite the excellent prodding backhands. 11-4. 11-6. Brooks is in control. Three games up and a decent haul of points. WHAT IS IT ABOUT THIS MAN? He doesn't have the power of Bevitt, or the youthful skill of Spibey, or even the lugubrious, dark veil of Lawrence. Experience. Knows his way around. Able to read the terrain like a discerning nomad. Not the last game (6-11) which included the best rally of the night – point to Smart – but it's a decent 41-32 win.

They've all had their first run out now. What follows is number-crunching madness:

Hilton	Spibey	25 – 41	(11-8, 9-11, 1-11, 4-11)
Bevitt	Smart	38 – 38	(11-9, 8-11, 8-11, 11-7)
Brooks	Lawrence	38 – 37	(8-11, 8-11, 11-9, 11-6)
Hilton	Smart	33 – 44	(11-9, 8-11, 11-13, 3-11)
Brooks	Spibey	28 – 36	(11-8, 11-6, 2-11, 4-11)

272-305 Gross. 309.5-305 Net (including the full handicap).

Heaton 'E' have a slight edge. It's all down to Bevitt and Lawrence; the man who mutters, curses himself quietly, chides his own play and the Assassin, deep in thought, mindful of his glasses not slipping down his nose due to the perspiration.

"Come on." "Watch the ball." "Nnnooooo." "Rubbish." A few stock Bevitt phrases.

None of the above from Lawrence. Just concentration. A mute, torpedo-like manner.

IT'S BEGUN!!!! 8-11. 4-11. 11-5. The Heaton E 'net lead' is down to an excruciating 1/2pt (yes – half of one point). Winner takes all: last game....

Landslide-like bombing forehands are woofed across the net. Amazing. Then greedy. Back to amazing. Lawrence into the net. 4-1 healthy start from the resurgent Bevitt. Wide Lawrence winner (4-2). Big miss from Lawrence... LOOONNNGGGGG. LOOOONNNGGGGGGGGG. 7-3. The Assassin finds something...draws on *some* latent gas tanks, super-chargers, vein-enhancers, mind-turning positivity. Four straight points. Alas...7-7.

Alan Ingerson is chewing my ear. Sat in the audience. Christ – back off. Back off. This is history. HISTORY. Has Bevitt thrown it away? Perhaps not. The gilded promise of yesteryear returns. A superlative forehand to his right. 8-7. But – ahhhhh! Inexplicable. AGAIN. A missed shot to the left. 8-8. Lawrence paws at his glasses amidst the sweat, the slippery focus, the mire before him. Back to level but can he even see?

A tragedy for either one of these gents, their teams, their kin folk. Whoever loses ought to be carried aloft, squeezed through the internal doors; into the car park and beyond, paraded around town as a giant of the table tennis community. YOU REMEMBER IT? THE 9TH MATCH, THE 36TH GAME AT 8-A-PIECE. THREE STEPS TO GLORY.

Bevitt stares out across the nine-foot swamp – Lawrence's bat has become a frogman, an able diver. LET IT BE, JOHN. JUST LET IT SINK. It does. 9-8 to Bevitt. The Assassin then somehow freezes – hits a short one into the net. 10-8. NEARLY THERE, DETROIT! A spinning, sliced shot to the left from Lawrence. Looks good. Looks.....OUT. OUT!! MISSED!! I hear you. 11-8. Bevitt has done it for Heaton 'E'. He has ridden the merciful yet torturous chariot over the line, shown his stamina to the crowd, regaled them with his vocal spasms. Hail Dave Bevitt! Hail John Hilton! Hail Mel Brooks! Respect to Hilton 'H' – gross masters yet unable to turn the tide (pulling back 34pts – four shy of a net victory). They must feel like Al Gore.

I look at the clock. 10.25pm. I have been here for three hours. An average of five minutes a game. THREE HOURS. Soporific. Tired as hell. Like watching *two* football matches. Or *Lord of the Rings*. Get in the car and don't come back. DRIVE. DRIVE!!!!

Index

Printed in Great Britain
by Amazon